Anatomy of a Hustle:
Cable Comes to South Central L.A.

Clinton E. Galloway

This book is dedicated
to Mother Dear and Daddy

It is also dedicated to my brother, Carl. I hope that you can see the battle was worth it, even if only for the right to tell the story of how the Constitution got lost in the hustle. You never had a gram of quit in you. Peace go with you, brother.

INVICTUS

Out of the night that covers me,
Black as the Pit from pole to pole,
I thank whatever gods may be
For my unconquerable soul.

In the fell clutch of circumstance
I have not winced or cried aloud.
Under the bludgeonings of chance
My head is bloody but unbowed.

Beyond this place of wrath and tears
Looms but the Horror of the shade,
And yet the menace of the years
Finds, and shall find, me unafraid.

It matters not how strait the gate,
How charged with punishments the scroll,
I am the master of my fate:
I am the captain of my soul.

William Ernest Henley

Anatomy of a Hustle

Chapter Index

Foreward

"As my brother and I were escorted past hundreds of citizens, on our way up the steps to the Supreme Court of the United States of America, we could not help but be affected by the fact that the highest court in the land was going to hear our case. Our small group of regular citizens had brought the second-largest city in the nation to task before the highest court in the land."

This is a story of how government really works. It is not a theoretical or abstract dissertation of my feelings about government. This presentation is a step-by-step playbook for how government pretends to assist their constituent communities and instead stifles growth and investment in numerous ways.

Cable television is the industry example showcased here. The story is based in Los Angeles, California, but translates to many other cities in the United States—perhaps even yours.

The entire cable television industry started in a fashion similar to what has happened in Los Angeles. The unconstitutional behavior on the part of various cities and local governments fostered an era of modern media ownership restricted to a few very wealthy individuals and groups. This consolidation of the broadcast media accelerated the decline of the independent press, which potentially threatens the freedoms we all hold so dear.

You may assume this is a story about cable television and an impoverished black community. It is actually a much larger story of an unholy alliance that has developed between the government and the media. I'm probably the last living person who knows the entire story and would want it told. This is a responsibility that I must fulfill despite the personal pain of telling the story.

This was not a game, but the life of a city and its constituents. We wanted to bring the same opportunity for economic progress to South Central that existed in the rest of the city. While the rest of America was exploding with international growth, Black America was imploding with crime and limited economic opportunities. It remained outside of the American mainstream.

My brother and I were successful, educated black men, a doctor and a CPA, respectively, wanting to give back to the community and enrich the lives of South Central Los Angeles residents—with a technology bridge to the future.

However, powerful, successful black politicians, their friends, and major campaign fundraisers, conspired, with great stealth and subterfuge, to prevent our efforts in cable television from ever getting started. They worked just just as hard to make sure their intentions and actions were never discovered by the public and the media.

Our cable television application process and subsequent court case in the City of Los Angeles and the U.S. District Courts, revealed the height of city government corruption, conspiracy, and judicial-biased activism, adversely affecting the neighborhood of South Central Los Angeles with broad media and civil rights implications. The effects would not be limited to South Central but would cascade through the entire nation regardless of economic, racial, or ethnic differences.

First Amendment rights, the expectation of judicial independence, and the telecommunication future of the minority South Central Los Angeles population were mashed and squandered in the process. City fathers heinously and thoughtlessly set an invisible, rippling tsunami wave of neglect on all the families living in the poorest community in Los Angeles.

This unabashed political grab for money and power in cable franchise licensing in South Central Los Angeles also became a two-pronged attack by the City of Los Angeles and U.S. District Court Judge Consuelo Marshall. These efforts were designed to hide detrimental information about Mayor Bradley and Los Angeles city government and suppress increased scrutiny in the periods of his two-time candidacy for governor of California.

Most of this reprehensible, nearly unbelievable process was conducted in a highly secretive manner in stark contrast to the public face his Honor, Mayor Bradley, and the City Council of Los Angeles put forth in his "glory days."

Anatomy of a Hustle outlines the illegal, unethical practices and misconduct of Mayor Tom Bradley, City Council members, friends, and benefactors of the Los Angeles city government.

Major American corporations and some of the richest people in the United States would receive special and favorable treatment at the expense of the most economically disadvantaged community in Los Angeles. In our case, Eli Broad and his company KB Homes would have special rules created that would apply only to them. These rules would allow him to receive millions of dollars while defaulting on the contract to construct a cable television network. When you are not a political insider, even the financial support of the richest man in the world is not enough.

This book also unmasks other examples by the burgeoning cable television industry of collusion with city governments, large and small, throughout our country—to the detriment of citizens and their communities.

This story takes you on our journey from Los Angeles City Hall to the United States Supreme Court and back to the Federal District Court in Los Angeles. We were to find that dealing with the government was not for the faint of heart.

Did these issues happen independently? We offer an emphatic no.

So we say, read and beware. An entire industry created and sustained itself based on government malfeasance and corruption. We fought with all the resources that we could muster.

This book is merely a continuation of the battle. And though we may have lost some battles within the war, we won some as well, and came out amazed and gratified that we fought for so long and so well. To be forewarned is to be forearmed.

I write these words on behalf of not only my brother and myself but on behalf of all African-Americans who have lost their rights and their ability to utilize media to improve their life situation.

While we knew the importance of cable television to the future of South Central and America, we were unaware of the massive future economic value of a cable television system. Even today I must smile as I realize that in the process we lost more money than we ever dared to dream of making.

We documented the entire process because of the constitutional issues we fought for in the federal courts. The documents have been made available at www.cablecomestosouthcentral.com to support what we have written here. Let the documents speak for themselves.

Today, the power of the cable television industry is massive. It impacts our everyday lives. Do you have a cable television connection, Internet cable access, or a satellite dish attached to your home and entertainment choices at this very moment?

Just who is influencing you?

Prologue

Diary of A Hustle

In South Central Los Angeles, opportunity knocks softly and leaves quickly. Sometimes, fleeting and fickle at best. Such occasions are as much about timing as they are about any idea.

Opportunities can be real or made to look real on the outside, but are something else altogether different on the inside—like a cardboard cake with real icing on the outside. It's a cheat that looks genuine...until you're deeply involved in the process.

Many times, if people could look on the inside they would see the beginning of the tragic confidence game, or "the hustle." It's an age-old ruse played on everything from a carnival table to a city council chamber. But that's not possible.

That's what happened to my brother and me in a cable franchise application "setup" at Los Angeles City Hall.

Let's look at the process. First, the perpetrator of the hustle must gain the confidence of the victim.

In the hallowed halls of the City of Los Angeles, the hustle was an art form like the magical shell game.

Look at the well-tailored French cuffs and gold cufflinks of the mayor of the second-largest city in the United States, as the pea darts among the three walnut shells.

Look at the hallowed halls and rich wooden podium of the Los Angeles City Council Chamber and all the esteemed council people as hands flash across the table top among the nut shells.

Look at the all the Los Angeles city departments with their frosted windows and wide customer counters as the barker asks you which shell holds the pea.

Where's the pea? Was there ever an honest chance to win?

Chapter One

The City Of Los Angeles Hustle — The Setup At City Hall

In December 1978, my older brother, Dr. Carl Anthony Galloway, presented me with our opportunity of a lifetime in the new and burgeoning media of the cable television industry. He persuaded me to help him pursue newly created cable television franchise opportunities in South Central Los Angeles.

We saw this as a great chance for business success and for black businessmen to inform and help Black America in the largest minority cable franchise area of its size in the nation. An entirely new industry within American media was opening up and we had a chance to be part of it. But I'm getting ahead of myself.

At the time, my brother and I owned Megavision, a big-screen and video specialty store in Studio City, California. This was before the industry became populated with the big-box store names like Best Buy.

We knew from our work at Megavision that the public's expectations for video programming were changing both dramatically and rapidly. We saw people responding to the opportunity to have bigger screens for televised programming, especially sports. At that time, consumers also enthusiastically purchased videocassette recorders (VCRs) and videotapes, both relatively new products in the marketplace.

Carl continually insisted these consumer actions indicated a new media revolution was coming. "You mark my words, Clinton. It's coming!" I knew Carl was an extremely bright man, bordering on genius, but I, as his brother, was of course skeptical at times of his pronouncements.

"I'm in with you, but I get fifty percent or I am telling Mother Dear," I joked with him, giving voice to my skepticism. Mother Dear was what we called our mother, and my older brother Carl would not want me to tell our mother he was trying to gyp me out of my share of *anything*.

Carl only smiled and explained he was interested in researching relationships with cable television providers offering valuable connections to the ultimate customer—way beyond the purchase of our new line of video products.

I can hear his words now, trying to convince me. "I know you think I'm crazy but cable television is going to replace the newspaper. You'll just sit there, watch, and turn the channels to see everything you need to know. Believe me!"

I still was as skeptical as Carl was confident. Despite my skepticism, Carl added more facts and figures to his arguments, which finally convinced me cable television, as an independent industry, would become a technology that would revolutionize how America obtained information. "Try to envision it again. It will all be right on the screen. Just by sitting there you'll get all the information!"

Carl also vehemently insisted Black America could, and should, not be left behind. "You know Black America is already behind the general population in so many areas within society. If we can help, we've got to try."

The last remaining neighborhoods without cable television in the greater Los Angeles area, included minority neighborhoods like South Central Los Angeles. In this application process, Carl identified these cable applications as the *only* opportunities left to get involved with this new technology—a chance to make sure black and other minority citizens would be treated to the very best this new technology offered.

Serving South Central Los Angeles would be a daunting task. The economic, social, and crime challenges in South Central were already widely known. The scourge of the 1965 Watts Riots had seen white citizens and businesses flee the area. We felt we could address those challenges and help to positively affect those problem areas.

"Are you sure we can get the Watts Riots out of people's minds?" I asked. At Carl's angry frown I changed my tone a bit. "I know you work down there at the hospital...and the riots were in 1965."

"These areas are stronger than people think. There are still plenty of people with money to spend in the Baldwin Hills and West Adams neighborhoods. You know that," Carl replied with feeling. "The manufacturing sector down there is staying steady... but I've got to admit there have been job losses with a few more businesses moving out."

Carl explained we only had a short time to develop our plan after the paperwork became available. This meant we needed to put our ideas together quickly, concerning: (1) the construction of a cable television system, (2) preliminary programming ideas, and (3) the financial package necessary to enter the application process proposed by the City of Los Angeles.

"I especially want to work on the programming aspect," Carl said with relish. He knew that with my background auditing major construction firms for an international accounting company I'd be of help with the construction and financing aspects.

First, we took a look at the business opportunity to see if the clearly identifiable and demographically unique community of this size made economic sense. The larger the prospective business area, the more we could address our goal to fund and develop programming for this special niche market from our franchise profits—educational programming for children and adults, community health issues, skill-related and counseling programs, as well as literacy training. I was particularly convinced the best way to influence economically disadvantaged neighborhoods was to provide economic and financial counseling programming as well.

We felt those in the South Central market would be willing to pay for this unique programming, which was not available on either the broadcast networks or cable television stations. We also visualized South Central Los Angeles as a beginning programming cornerstone in the development of a regional system to address the problems of other inner-city areas beyond the city of Los Angeles.

Second, we were told by city officials that the applications were for non-exclusive franchises, and we were under the impression that *more than one* company could receive a franchise. The language in the paperwork was clear.

The term non-exclusive appeared to be straightforward in its meaning and intent. The City of Los Angeles could *not* grant only one license for the issuance of cable television franchises. That would be a monopoly, and it seemed incomprehensible for the City of Los Angeles to come up with a plan to award a monopoly license given the wording in the application and the concept of non-exclusive licensing stated *in the application instructions*.

Fortunately, I had worked as a financial consultant specializing in the placement of utility stocks and direct participation programs for the Beverly Hills office of Smith Barney and was somewhat familiar with cable television as a quasi-public utility. Direct participation programs differ from common stock because they invest in a specifically defined group of assets.

The most common program of this type is a real estate limited partnership.

We were aware of the difference between a *standard* public utility (gas, electric, water) and cable television. Electricity and water, unlike cable television, were the same everywhere. There was one type of water, gas, and electricity offered through a pipe to your home.

Cable television was very, very different. Although it came through one wire to your home, you could select and pay for various "packages" of programming. There were a myriad of choices and opportunities for the consumer to select.

Although both categories were government-sanctioned monopolies, the standard public utility, as a *regulated* monopoly, had its services and rates supervised or controlled by the government—one price for the unit of water and one price for the unit of gas. Cable television had many different choices and packages and most of their activities were *unregulated*.

As an unregulated monopoly, cable television had few restrictions upon its pricing or services offered. In the case of cable television, the *competitive marketplace* controlled the prices and services, as in most industries in the United States. Without competition, there would be *no control* over the cable television market.

Carl and I knew this was both a competitive business opportunity and, as indicated before, an opportunity to bring quality programming to the black community. We felt *no one* could dispute the need for programming responsive to the needs of South Central given the economic and social conditions there.

"Just think!" Carl said. "We can use some of our profits to produce quality programming to benefit the South Central community. This is something that's never been done before!"

Carl, as always, was thinking big. He outlined educational, television series, and news programs for the black community with special emphasis on the medical and financial needs within our expertise.

———

On November 30, 1978, the Board of Public Utilities and Transportation of the City of Los Angeles (later to become the Board of Transportation Commissioners or BTC), had recommended the Los Angeles City Council offer the final two undeveloped cable television franchises for applications. One franchise was in the West San Fernando Valley, and the other was the South Central-Harbor area of Los Angeles—the one we wanted.

While the process was routinely called a "Notice of Sale," nothing was being sold. The Notice of Sale was a public invitation to submit an application for either or both of these franchise opportunities. "Paperwork for the franchises will be available probably in four to six weeks," the clerk said.

I shrugged my shoulders and looked at Carl. "We'll just have to wait, but we can continue to do research."

In December 1978, weeks before the application process paperwork became available, Carl went to the National Cable Television Association (NCTA) tradeshow in Anaheim, California, with the original purpose of finding new customers for our Megavision line of video products, including big-screen televisions.

Carl met Paul Skulsky, the president of Six Star Cablevision, a multiple-system cable operator with properties in several states, including several operating cable television systems in the Los Angeles area. Carl found out that Paul's company had an application pending for the Hollywood-Wilshire franchise area in the City of Los Angeles and Six Star also intended to submit an application for the South Central-Harbor franchise area.

As Carl and Paul both told me many times, Paul and Carl immediately liked one another. Paul, coming from New Jersey, and Carl, being from New York, managed to strike up a mutual respect for each other based on similar experiences and interests. They both foresaw the coming revolution of media in the United States, which would rely heavily on the cable television industry.

In their first conversation, Paul reaffirmed Six Star knew the City of Los Angeles was soon going to accept applications for the largely African-American and Latino-populated area known as the South Central-Harbor franchise area. According to Paul, the City of Los Angeles was set to announce the date to accept applications in January 1979.

Paul asked Carl if he would be interested in submitting an application for the South Central-Harbor franchise area, in conjunction with Six Star.

"These kinds of opportunities are about *all* I've been talking about with my brother," Carl replied. Carl told Paul he was *very* interested in the opportunity.

——————

A week after Carl met Paul Skulsky, I was having dinner at Carl's house. Carl continued to expound with his original enthusiasm on how we were going to become successful as cable television providers and his ongoing conversations with Skulsky.

I was pretty smug when I laughed at the prospect of people actually *paying* to watch television. There were at least eight television stations in Los Angeles, an international mecca for both motion pictures and television. I thought we needed to be cautious because everyone seemed to be satisfied with those television channel choices, especially relying on the three major broadcast networks of NBC, ABC, and CBS.

Again, in three hours, Carl emphasized how committed he was to the idea of cable television changing the way information was disseminated in the United States. Carl reiterated that if we failed to take advantage of this opportunity it would never come again. "Opportunities have an expiration date," he said.

Carl talked about how the City of Los Angeles had *created* the "Community Antenna Television Master Plan for the City of Los Angeles." For the City of Los Angeles, this document and its subsequent ordinance controlled what has come to be known as "cable television," initially defining any cable television system as a *community antenna television system*.

The original intent for cable television was to cater to each individual community's needs and preferences, not the giant media conglomerates that now run the cable television industry.

Carl understood and embraced the concept of cable television, near its industry inception, not only to give the community information but also as a method by which communities could be proud of their neighborhoods, themselves, and a way to bring people and their thoughts and ideas together. It was a community builder.

The city's master plan also specified that *minority ownership of cable television* in minority communities should be *an important factor* in determining the award of the remaining franchises, since these remaining franchises were largely minority neighborhoods. This report was done in 1974—almost five calendar years before the South Central-Harbor franchise came to our attention.

Carl said, "Let's work out a plan." He grabbed a paper tablet and a pen. "Since I'm the one who's most interested in this business, I'll go to the meetings and get the information. You'll be my backup and manage Megavision. You'll take care of the financing and we'll split up the research and writing the application. Fair?"

I nodded. "We'll see each other every week, and after any meetings, to go over our progress?"

"As close to that as possible," Carl replied.

————◆————

As franchise application bidders, and members of the public at large, we thought this was the *first* time applications had been submitted for these franchise areas and assumed there were no other franchise applications pending.

"I can't believe it, but it's all new down there," Skulsky said in a phone conversation. "There's not another application on the books...and in the media capital of the world, to boot! Unbelievable!" Skulsky's gruff laugh echoed in the phone. "That's not all! You're fortunate to have heard about this opportunity...at all."

Up until these two franchises (West San Fernando Valley and South Central-Harbor) were opened to bids for cable television applications, such applications were submitted with little or no public notice.

We couldn't believe our luck.

———————

A few days later, we got another phone call from Skulsky. "I try to be accurate with information but I've made a mistake in what I've told you." Carl and I looked at each other.

"Seems I was inaccurate about saying there weren't any other applications for the franchise, but they're from ages ago and aren't active anymore, according to the people down at city hall," he informed us. "Just thought you should know."

So those first assertions by the city were false. These franchises, which we thought had never been offered or applied for before, had actually been previously sought by at least one other applicant.

"Does that affect us?" I asked.

"No. No, not as far as I can see, but I wanted to tell you because I had said...and thought something different," Skulsky replied.

"OK. OK," Carl said. I could see his mind mulling over the information. "But the application structure is still the same?"

"Unchanged. I've checked twice. You do the same to assure yourselves," Skulsky advised.

We did. What Skulsky said at the time was true. Some applications that had been previously filed were held without processing or explanation.

———————

Now there also were rumblings, within the Los Angeles city government and the departments responsible for looking at these cable franchise applications, that things might be different with these two remaining franchises being put out to bid.

"Seems like I'm always calling with bad news," Skulsky said. "We've all got the paperwork and it's never happened before, but some of the people down at city hall say there might be changes." He stopped for a minute. "Nothing specific...but I've got a feeling. I can't pin them down and they're evasive when I ask questions."

Skulsky said there was also no explanation in what turned out to be a *distinctly new and different* application process as well as changes in every aspect of the cable television application process.

Ever so slowly, the Los Angeles cable television hustle began.

———◆———

On January 16, 1979, the Los Angeles City Council approved the West San Fernando Valley franchise for sale but decided not to set a date to accept applications for the South Central-Harbor franchise. They delayed offering the South Central-Harbor franchise for *six months.*

"It's strange. A first time here," Skulsky shrugged. "But I've seen it happen other places...and things usually work out."

Five years since the completion of the Community Antenna Master Plan and now six months more? The authorities' pretense, they explained, was to conduct an investigation into the availability of minority-owned cable television operators.

The city was, once again, proclaiming its desire to seek out minority-owned cable television operators to develop the South Central franchise? According to what the city was saying, we had arrived at the right place at the right time.

This was the beginning of the city government setup—a number of clean, polished, and systematic steps leading away from a fair and open process. We, as first-time franchise applicants, were unaware of this first sign of trouble.

This decision to postpone the application process for South Central cascaded into a series of delays in cable television installation in South Central Los Angeles. This was a clear derailing of technology opportunities. But for what reason?

———◆———

Carl tried to find out when they would conduct this search for minorities who were interested in building a cable television system in South Central. "We're right in front of them and they know it," he scoffed.

Carl discovered other black entrepreneurs, as far back as the 1960s, who might have tried to obtain a cable television license to build cable in South Central, but the city had always refused to process their applications. "I don't have time to poke around now. Things are pretty hectic with my work with the interns," Carl informed, explaining why he hadn't found the full explanation for why this processing problem had occurred. Carl was the chief resident at St. Francis Hospital in Lynnwood. "Give me time. I'll find out later."

Then we heard the City of Los Angeles had an application from at least one minority-owned company since 1975, that was still pending. The application had been held, without processing, and the city repeatedly declined to make the franchise available for application submission. *Repeatedly declined?* This, even after the city had the guidelines from the Community Antenna Master Plan in place.

With this disturbing evidence that other black entrepreneurs had submitted cable franchise applications and had been denied, we began to wonder if this indicated a pattern for the future of South Central.

"I'm going to find out when and how city officials conducted the application process in the South Central cable franchise back then," Carl said. During the six-month wait, we would discover that more changes in the current cable television process were in store as well.

———◆———

Carl and Paul Skulsky, from Six Star, kept in contact during the early months of 1979. Skulsky told Carl more alarming news. Paul said he had met with both Mayor Tom Bradley and Councilman Dave Cunningham. The mayor's office provided Skulsky with a list of potential minority investors for the other franchise Six Star was bidding on, the Hollywood-Wilshire franchise. *Was it standard practice for the mayor's office to give lists of investors to an independent businessman and his company? Did this affect the unbiased independence of the council in this matter? Was this ethical? Would anything happen to the Six Star bid request if Skulsky didn't call the people on the list?*

"Cunningham really pushed the mayor's list in the meeting... and called the people on the list about the Wilshire deal," Skulsky reported.

"So they've given you at list of potential investors for the Hollywood-Wilshire franchise...and nothing about the South Central-Harbor franchise?" Carl asked.

"Nothing about South Central-Harbor, but I thought they would," Skulsky replied. "If they were interested in doing it that would have been the perfect time. But I'm not going to say anything. I don't want to give them any ideas to muck up the process."

Skulsky said he called all the people on the list, and the only person who responded to his inquiries was a Mr. Edgar Charles. Skulsky said Charles seemed a bit reluctant to talk about the cable television industry.

"'Please call me Edgar,' was all Charles said in the phone conversation," Skulsky reported. "Thought we were getting off to a good start, but once I told him I was from Six Star, he stopped talking." Skulsky shrugged his shoulders. "That's about it."

In future conversations, Charles admitted his initial reluctance to talk to anyone about cable television was based upon Charles's previous involvement with the city and the cable television licensing process since 1966.

———◆———

"I've *finally* got a face-to-face meeting set up with Edgar Charles," Skulsky said a week later. "I want to at least try to talk to someone from the list I got."

———◆———

Skulsky went to the meeting to discuss Edgar's potential participation in Six Star's franchise applications for the Hollywood-Wilshire franchise area per Councilman Cunningham's instruction.

Edgar Charles didn't show up.

On May 20, 1979, Skulsky contacted Carl to tell him he tried to contact Edgar Charles, again, to determine his interest in the Hollywood-Wilshire franchise. Skulsky was concerned because he did not think he would receive the Hollywood-Wilshire franchise without some degree of local participation. "Cunningham seems to want this. Will you work with me...and get a meeting with Edgar Charles?"

Carl contacted Edgar Charles. Charles said he could not meet for one week because of other business plans and they set up a meeting for May 30, 1979.

During that week, on May 24, 1979, the Hollywood-Wilshire franchise was awarded to Six Star Cablevision, the largest single cable television franchise within the City of Los Angeles.

At the prearranged May 30, 1979, meeting with Edgar Charles, Charles also told them he was one of the people who had tried and failed to become a minority cable franchise owner for many years.

Carl informed Charles the Hollywood-Wilshire franchise had been awarded to Six Star. Charles became very upset.

"I spoke to Mr. Skulsky a few weeks ago," Charles sputtered. "Not one of my contacts at city hall said *anything* about the franchise being even *near* a franchise award."

Interrupting the meeting, Edgar Charles called Mayor Bradley and Councilman Robert Farrell and left messages saying he wanted to discuss the award of the Hollywood-Wilshire franchise.

"I've been fighting to get a hearing...and a franchise since 1966." The utter frustration seemed to almost overwhelm him, according to Carl, as he tried to calm the older man down.

———◆———

"We're now on a first-name basis and we can call Mr. Charles by his first name, Edgar," Carl said. "If we could, I'd like to consider adding him to our board of directors or...maybe even as an investor."

"Are you sure?" I asked. We needed investors and Carl had already lined up some doctor friends who were willing to invest. I was working on getting investment commitments as well.

"It might take a few more meetings to decide to include him... but I think so," Carl replied.

———◆———

Edgar called Carl several days later and said he had received a call from Councilman Farrell. According to Edgar, Councilman Farrell said he had been absent on the day the Hollywood-Wilshire franchise was awarded...and nothing more could be done on the issue. Even though Councilman Farrell admitted Edgar's interest in a cable television application started in 1966, Farrell was sorry—Edgar was "out of the Hollywood-Wilshire deal."

Edgar went on to say Councilman Farrell recommended Edgar look at the South Central-Harbor franchise area, which Farrell said they were planning to accept applications for in September 1979—*three months longer* than the original six month delay day. *Why wasn't this further delay public knowledge, and why weren't the prospective franchisees aware of this change?*

———◆———

Now that Edgar and Carl had become aware that the South Central-Harbor franchise was going to accept applications in September 1979, we, along with Skulsky, agreed Edgar was a good fit in our franchise effort and we asked him to join in our pursuit for the South Central-Harbor cable franchise.

There were mutual benefits for this strategy. Edgar was supposedly a friend of Councilman Robert Farrell and knew the ins and outs of City Hall and Los Angeles city government. His company, Ebony Cablevision, also had a history in documents and submissions with the city.

From June 1979 through December 1979, Carl and Edgar conducted our efforts through Ebony Cablevision. Carl and Edgar wanted to continue to use the name because of the history Ebony Cablevision, a minority-owned company, had in submitting previous cable television application filings many years prior. Edgar dug up all the previous paperwork to authenticate his claims, documenting thirteen years of dedication to seeking to provide cable television service to South Central.

In February 1980, Carl and I formed a new company, Universal Cable Systems, Ltd., to legally pursue a cable license. Universal Cable Systems, Ltd., would be formed to replace Ebony Cablevision. We would hold sixty percent and Six Star would have forty percent in this joint venture—South Central CATV Associates. The equity to finance this joint venture would be provided In the same ratio as the division of ownership.

———◆———

During this time, I was already using cable television to provide financial information and education to the public. From 1979 through mid-1981, I hosted and did segments for a cable television show called *Utilities Outlook* out of the Beverly Hills office of Smith-Barney on the local financial channel.

The broadcast version of the show, on a small UHF station, Channel 22, was enhanced because of cable television. Although the broadcast signal was limited to Los Angeles County, our show was seen by viewers in San Diego, Orange, and Riverside Counties on cable television. With the assistance of cable television, I reached a much larger audience than I could ever have met with only broadcast television. I understood the power of cable television to expand your distribution of information beyond a smaller geographic area than was covered by broadcast television.

I saw the power of cable programming to enhance investment and financial decisions within the viewing audience. I wanted economic opportunities to come to South Central and I now believed such investment could be *generated* from the South Central community for its own development. I believed a community that has an investment in itself is less likely to attempt to destroy itself, as we'd seen in the riots. Carl had been right.

———

Edgar said, in his monitoring of city hall, that he'd told Councilman Farrell of his conversations with Carl, who Edgar identified as a doctor interested in filing an application for the South Central-Harbor franchise.

Councilman Farrell said he was glad to hear it and would personally assign his deputy, Channing Johnson, to assist Edgar and Carl with the cable franchise application process. "Let's set up a conference call."

———

During the second week of June 1979, Channing Johnson, Councilman Farrell's deputy, contacted Edgar and Carl on a conference call. "Councilman, are you there?" Carl asked.

Johnson stated that Councilman Farrell had been "too busy" with budget hearings to follow up with Edgar and Carl personally that day and sent his regrets. But Johnson went on to say Councilman Farrell had indeed directed him to assist Edgar and Carl in the application process for the South Central-Harbor franchise area in any way possible. So Edgar and Carl spent a few more minutes answering Johnson's questions and hung up.

———

Skulsky and Carl continued their in-depth conversations regarding our business plan for a successful cable franchise application for South Central-Harbor. With the strength of our business plan and programming ideas, Six Star agreed to be the construction and financing partner for our application.

During our company's meetings with Channing Johnson, Johnson continually told Carl and Edgar he had contacts with venture capital organizations. Johnson also said a local businessman involved in cable television, Moctesuma Esparza, owed Farrell a favor because of Farrell's assistance with Esparza's Buena Vista Television's (BVT) Los Angeles County application. "He's got a Los Angeles County cable franchise, which he hasn't built yet, and he's also a friend of Councilman Snyder," Johnson told us.

We were never interested in any new partners and we were a company comprised of three local minority businessmen as the management team of our company.

We were providing our own financing package and had successfully done so with the agreement with Six Star. We did not need venture capital organizations and we did not want the favors of political friends of elected officials. We were offended that they thought they were doing anything other than trying to strong-arm us.

Several weeks later, Esparza contacted Carl. Carl remembered his name being mentioned during a meeting but had never asked for this man to contact him, or for Johnson to give Esparza Carl's phone number.

Esparza was a Latin film producer whose film *The Milagro Beanfield Wars* would be nominated for several Oscars. Esparza related that as a favor to Farrell, he would assist Carl and Edgar with their cable television application, providing technical assistance. We were curious as to why Johnson thought we would need the help of Esparza, since we were already partners with an operating cable television company.

We didn't know.

We met with Esparza as a favor to Johnson, but it soon became clear, even at this early stage, we were as expert as Esparza in matters concerning the cable television industry.

In our conversations, Channing Johnson knew our level of expertise. Johnson clearly didn't help us with this introduction to Esparza, and we were disappointed that Johnson was unable to appreciate our level of cable television expertise and that he was foisting Esparza on us.

———

Later in June 1979, in Councilman Farrell's office, Johnson arranged a meeting with Pierpont Laidley, Councilman Farrell's personal attorney. The meeting was arranged because Laidley was recommended by Johnson to help us with the "application and licensing process."

After the June meeting with Laidley, Carl and I met to discuss his meeting with Laidley. "If he's as helpful as Esparza," Carl remarked, "we've got another dead weight on our hands and that's *two people* we'll need to part company with."

———

The interaction with Johnson, and now Laidley, was strange at times. Carl and Edgar educated Johnson and Laidley about a variety of things, including the trends in the national cable television arena, the cable television application process, and the necessary steps to go through the application process. Why didn't Johnson already know these things if he was supposed to be helping us? Why wasn't Laidley informed as well?

Carl revealed to Laidley and Johnson that we had already reached an agreement with Six Star to form a joint venture. Universal Cable Systems, Ltd., was slated to retain sixty percent of the joint venture and Six Star would have a forty-percent interest.

We also wanted to talk about our programming ideas.

"We've done our research," Carl said. "South Central *badly* needs technology advances. They're years behind other neighborhoods in the city."

Edgar and Carl also discussed the entire cable television industry and the dramatic potential for the expansion of programming opportunities to uniquely serve the residents of South Central. Among these new programming ideas were special medical and financial programming Carl and I felt met the unique needs of South Central.

The facts spoke for themselves. In South Central, the advances in technology were restricted like most other advancements in education, health care, and economic opportunities.

In a technological example we mentioned to Johnson and Laidley, cable offered an opportunity to level the educational and economic disparities that existed in communities like South Central. Depriving the people who had the least resources of this coveted access to technology, put them, once again, at the bottom of the learning curve. Carl and Edgar went on to explain that cable television, at a lower cost to households and schools, offered a unique opportunity to access information and some of the latest technological improvements, without having a computer. Cable television could be packaged in a unique way to provide some of these same services to citizens and communities who could not afford to come into the computer age.

About halfway through the meeting, Councilman Farrell joined us for lunch and joined the discussion. Johnson gave a summary to Farrell about our joint venture and the key points of our programming ideas before the group discussion returned to general topics of cable television and the South Central area.

Since we previously had seen the lack of Johnson's expertise in our cable television efforts, Carl tried to get some indication of how much more time was going to be devoted to coming to city hall. "How many more meetings do we need before the application process starts?"

Even though all attendees knew we had our company's business plan and joint venture completed for the application process, Councilman Farrell insisted that Carl and Edgar still needed Channing Johnson to help with our cable television application and that we needed to continue meeting with Johnson. "You know he's a graduate of Stanford and trying to pass the bar after graduating from Harvard Law. Why wouldn't you want his help?"

Carl and Edgar didn't know what Farrell's bragging about Johnson's academic credentials had to do with the conversation but they acquiesced to Councilman Farrell's pointed request to continue working with Channing Johnson—a good faith measure.

According to Farrell, now that Johnson would be helping us, he should be given all the information that was available. At Farrell's recommendation, Carl gave copies of all information he had obtained from the FCC and the city to Johnson. Carl did not object to this because, as he told me later, "It's all a matter of public record and it shows we're going about this all in good faith."

"A second good faith measure," Edgar remarked. "I'm keeping track."

Before the meeting ended, Johnson suggested that it would be good to retain Laidley to represent our company in the franchise process.

After Farrell left, Edgar convinced Carl to retain Pierpont Laidley to represent them in the upcoming cable television application process. Carl gave Laidley a retainer check for $1,000.

———

Near the end of June 1979, Johnson called Carl. During the conversation, Johnson said he'd recently met with Herb Wilkins, president of Syndicated Communications, Inc., (SYNCOM) and talked about how Wilkins's company would be able to help us secure the franchise because of their contacts with Los Angeles city government. Johnson, Esparza, and Laidley had previously told us that they would be all the help we would need in City Hall.

It seemed that Wilkins's company, SYNCOM, supposedly specialized in assisting financing for minority investors in the media industry in Los Angeles and was a Minority Enterprise Small Business Investment Corporation (MESBIC).

As we found out, a MESBIC received its financial backing from a federally chartered-and-sponsored venture capital fund that specialized in making investments to minority businesses and assisting in financial development within minority communities.

Since their conversations were wide-ranging, Carl didn't think much about Wilkins or SYNCOM until his next meeting with Johnson.

On July 10, 1979, when Carl and Edgar met with Channing Johnson, Johnson stated he wanted Carl and Edgar to talk with Wilkins to discuss possible participation by SYNCOM in our South Central application—trying to join Ebony Cablevision and SYNCOM in a single application. Carl and Edgar were stunned.

In the heated conversation that followed, Carl and Edgar repeatedly explained to Johnson that Six Star was committed to support their South Central application. Carl and Edgar would have majority control through a company formed at the time when the City of Los Angeles would actually begin the process to accept application submissions—February 1980. They'd already clearly told Johnson and Laidley those facts in previous conversations.

"This is the *first cable television deal in the United States* where a multiple system operator (Six Star) has *ever agreed* to allow a minority-controlled company to *have majority interest and run a franchise in a minority community!*" Carl exclaimed. Why wasn't that good enough?

"We don't want to work with MESBICs. Our company will put up sixty percent of the equity capital with investments from me, Carl, and his family and friends and Clinton's investor relationships...and Six Star will put up the other forty percent of the equity capital. We get sixty-percent ownership and Six Star gets forty percent," Edgar explained. "The documents are all finished. We've talked about it with you already! Many times!"

Edgar carefully outlined his previous dealings and experience with two particular MESBICs as unpleasant and unsuccessful experiences because of the time and government paperwork involved. Although his prior dealings with MESBICs did not have anything to do with cable television, Edgar was adamant that his prior attempts with MESBICs had proved very troublesome and the paperwork involved was "beyond cumbersome."

Carl and Edgar didn't encourage Johnson in his MESBIC plan, but Carl asked me to investigate MESBIC financing to truthfully understand and identify to Johnson why we already had a superior financing plan.

21

As we investigated MESBICs, we found additional government restrictions and investment limitations on the MESBICs beyond what Edgar had outlined in his conversations, which made them almost impossible to work with on large business ventures like the South Central-Harbor opportunity.

When confronted with these problems, neither Johnson nor Wilkins could deny these cumbersome government-imposed aspects we found in our research. MESBICs did not have the capital base necessary to fund the major investment capital required for this franchise. It would take ten or eleven different MESBICs, like SYNCOM, to get the capital needed to fund the South Central franchise. The logistics of such a transaction with such small financial entities could only have a negative impact on our business plan.

Johnson stubbornly and continually persisted in saying that working with the MESBICs, no matter what the number, would be preferable to working with "a white partner." We were chagrined by his racist comment.

"You know what you're saying?" Carl said. *Could we call this black man who represented a councilman a reverse racist?* Johnson silently looked Carl straight in the eyes and gritted his jaw. We had our answer.

Edgar wasn't going to give up on the conversation. He kept talking. "We're here now and there're a few more things to cover, Channing." Edgar wanted to talk about Johnson's persistent interest in utilizing a more risky financing concept such as MESBICs from another angle. *Was there another motive for Johnson's insistence?*

"Seems to me you're a bit too concerned about the 'who-and-why' of this thing, Deputy Johnson. We've got a clean deal and a good plan. Do you have any cable television plans going for yourself?"

Edgar broadened his question, asking Johnson whether he had any financial interest in any MESBICS or joint ventures in commerce in Los Angeles—especially any interested in the cable television industry. "You keep talking about venture capital. Are you going after this franchise?"

Johnson's iciness from the previous comment disappeared. He became defensive and aggressive at the same time. Johnson stated he did not have any financial interest in a MESBIC or any interest of any kind in the cable television business. "But you *do* need my help."

Johnson changed the direction of our questioning and went on to say we should avoid Councilman David Cunningham because he was "too greedy."

"I'll take care of things." Johnson ended the meeting by walking out the door and said, as we looked at his back, "That's it."

———————

The following week, a secretary from Councilman Farrell's office called Edgar and Carl and asked them to meet with Moctesuma Esparza on July 18, 1979. The July 18 meeting was held at Esparza's office on LeMoyne Street in East Los Angeles.

When Carl arrived, Esparza was talking on the phone with Herb Wilkins from SYNCOM. Carl joined in the conversation on a speakerphone. In response to questions that had been raised by Carl, Wilkins stated he had received the materials from Johnson that Carl had provided to Johnson and Laidley at a previous meeting. *Without our permission, Johnson had given our research work to a potential franchise competitor.*

Wilkins went on talking, unaware of this potential conflict of interest, saying he thought the South Central-Harbor franchise was viable but the area was too large. Wilkins suggested the San Pedro-Harbor part of the cable franchise should be separated from the South Central franchise, thereby reducing the financing package required to run such a large company.

We already had the business plan, financing, and expertise for the *entire franchise area*. "The only reason to decrease the size of the South Central franchise was to allow Wilkins's idea for MESBICs into the application process," Carl said after the meeting.

"What can we do?" I asked.

"Wait...and hope that's not what they're doing," Carl replied. "Call Paul at Six Star and tell him what we've learned.

In a subsequent meeting with Johnson at Laidley's office a few days later, Johnson stated Esparza and his company wanted twenty to thirty percent of the northern area of the South Central-Harbor franchise for his company in return for his support of our application.

We were dumbfounded. Thirty percent of the South Central-Harbor franchise carved out for Esparza? As far as we were concerned, Esparza had no technical skills that could be of *any* benefit to us, and we didn't need his money. The price of his "support" was unconscionable.

Johnson also said Wilkins and SYNCOM wanted to cut the size of the franchise to facilitate the funding Wilkins could get, and now Esparza wanted about thirty percent of the deal.

"So as a government official, you're representing the interests of Wilkins and Esparza! Anyone else?" Carl fumed as he looked at Johnson. Johnson just smirked, folded his hands, and stayed silent.

Edgar and Carl strongly opposed any division of the franchise and stormed out of the meeting. The division of the franchise seemed to be another ruse to delay the actual franchising for South Central. It had now become clear that Johnson was working his own program in regards to cable television.

After finding out about Johnson's and Laidley's plan to hijack the franchise process, Carl and I met for a drink. Carl was so mad I could almost see all the veins pulsing in his neck. I asked Carl to give me a visual picture of Johnson, since I had never met him.

"He's a medium-height, brown-skinned, swarthy, bearded man in his mid-thirties." In a doctor's fashion, as if he were doing a physical assessment, Carl continued, "He's got sharp angular features and a full beard. He always looks angry and his large eyes seem to be without pupils." Once I met Johnson, I saw Carl's description was very apt.

Carl also summarized his opinion of Johnson's behavior. "He looks like all he's doing is training to be a bigger politician."

Carl frowned. "I know a few more things. We're cutting ties with Esparza." Carl looked determined as he continued, "He's not going to get anymore information from us. The same goes for Wilkins."

Carl recognized these other men were really working for Johnson.

———◆———

Carl and Edgar met with Esparza to inform him that his technical and financial support would not be needed. Period.

Carl and Edgar also felt that it was important to maintain the South Central-Harbor franchise in its current state to avoid future delays—no more talks about cutting it into smaller pieces.

———◆———

On July 20, 1979, Johnson called a "cooling off" meeting with Esparza, Carl, and Edgar at the offices of Pierpont Laidley. Esparza arrived late. During his absence, Carl and Edgar met with Johnson and Laidley.

Carl and Edgar continued to express their displeasure with the concept of working with a group of MESBICs, instead of working with Six Star to arrange financing for the franchise construction. Six Star's financing had already been approved for the Hollywood-Wilshire franchise in the City of Los Angeles, and no one in city government had any problem with Six Star's arrangements before dealing with the South Central franchise.

Carl and Edgar identified that working with one company, such as Six Star, was preferable to working with ten or more different MESBICs. Six Star had already financed a number of successful existing franchises and retained numerous strong banking contacts.

Johnson became agitated with Carl and Edgar as they continued to express their dissatisfaction with the MESBIC financing idea.

"I'm not going to sit here and listen to this," Johnson bellowed. Johnson warned Carl and Edgar as he wagged his hand, "Farrell says you need to go along with MESBIC financing because you and your company are *asking for a political favor* in all this...or you and your company are out. No Six Star." The position had been previously insinuated but never stated overtly.

To be clear, according to Johnson, who was employed as a representative of Councilman Farrell and Los Angeles city government, Carl and Edgar needed to agree to Johnson's terms or Johnson and Laidley would continue in the process and cut Edgar and Carl out entirely.

"Here's the deal." Johnson's proposal called for Carl and Edgar to split forty percent of the company between the two of them. The remaining sixty percent would be split between Johnson, Laidley, and *an unnamed third party*. Could the third party be a councilman or someone else in city government?

From that time forward, the tone of the conversation with Johnson and Laidley *did* lead us to believe the unnamed third party was actually Councilman Robert Farrell, although no such direct statement was ever made.

Sixty percent for them and forty percent for us?

This was the first time Johnson and Laidley had directly expressed their desire to receive *any* interest, much less controlling interest, in our cable television application. Carl quickly raised the obvious "conflict of interest" question, clearly prohibiting Johnson, as Councilman Farrell's deputy and an employee of the City of Los Angeles, from having an ownership position in a city-sponsored licensing process. With no honor among thieves, Laidley agreed that Johnson did have a conflict of interest but he, Laidley, Farrell's attorney, did not.

Undeterred by our objections, the two men also proposed dividing the South Central-Harbor franchise into *three separate areas*: Boyle Heights, South Central, and Wilmington-San Pedro.

"You already know about Boyle Heights. It borders Esparza's Buena Vista Television's (BVT) Los Angeles County franchise and Wilmington-San Pedro will be a no-profit nightmare when we separate it from everything else, so we'll just bid that out to anyone who wants it," Johnson said.

Esparza arrived as these "divisions" were being discussed. Esparza proposed he should receive an area larger than "just Boyle Heights."

The Boyle Heights area would consist of approximately 15,000 homes out of the approximately 250,000 homes in the South Central-Harbor franchise area. "Why only these specific 15,000 homes?" Edgar asked.

"These additional homes help my Los Angeles County franchise," Esparza replied. Two years earlier, Esparza had already received a cable franchise from Los Angeles County under the name of Buena Vista Television, and these additional homes from Boyle Heights were contiguous to his existing franchise. Esparza was, at the time of this conversation, in default on his Los Angeles County cable television franchise. He had built nothing in two years.

———————

After Esparza left the meeting, Johnson and Laidley rejected Esparza's idea for a larger franchise area other than Boyle Heights.

When Carl and Edgar asked for their reasoning and more details, neither Johnson nor Laidley would explain their reasoning behind excluding the Wilmington-San Pedro area in this conversation.

While they were talking, Carl surmised that the Wilmington-San Pedro partitioning had to do with Herb Wilkins's idea for reducing the size the franchise. *What other plans did they have? Could these men really carve out franchises and railroad the process?*

We needed more information, so Carl tried to broaden the discussion.

Carl asked to have Councilman Gilbert Lindsay join the discussions. Lindsay was the senior black City Councilman in the City of Los Angeles and his district was also impacted by the South Central-Harbor cable franchise area. Carl hoped Councilman

Lindsay would object to Johnson, Laidley, and Esparza's brazen "reapportionment" ideas.

Johnson's reply to Carl's suggestion was succinct and rude. "Lindsay's old and we can control him."

———◆———

On July 26, 1979, the Council approved the Notice of Sale for the *entire* South Central-Harbor area, and set September 26, 1979, as the date to receive applications. In the course of normal Los Angeles City business, the approved Notice of Sale meant no application could be accepted before September 26, 1979.

Now that the formal application date had been set, Carl and Edgar, who had expressed their intention to apply for the franchise, knew when they could submit their application.

———◆———

On August 2, 1979, Laidley called Carl and informed him he and Johnson were "putting a *new* group together" since Edgar and Carl would not accept their terms given at the July 26, 1979, meeting. *Would the "new" group still contain the deputy for a Los Angeles City Councilman and the councilman's lawyer?*

We wanted to stay as far away as possible from these men who represented themselves as "men of the people" but who were willfully subverting the franchise rules and ethics of the City of Los Angeles.

As Carl would later describe it, "It seems like a bad script from a black-and-white movie." But in fact, we were to find out later, this was everyday insider politics in Los Angeles.

"I don't know but it seems like this could easily end up as a criminal matter, if we don't watch our step," I cautioned Carl. As a CPA, I was extremely concerned about the illegality of government employees being paid by applicants for franchises.

"If we're able to state our case with our programming ideas and solid financial and technical backing, I think we should stay in the application process," Carl said.

I wasn't going to leave him alone in the process.

———•———

On August 9, 1979, another new cable company, Community Telecommunications, Inc., (CTI) submitted a letter to Councilman Farrell asking for the division of the South Central-Harbor franchise area into three new franchise areas. *The very same division of the franchise Johnson and Laidley had proposed on July 29?* Yes, the very same proposal in every aspect.

A Mr. Robert Davidson had signed the CTI letter. This was the first time we had heard of Robert Davidson. Davidson, we were told, supposedly owned a small paint manufacturing company in East Los Angeles. In subsequent franchise hearings, Davidson identified himself as a friend of Channing Johnson.

Davidson never appeared in any hearing or meeting without Johnson and never really spoke. Johnson was *still* a city employee at the time the CTI letter was submitted. Was Davidson the surrogate for Johnson in all filings and documents while Johnson continued in his position as a city employee in Councilman Farrell's office?

"Let's see who's in CTI," Carl said. "We can check with the Secretary of State" he added.

A review of the records of the Secretary of State of California indicates CTI was *not formed until September 18, 1979*—over a month after the letter was submitted to Councilman Farrell. The City and County of Los Angeles and its taxpayers had been duped. A company that *did not exist* submitted a letter to reconfigure a Los Angeles city franchise map.

———•———

About that time, Edgar heard Johnson was going to resign as Councilman Farrell's deputy. "Seems Johnson's finally passed the bar exam or something."

"Johnson might be leaving Councilman Farrell's office but he's still got the power of being a former deputy," Carl replied.

For the next decade, after his resignation from office, Johnson's name would always appear in conjunction with the South Central franchise. So would Pierpont Laidley, as shareholder and a director at CTI.

On August 13, 1979, BVT submitted a letter to Councilman Farrell asking for the division of the South Central-Harbor area into three new franchise areas. The boundaries of the franchise areas were exactly the same as the boundaries contained in the August 9 CTI letter. The letter was signed by Moctesuma Esparza.

Upon inspection, the "boundary change" letters submitted by CTI and BVT consisted of little more than a one-page letter and a map asking for the franchise area to be divided. One company, CTI, did not legally exist, and the other, BVT, had no employees and was in default of requirements to start building its Los Angeles County cable television franchise.

Interestingly enough, there are no records to indicate that any official, department, or employee of the City of Los Angeles checked to identify the existence or viability of CTI or BVT in their presentations or requests for franchise changes affecting 250,000 homes and more than half a million people!

"I've looked at the maps with the CTI and BVT submission letter and the division would mean ninety-nine per cent of the black population in the area would end up in the South Central franchise," I said.

"You mean it's segregation all over again!" Edgar gasped.

"Can they do that?" Carl asked. "In this day and age?"

"They can do whatever the city council and mayor want to do. Whether it is legal or not is another story. We'll have to see what the city council does," I replied.

At the August 13, 1979 meeting of Los Angeles City Council, with the applications due for submission for the South Central-Harbor franchise due soon thereafter (on September 26, 1979), Councilman Farrell and Councilman David Cunningham introduced a motion to rescind the published Notice of Sale of July 16, 1979. There was little discussion and the council voted to rescind its previous Notice of Sale on the South Central-Harbor cable franchise area.

It was as if the clock was legislatively turned back, the slate was wiped clean, and no one and nothing had happened—except CTI and BVT had the benefits of our knowledge and expertise to continue their scheming...and the South Central cable franchise was to be resegregated!

———◆———

Carl, Edgar, and I met to evaluate our business plan in light of these changes. Fortunately, Skulsky and Six Star were still willing to participate with our deal, despite the franchise border changes and the threats from Johnson. We were encouraged with Six Star's loyalty and hoped to overcome the insider dealing we saw going on at City Hall.

"We'll just keep going," Skulsky said. "There are several next steps. The cable application has to go before the Department of Transportation and the Board of Transportation Commissioners."

———◆———

On September 21, 1979, the DOT, in a complete change of previous protocol, issued "new" recommendations to the BTC. DOT recommended the South Central-Harbor franchise area be divided into three separate franchise areas.

According to the DOT report, "*Both applications* have agreed on a boundary line for the franchises." "Both" referred to CTI and BVT. What about our application—or any others?

We were speechless. The application date had not even arrived. The actual applications would exceed 350 pages each! How did a one-page letter from two potential franchise candidates constitute an application—and a change in boundaries?

"Can they do that?" Carl exclaimed.

"I'll check with my legal department," Skulsky said. "But my feeling is that the City thinks they can...or they can hold up the process even longer."

"I've seen it done before in other cases, not franchising ones, mind you. But they throw you out of the process if you file suit in court," Edgar remarked.

Throw us out? Court?

"OK. Let me check with the attorneys before we say anything more publicly," Skulsky replied.

———◆———

On September 26, 1979, it became official, the Los Angeles City Council voted to accept a motion to separate the South Central-Harbor area into three franchises—designed exactly as Channing Johnson and Pierpont Laidley intended.

Individuals working in the offices of elected officials were now going from *regulator* to *direct competitor/owner* in an area where they were responsible to legislate city business. In our case, we were directed to a government official under the guise that he would provide assistance in dealing with the government bureaucracy. The same government employee who had the job to regulate us as a company was now competing with us.

———◆———

In the days after this splitting of the South Central-Harbor franchise area, we asserted to everyone and anyone who would listen that splitting the franchise was an illegal attempt to cut our company and Six Star out of the process and amounted to a step back toward segregation.

"How was the legislative segregation of the South Central cable franchise any different than the prior legislative segregation accomplished in Mississippi or Alabama?" we contended.

The entire process indicated these actions were not in the interest of free enterprise, the black citizens of South Central, or the greater City of Los Angeles; these tactics only delayed accessing the technology that was readily available in most of other communities.

———◆———

Leaving the serious moral issues of the government activities aside, competitively, our company couldn't allow this illegal process by city officials to continue. Our bid, along with our business, would be dead—and so would our plans for the South Central community. It was time to reevaluate and reassess our objectives. "I know we don't have much time between us with my work as a doctor and you in your securities work," Carl began. "But we've got to get into the South Central neighborhood, the offices of any available media, and everywhere else we think might help to tell everyone what's happening here."

"Don't forget we've got Megavision," I replied, wondering how to carve out time for this new strategy.

"I think we should close the store if we're going pursue cable television," Carl replied.

In November 1979, we closed Megavision.

Chapter Two

The Cheaters Continue The Setup

Now that we had committed ourselves to the cable television industry, we fought to publicize what had now become city law. We started to spotlight what we thought was the illegal and unethical behavior of all the elected officials and their associates; tracking the political moves in breaking up the South Central-Harbor franchise area, which was so wrong on many levels.

We stated that Councilmen Farrell and Cunningham were instrumental in the resegregation and isolation of black citizens of the franchise area into a new area known as the South Central cable franchise. When had a government for the true benefit of the black community segregated black people from the larger community? Never. And we vowed to fight to rectify this "artificial segregation."

In answer to our company's objections on this issue of "artificial segregation" or "resegregation," black politicians continued to say this action was undertaken to give minorities a chance to put together an application.

The disingenuous intent of the members of the Los Angeles City Council, and especially Councilmen Farrell and Cunningham, would become abundantly clear, as South Central was treated differently from any other franchise area for cable television by the City of Los Angeles.

———◆———

At the Los Angeles City Council hearing on September 26, 1979, we made the councilpersons in attendance aware of three things. First, that Councilman Farrell's deputy, Channing Johnson, and the councilman's personal attorney, Pierpont Laidley, had told us they wanted sixty percent of *our* franchise deal with no business plan or financing of their own. Second, we explained that when we, another minority-owned company with a viable business plan and financing for the entire area, refused to agree with their plan, the franchise was broken into three parts. This is what had been threatened by Johnson and Laidley. Finally, we reminded them that the winning plans were promoted and adopted without dispute or investigation by the Los Angeles City Council.

So everyone knew all the facts, on the record.

We also made it known that the division of Boyle Heights was economically unviable. With only 15,000 possible subscriber homes in the franchise area, the only possible successful business alternative, with this forced division, was to join this newly-legislated area with some other franchise. The only company interested would be the one Esparza owned: a Los Angeles County cable franchise for East Los Angeles County exactly bordering the Boyle Heights franchise opportunity, and owned by the same person who submitted the "other" one-page letter asking for the South Central-Harbor franchise to be divided into three franchises.

——◆——

There was no response from the Los Angeles City Council. This—their silence—was how the setup was assisted by elected officials.

——◆——

We were now learning, first hand, how the *real* legislative process worked in the City of Los Angeles and wanted everyone to know on the public record how things were run as well.

They didn't think we would object because they deluded themselves by thinking they were the law and could alter things as they saw fit, and that they could use the size, legal staff, and money of the City of Los Angeles to hold off any objections in the court system.

——◆——

Now a wider concern presented itself. The committee hearings were coming up. Just how dishonest were the supervising departments and committees?

"Since they've changed the franchise boundaries, I'm concerned about DOT rejecting our applications. I don't want our company to be added to the pile," Carl said.

In another troublesome move, DOT also changed their policies to endorse the three-franchise idea for the South Central-Harbor cable franchise. Inexplicably, DOT began discussions with two applicants—CTI and BVT—before the application process was started, saying, "Both applicants have agreed on a common boundary dividing the original area."

The decision to describe CTI and BVT as "applicants" was a true stretch of the imagination since each company had only submitted a one-page letter, as opposed to an actual application required by law and past action, which generally required 300 to 400 pages.

Changes implemented by Councilmen Farrell and Cunningham at the city council level were endorsed by DOT, which changed its procedures and policies.

"Their report doesn't help matters," Edgar said.

According to the DOT report, "BVT currently holds a Los Angeles County franchise, in an area adjacent to the area they are requesting. The company has indicated that the city and county franchises will provide a total area sufficient in size to provide for a viable cable television system." The DOT report neglected two important facts: (1) BVT had failed to construct the franchise for two years, and (2) BVT was currently in default on its Los Angeles County franchise.

This DOT acknowledgement indicated that the Boyle Heights franchise was not viable by itself and could only survive with the existing Los Angeles County franchise that had been awarded to BVT. DOT providing a special franchise area for a company that had defaulted on a continuous county franchise seemed contrary to the best interests of the citizens of that area and the City of Los Angeles.

The assumption that DOT was an impartial independent evaluator of the information was suspect before the application process even got underway.

———————

The challenge was clear. In political power and maneuvering, our company was way behind. So, the race was on to assemble the political and financial power necessary for constructing a cable franchise covering more than half a million people.

Carl told me he was going to need my direct involvement after watching the actions of Councilmen Farrell and Cunningham—and Farrell's deputy Channing Johnson. "It's going to take a lot more time," Carl said.

"Staying in this process is going to eliminate any free time we had," I agreed. This was going to be my second full-time job.

On the other hand, Johnson, Laidley, and Esparza had played their patronage cards and now they needed to show the business acumen and financing ability to make their own application a reality. We thought they were behind in business and financing know-how and we were behind in gaining patronage.

"Can this be more fun? Let's make this happen," Edgar remarked.

We gained many relationships that became important in our attempt to enter the cable television business. Carl and I met our lawyer, Ted Eagans, through his brother Jesse, who'd come to my company's Beverly Hills office and wanted to discuss financial leveraging techniques. This Marine veteran impressed me with his knowledge but he lacked the resources and licensing expertise to implement his financial plans—a common occurrence in black America.

"Sometimes, it is better to be lucky than good," Ted Eagans said, as he started working on our team. Eagans's knowledge of the players in the political process was crucial because he was a native of Los Angeles and familiar with the local political history—and we were not.

Ted introduced us to two men who would become integral parts of our cable company: Perry C. Parks, a seventy-five-year-old retired postal supervisor, and Albert Watson, a South Central meatpacker, both well-known and respected people in the South Central community. Although Perry Parks asked us to call him by his first name, I could never do it out of my admiration for him. The best I could do was to shorten his name to Mr. P. Mr. Parks, as a more than forty-year South Central resident, never let us forget that our first and foremost responsibility was the well-being of the South Central community, and any financial gain was always secondary to the needs of the community. Mr. Parks represented the consummate community activist. When we met him, he devoted his great energy working tirelessly for political candidates who gained his respect. Every politician in the Democratic Party of Los Angeles—and the Republican Party, as well—knew Perry Parks.

In December 1979, Ted introduced us to Albert "Al" Watson. Al owned a South Central meat processing plant, which employed 200 people. Watson needed help with tax concerns and Ted asked me, as a CPA, to assist him.

When Al Watson decided to join our fight, he said, "You know why I'm in this with you?" He smiled broadly. "If South Central and the other minority neighborhoods can't get the same flow of information as the rest of the city, that's just another form of discrimination, in my book." His smile faded. "And it pains me that it's all at the hands of our black mayor and his cronies down at city hall." He pointed his finger around his office. "We care about a free marketplace and we've worked at it all our lives, some longer than others. But we also care about freedom and money coming into the neighborhood to keep those freedoms and opportunities alive. Am I right?"

"Without free speech, there can only be the appearance of freedom," Mr. Parks said.

"Knew that *all* in the South when I was a boy." He waved his long-fingered hand. "All secrets and hidden agendas kept by those white judges and politicians."

"Don't get me started about here in Los Angeles. If it's not those downtown messing with things, it's the gangs starting to take hold and messing things up," Al Watson said. "They don't care about anything long-term. They're stuck on stupid." His arm slashed the air. "Big money for a while, if they don't get killed. If they get caught and go to prison, it's like a leash around their neck for the rest of their lives, taking down everyone and everything close to them."

"Can't get a job, let alone a future and some security like my career at the post office," Mr. Parks agreed.

"Stuck, and a prisoner of the government dole or the illegal system. Do men really want that?" Mr. Watson asked.

"No," Mr. Parks said. "They get frustrated and burn the place up like they did in Watts in 1965."

"Seeds of discontent planted by poverty or all those politicians messing things up in city hall—both as bad, both the same," Mr. Watson replied.

I was happy these men saw what needed to be done but I wanted some clarification of Mr. Watson's point concerning money. We wanted to plow a lot of our profits into programming, so the decision of how much money to return to the owners of the invested money needed to be clarified. Like Mr. Parks, we were interested in the benefits of what programming could do for the neighborhood.

"Maximization of profit is not always your best return on investment. This is especially true when you are black and you always remember the stories of your father about the treatment of black Americans in Alabama from the '20s though the early 1950s. Here in South Central...the color of the skin has changed from white to black," I said.

"Clint's got the statistics," Carl said. "We're interested in *financing* programming for the neighborhood...in many different areas."

"We understand that," Mr. Parks said, and Mr. Watson nodded. "Now, what's the statistics you want to talk about? Want to share them with the people from the neighborhood."

I swallowed and started talking. "The rule of thumb is, a new job is created for every $10,000 of capital invested in a new business enterprise. In addition, three additional jobs are created to support the new job. A $50 million investment would, at a minimum, create 5,000 new jobs within a community that has long suffered the highest unemployment rate in the city."

"So, with our figures, the 5,000 new jobs created by direct capital investment would in turn create 15,000 additional jobs for goods and services within the community. This would represent a total of 20,000 jobs created by a capital investment of $50 million for putting the cable system in the ground," Carl mentioned, keeping the topic going.

"That's impressive considering we've been told the unemployment rate for some neighborhoods in South Central has ranged from fifteen percent to twenty percent lately," Mr. Parks said.

"It will get higher quickly if something isn't done," Carl replied.

"The creation of an additional 20,000 jobs in a poverty-stricken community represents potentially life-changing situations, as more families would have been able to support themselves through new employment opportunities within their own community. These newly created jobs, which could not be easily outsourced, would exist mainly in the semi-skilled area, with additional positions requiring as little as a high school diploma," I said. "These were *good entry-level jobs* that will be created within a community based on capital invested by members of the community."

"Impressive," Mr. Parks commended. "We will show the powers that be that we can create jobs in our own community without government money."

"He's done his homework," Mr. Watson said. "That matches my figures and I'm satisfied."

We all kept talking. We were all enthusiastic agreeing about the cable franchise opportunity. "Now let's talk about my relationship with Councilman Lindsay," Al Watson said.

"Everyone goes down to city hall, hat in hand, to ask for things," Mr. Parks said. "If we don't get some political clout, all the stuff about programming for South Central will stay a pipe dream."

Mr. Watson rubbed his chin. "Johnson, Laidley, and the councilmen are showing they're ready to play hardball."

"We've got to gain some influence in the city council or we're through," I admitted. It seemed quite obvious after all the in-roads and changes Johnson, Laidley, and Esparza had obtained through their political influence. "We won't have a chance otherwise."

Mr. Watson would talk to Councilman Lindsay, introduce me, and find out if Lindsay was interested in our franchise efforts, objectives, and programming ideas. This *might* give our company another chance in getting the South Central franchise area.

Councilmen Farrell and Cunningham successfully had divided the South Central-Harbor franchise, belittling and negating Councilman Gilbert Lindsay, whose district now contained a substantial portion of the "new" South Central franchise. *Was Johnson right when he said "they" could control Councilman Lindsay?*

———————

In late December 1979, Al Watson arranged a meeting with Councilman Lindsay and our group.

Councilman Lindsay, a smallish man in his mid-seventies, controlled one of the richest financial districts in the City of Los Angeles. While the residential portion of the district was comprised of mostly low- and middle-income African-Americans, the downtown portion of Los Angeles was going through a major commercial redevelopment and building phase.

We explained the cable television industry to Councilman Lindsay and the ongoing delays in providing service to South Central. Councilman Lindsay became concerned, saying he never heard anything about this important technology coming to his district and its implications.

Then we explained we had previously talked with Councilman Farrell and Channing Johnson about developing the South Central-Harbor cable franchise and how the franchise was now in three pieces.

"They've left me out!" Lindsay became infuriated. He now knew Councilmen Farrell and Johnson had gone behind his back to take resources from his district without even the consideration of discussing the matter with him.

As Lindsay stated, with his Southern drawl, "They didn't even buy me a cup of coffee."

Councilman Lindsay explained he would like to help us but the size of the cable franchise deal was so small compared to the high-rises being developed in his downtown district he could not commit too much time to our effort. "Takes lots of jawboning...and it might not get you much."

While the deal was a large deal to us, the new high-rise construction in downtown Los Angeles would cost millions of dollars, generate business dollars and jobs, and be Lindsay's primary focus and legacy in downtown Los Angeles.

We told Lindsay about our deal with Six Star and he was impressed that we were working with an existing and operating cable television company. When we showed Lindsay a copy of the December 17, 1979, front-page story from *Variety*, the entertainment industry daily publication, the *Variety* headline on page one read, "Six Star Becoming Big Cable Force." Publicity from such an important source went a long way in getting Lindsay committed.

"Think I know what's wrong. Not much money going down to their districts in comparison to downtown," Lindsay explained, referring to Farrell and Cunningham. "They're jealous and thought they could ignore me on this."

Councilmen Farrell and Cunningham had little economic development occurring in their districts and this cable opportunity constituted a major chance for business and money for them and their districts. But they hadn't paid attention soon enough.

"There's another reason I want to help you." Councilman Lindsay went on to say that in all his years at the Council, he had never been able to assist a black person in obtaining any significant economic venture in the South Central area. Lindsay explained he had been on the Los Angeles City Council for nearly twenty years and no major project had ever gone to a black-controlled company. *Twenty years*.

According to Lindsay numerous minority entrepreneurs had come to city hall with great ideas but no capital. Lindsay now understood that we had the capital and the time for the technology had arrived. "Exciting! Exciting!" Lindsay said.

We told Councilman Lindsay we understood his limited time commitment and reiterated that, with his help, we might be able to bring cable television to South Central to improve the economic and social conditions within the community.

"I'd *really* like to do that," Lindsay replied. He sat and continued to listen carefully.

In our conversation, Councilman Lindsay could see we had no political connections within the Los Angeles city political structure. "You won't get anywhere without help from someone on the Council."

Councilman Lindsay started to help immediately. "Call me Gil and use that name when you're talking about me or need something from someone around here, so they'll know, too."

Lindsay arranged for additional meetings with other members of the Council, so that we could inform them of our plans for South Central. Among the meetings arranged by Lindsay was John Ferraro, President of the Los Angeles City Council. Lindsay also arranged meetings with Pat Russell, who we would see later was on the City Council Industry and Economic Development, the subcommittee that was responsible for the regulation of cable television. We also met with Peggy Stevenson, another councilwoman.

After our meeting with Mrs. Stevenson, and telling her about dealing with Channing Johnson, she said that she was obligated to call the district attorney and the police department. Mrs. Stevenson said the behavior of Johnson appeared to be in violation of the law regarding persons working for elected officials.

The LAPD assigned two detectives to investigate Channing Johnson and Councilman Farrell. We were interviewed by Detectives Domino and Ramirez. The LAPD provided a report to the district attorney's political crimes division. The district attorney would close the case because Johnson and Councilman Farrell refused to assist the investigation by the district attorney, according to an internal memo obtained from the district attorney.

———

We were somewhat dismayed when Councilman Lindsay offered us a list of people who he thought might be interested in investing in the cable television opportunity. *Was this standard practice?*

We explained we already had the business plan and financing necessary with a current franchisee, Six Star, who was already doing cable television business in the City of Los Angeles.

Out of respect, we accepted the list of potential shareholders Councilman Lindsay asked us to consider because of their interest in investing in city projects and their political influence downtown. "It's the way things are done here," Lindsay said. *But was it right? Was this the kind of behavior the constituents of these councilmen expected?*

At the top of Councilman Lindsay's list was the name Danny Bakewell. As Lindsay explained to us, little got done in the black community if Danny Bakewell was not involved. According to Councilman Lindsay, Bakewell was Mayor Bradley's boy. "You know what I mean," he winked.

From our life-long experience within black communities, we knew Councilman Lindsay meant Bakewell was one of the "good old boys" who had the mayor on his side and the ear of Mayor Tom Bradley on issues concerning the black community and beyond.

Lindsay went on to say it would be very difficult, even as a councilman, to make any venture happen in South Central without the support and approval of Mayor Bradley.

"Don't let the black fool you," Councilman Lindsay said. The fact that Bradley was black did not mean that he had an interest or concern for the black community. Lindsay would explain that even though Bradley was black, he had done little for the black community.

———◆———

We started on the list. As Lindsay suggested, we contacted Bakewell and informed him Councilman Gil Lindsay had asked us to call him regarding cable television. His representative informed us that Bakewell had already been contacted by Channing Johnson and agreed to work with their group.

We met with Lindsay again and told him Bakewell was aligned with Johnson. "That's a problem but we'll keep working," Lindsay said.

Despite the added difficulty involving the allegiance of the mayor's friend, Councilman Lindsay said, "I like your plans for the South Central franchise and what it could mean to the community."

———◆———

Now, with Councilman Lindsay's support in our franchising attempt, Councilmen Farrell and Cunningham might not get their way in changing any more of the franchising process, as they had done in September 1979.

Secondly, Councilman Lindsay began to make inquiries of Councilmen Farrell and Cunningham about their behavior regarding the division of the franchise without consulting him. As the most senior black councilman, Lindsay felt he deserved the respect of at least being consulted regarding something that could have such an impact upon the residents of his district. "You'd better not do it again. I may be older but I've got a sharp, long memory."

At the same time we were trying to block Councilmen Farrell's and Cunningham's hijacking of the franchising process with Lindsay's influence, there were other aspects of the process where we wanted to stay ahead of the other applicants. We spent large amounts of time heavily involved in understanding the cable television industry and the technology required to implement our business plan. We met frequently with the Six Star Cablevision engineers trying to increase our knowledge of this emergent technology and the cable industry.

———◆———

"I think we need to submit applications for every franchise we can in the City and the County of Los Angeles," I said.

"Why should we waste our time on the small cities and Wilmington and Boyle Heights when it's South Central we're interested in?" Mr. Watson asked.

Due to the instability of the situation in the City of Los Angeles and the programming opportunities we envisioned, Edgar and Carl agreed they wanted our cable television company to develop a broad cable service plan. If our other strategies failed and we couldn't win the political battle for the South Central license, we could get *county franchises* near South Central and enter South Central as a competing cable company.

"We might be able to get something going in Compton or another small suburb but I hear they're a mess down there...and they're trying to be as corrupt as they are here in the City of Los Angeles," Mr. Parks remarked. "Can't tell the gangs on the street from the elected 'gangs' in their city halls."

"If you think it will help, let's try." Mr. Watson shrugged. "Just more paper and a few trips up and down the freeway."

To fulfill this goal, we filed applications for franchises in the City of Compton, the City of Inglewood, and various unincorporated sections of Los Angeles County contiguous to the South Central franchise.

Just as Mr. Parks predicted, we found elected officials in these adjacent communities acted like the politicians serving the City of Los Angeles. Once again, elected officials had no understanding of cable television, and seemingly little concern for the benefits they could bring to the citizens of the community beyond their own re-elections and influence. Their main concerns were the effect on their campaign contributions and their future political aspirations.

We were told the process of awarding the franchise in Compton was done without even bothering to open the application packages for anyone other than the successful bidder. The successful applicant was a garbage company.

Mr. Watson's inside sources were correct. After the Compton franchise was awarded, we examined our application, which had never been unsealed from the time it was filed with the City of Compton. "Well, that was a bust," Mr. Watson remarked with blunt sarcasm.

"Taking Compton to court is our only avenue there," Mr. Parks said. "Do we have the time?"

"I'd like to but it would take too many resources to dispute Compton's corruption and the application process," I admitted.

"Let's focus our efforts on South Central," Carl said. "South Central's in three pieces and worrying about Compton and Inglewood would only reduce our resources. I say that's the right strategy and there's no turning back at this point." Carl looked at me and took a deep breath. "All future dealings with the City of Los Angeles will probably be adversarial. This could all end up in court so let's save our time and save our dollars with facing one opponent instead of several."

"That's a sad, daunting prospect but we have to be smart," Mr. Parks said with a sigh.

We didn't want to go to court, but we wanted the award of the cable television system to be done in accordance with the laws of the city as well as compliance with the Constitution of the United States.

"Gotta' serve South Central somehow with this, " Al Watson replied.

Mr. Watson was right. We wanted to serve South Central as the largest black cable television franchise area west of the Mississippi. We felt South Central could act as a pivotal element for the development of programming especially targeted to address the needs and concerns of Black America. Without a distribution conduit we knew we'd have no ability to implement our ambitious programming for the neighborhood.

Carl ran his hand over his face, and then looked at his notes. He located the calendar. "Our next hurdle is the Board of Transportation Commissioners in October."

———◆———

On October 25, 1979, the Board of Transportation Commissioners (BTC) approved the division of the South Central franchise under the guise they had been promoting—this "change" would give minorities an opportunity to become involved the cable television ownership of South Central. As we'd seen before, the wheels of the government bureaucracy could move quickly and in the direction the politicians wanted when someone inside city hall wanted something.

———◆———

On November 9, 1979, the city council approved the division of the South Central- Harbor franchise.

With this decision, the Council had decided for the third time in 1979 that they would delay the application process. Councilmen Farrell and Cunningham were principally responsible for these delays. This meant the process of meetings, hearings, and applications would be tripled. Progress for South Central would be delayed again.

"Things need to be started now in the neighborhood!" Al Watson fumed.

As we all knew, the educational levels in South Central were the lowest within the City of Los Angeles. The deprivation of this lower-cost technology, as indicated in our argument of cable versus computer, meant the deprivation of information and educational opportunities that could be delivered by electronic media via the cheaper cable television system—a technology available to most of the city and the county at this crucial time.

"What a needless waste of time," Mr. Parks said, shaking his head.

"Nothing to be done. The city council's had a long history of deferring to the councilmen from the effected areas," Councilman Lindsay said. "Not the right ground where we can stop them."

By blocking cable television in South Central, elected officials and their staffs made it clear they were willing to sell out the best interests of an entire race of people in Los Angeles area. Those people directly affected by their maneuvering were black people, the same race as Johnson and Laidley.

———

The setup perpetrated by Channing Johnson and Councilman Farrell was now complete. The next step was to see if they could back up their setup with an actual franchise award.

Chapter Three

Applications Hustle

As the 1980s loomed ahead, the influence of cable television that Carl predicted dawned in Los Angeles and other towns and cities in the nation.

We took what we had learned independently and from our partners at Six Star, to organize our plan and resources to write our cable application for South Central Los Angeles. Beyond the need for expert and legal advice, we remained entrenched in an all-encompassing war with the machinations and the complications of dealing with local politics.

— ◆ —

On December 15, 1979, our plans, and especially Carl's life, were thrown into turmoil by the power of the television media. That Sunday evening, in a segment of the popular CBS News program *60 Minutes*, Dan Rather falsely accused Carl, in his work as a doctor, of aiding insurance fraud.

Carl was totally blindsided, unjustly accused of a felony on national television, with no chance to defend himself before the broadcast. To be very clear, Carl never met with Mr. Rather, nor was he contacted by Mr. Rather or any representative of Mr. Rather, *60 Minutes*, or CBS before these slanderous accusations were broadcast for everyone to hear that December evening.

Carl was accused by *60 Minutes* of signing fraudulent insurance claims to bilk insurance companies when he worked part-time at a medical clinic for only several months. With those accusations, Carl's reputation had been ruined in one hour. Those sixty minutes—just one hour for Mr. Rather and his team at CBS—would mean a lifetime of needless repercussions for Carl.

The false allegations led to a lawsuit by Carl against CBS, *60 Minutes*, and Dan Rather as well as years of trying to regain his good name. The case would be one the first trials carried from beginning to end on CNN. Those false charges created great damage to his career and reputation, expensive years in court to try to clear his name, and unnecessary strain on his family, financial resources, and health to fight accusations that would come back time and again to affect his career.

"We're with you on this, Carl," Mr. Parks said. "Just tell us what we can do."

"Damn shame they'll come and mess with a man's life like that." Mr. Watson paced up and down the floor. "Must be something to do about it."

———

While still reeling from answering personal and professional inquiries, and as all of our family members and friends made every effort to proclaim Carl's complete innocence and save his career, another tragedy struck.

In the second week of January 1980, Edgar Charles was killed in Las Vegas, Nevada. In a freak stage accident, while Edgar was working on a charity benefit show, he was crushed by equipment meant for the exhibition.

———◆———

For the first time in his life, Carl admitted he felt completely overwhelmed. I couldn't blame him.

We gave very serious consideration to ending our involvement in the cable television application process. I could see on Carl's face the weight of the upcoming legal proceedings against CBS and his grief concerning Edgar's death. "Should we go on with this?" Carl asked.

I didn't want to disturb his thought process. I could see he had something more to say.

Carl asked another question. "What are the chances that one of the two principals on a minority cable television project would be accused of a felony by a major American television network while the other would die in a freak accident in a thirty-day time span?"

I looked at Carl silently because I did not have an answer to either question. I was asking myself questions as well. *Had the* 60 Minutes *supposed exposé merely been a coincidence?*

Carl looked at me and told me that if we were going to go on with the cable franchise application, "Clint, you're going to have to take charge of the *entire cable business.*"

I understood. Carl couldn't take the time now to have primary responsibility for our cable television application. He had a full-time medical practice, a wife, three children, and the horrid prospect of dealing with a lawsuit against CBS and *60 Minutes*.

"I'll do whatever you need," I replied.

Our emotions and family life were being rocked by grief for both of us and professional chaos for Carl. What would I do with this cable opportunity?

I was only twenty-eight years of age, and yet I'd been given the responsibility to manage a company that could make a dramatic difference in the quality of life of so many people in South Central.

Since I was used to working in the international accounting and investment banking fields, I felt I was capable of the cable franchise responsibilities, especially in financial matters. If we decided to continue pursuing this cable television franchise opportunity, I was ready.

But it was one thing to deal in a quantifiable commodity such as dollars, and it was another thing to deal with a completely arbitrary political system. Dealing with a Los Angeles city bureaucracy, which sought to deny the rights of qualified black people to participate in the development of new technology, would not be an easy task. It was a case of fighting city hall for our rights.

With a flash of humor, Carl quickly reminded me I had claimed a fifty-percent interest in the cable television project in the spring of 1979, after he convinced me of this "great opportunity" in cable television. "Remember?"

This was, of course, before we became aware of the Los Angeles City Hall shenanigans and how Councilmen Farrell and Cunningham and Channing Johnson, in particular, would make good on Johnson's threat to lock Carl and Edgar out of cable television in South Central if they failed to accept Johnson's "offer."

I also needed to support myself with my CPA and securities work and continue my cable network show.

Carl summed up his feelings by saying, "You may not be able to beat the bully but you can sure make sure that he's sorry he started bullying you."

"You know I'll do it now that you've asked," I replied, now realizing that I'd just saddled myself with pursuing a cable franchise, speaking out about nefarious bidding and political practices within the City of Los Angeles, and protecting our constitutional rights.

"So it's starting a business or going to court if they try to steal the franchise," Carl stated bluntly. The task consumed my life.

———◆———

Once we decided we were ready to move forward, I began to assemble our battle team and understand, if we could, why Los

Angeles, with a black mayor and several black city councilmen, had let the black community languish without the benefit of the latest technologies.

One of the first people I contacted was our attorney, Ted Eagans. Besides our friendship, his cable television consultations, and getting us an introduction to Councilman Lindsay by way of Al Watson, Eagans had served as General Counsel to the Cable Television Information Center in Washington, D.C. Eagans was one of the most knowledgeable black men in the United States when it came to cable television and, as stated before, he had an extensive knowledge of Los Angeles city politics.

Eagans, Carl, Mr. Charles, and Paul Skulsky envisioned the great potential for the industry, although Eagans said he also knew the City of Los Angeles had a long history of preventing the development of cable television in the South Central community.

We all bemoaned the dismal history of blacks attempting to gain cable television franchises in different minority areas, especially South Central since Edgar Charles had approached the City of Los Angeles authorities as early as 1966 to obtain a cable television franchise to provide cable television service in the South Central Los Angeles area. This foot dragging by the city was an opportunity for us, and it was something long overdue for the neighborhood.

In 1972, Eagans, as a member of another minority company, sought to construct a cable television system in South Central. This company, Eagans recalled, was known as Holoband. Once again, the city refused to even consider allowing minority-owned companies to develop a cable television system in South Central.

Eagans was angered and saddened that these efforts, based on good business and financing plans, were ignored and nothing had been done to benefit the community with cable television. Was ours one of the next batch to add to that dusty pile or would city hall insiders steal the opportunity.

"Remember, the black church was the only game in town for the black citizen but that's expanded to Los Angeles city government here now that black people can be politicians, and the black politicians are proud of their positions. That's a powerful and heady thing. Just don't try to tell them they have to share things with other opinions and other voices. They don't play by the rules like the church does. They'll never give up anything without a good long fight," Eagans said.

Eagans recalled that after the 1972 cable television applications were submitted to the city, City Councilman Tom Bradley advocated and obtained a citywide moratorium on new cable television franchises. Why? This moratorium was put into effect despite numerous cable television franchises having already been awarded in all other areas of the city, and most were built out or being constructed. But cable television was nowhere to be found in South Central Los Angeles.

Eagans recounted how Bradley said he wanted a master plan, so the Community Antenna Master Plan was researched and a master plan for Los Angeles was completed. Nothing was done. Still more delays. Why? "I've got a hunch," Eagans said. "Local black politicians, including Bradley, fear their political power base might be adversely affected if cable television isn't controlled within their personal sphere of influence and dictates."

"What?" I exclaimed. These were the excuses for grown men acting corruptly.

"They came up the hard way with segregation and all," Eagan recounted. "They don't trust anyone they don't know or don't control, because if they get kicked out of office, they'll never have such power and influence again."

By the beginning of 1980, Eagans said, "You and Carl have become some of the most knowledgeable black men on the cable television industry in America...and in dealing with the political pitfalls of Los Angeles city government." He turned and said more softly, "Politicians don't like knowledgeable men they can't control."

Seemingly an indication of Eagan's observation, we received a check from Pierpont Laidley's office. Carl and Edgar had given Pierpont Laidley a retainer of $1,000 to represent them earlier in June 1979 after their initial meeting. In February 1980, Laidley would return to Carl the balance of the retainer of $146. There seemed to be no such thing as a conflict of interest in Los Angeles.

I continued to enhance my knowledge of cable television, especially in the area of finance, as I worked for the Beverly Hills office of a major international investment banking firm. I had access to some of the leading financial analysts evaluating the cable television industry. My specialty was direct investment programs such as real estate and cable television limited partnerships, investments, and public utilities—just the industry we were dealing with in our efforts for South Central Los Angeles.

With our new team and the principal shareholders of Carl, myself, Albert Watson, and Perry Parks, we formed Universal Cable Systems, Ltd. (UCS), as a California corporation in February 1980. UCS then formed a joint venture with Six Star Cable, which was known as South Central CATV Associates.

After UCS was formed, smaller interests were provided to Virgil Roberts, one of our attorneys, John Mack, President of the Los Angeles Urban League, and Ernest Shell, Vice President of Golden State Mutual Life Insurance Company. The shares for Roberts, Mack, and Shell were provided as compensation for being on our Board of Directors. Each person was granted an option to acquire up to approximately a one-percent interest in the equity shares of the company.

Now, as a newly formed company, we started dealing with city authorities. For example, when we met or spoke with the officials and employees of the Department of Transportation (DOT), even before the applications were submitted, we encountered misman-agement, corruption, and caving in to political pressure time and time again. Not only that, their representatives continually tried to discourage us from pursuing our franchise efforts.

The DOT officials told us in our conversations at their offices that South Central simply could not economically support a cable television system, and therefore was not economically viable for the winner of any of the franchise battles. Secondly, DOT continually told us that the citizens of South Central could not afford cable television and we would lose all of our investment.

We were incredulous. DOT authorities continually used the 15,000-home franchise (Boyle Heights), cut out from the original 250,000-home franchise (South Central) as their example of economical non-viability as a stand-alone franchise. The very same franchise they DOT and the Los Angeles City Council had created themselves. It was a political gift to BVT.

They were clearly wrong, both out of stupidity and with intention. The attempt by government agencies to discourage economic development in minority communities with misinformation was, in our view, an attempt to distort the free market and limit competition.

———

During this time, we heard from reliable sources that the city council consulted with various political allies to see who might be interested in getting the South Central franchise. We also heard that the DOT report of the franchises not being economically viable had an adverse effect on big business interests pursuing cable television investment.

These big business investors, as I previously thought, considered cable television a unique and risky industry. The DOT report only validated that opinion. Little interest came from the business community or big-time political contributors. City Hall had scared away their allies—along with their money.

Beside the political pressure to end our franchise bid, there was competitive pressure as well—this time from an economically viable competitor.

We were told American Television and Cable Corporation (ATC), the largest cable television operator in the United States at that time, wanted to submit a bid for South Central. They would, no doubt, submit a good business plan and a solid financing package.

Only two things beside our tenacity were in our favor—the calendar and ties to the community. There were only a few weeks before the franchise application deadline and we didn't know if ATC had any South Central community support for their application. The master plan that had been developed by the City of Los Angeles for the award of cable television franchises specified that the South Central franchise should be awarded to *a minority group* that represented the demographic makeup of the community.

Knowing this, ATC, who needed some minority participation in order to satisfy the political forces in Los Angeles, sent their representatives to Mayor Bradley's office in the last week prior to submission of applications and got a list of black businessmen whom Mayor Bradley recommended as possible participants.

———◆———

The applications for the three new franchise areas were scheduled to be received on March 30, March 31, and April 1, 1980, for the Boyle Heights, Wilmington, and South Central cable television areas.

The 300-plus-page bids were received and sealed after the appropriate fees were paid for processing on each day, respectively.

We decided to submit bids for all three franchises. The decision to bid for all three franchises was based on a goal to develop the entire franchise area as a single franchise, as the City of Los Angeles had *originally* planned. Additionally, since we had no operating cable television franchises, we felt it would be better to have something as opposed to nothing. We felt we could build from something but that was very hard to build from nothing.

"Well, we've done our best," Al Watson said. "Let's hope they don't monkey around with the process."

———◆———

On April 1, 1980, bids for the South Central franchise were filed and accepted by DOT. In addition to our company, CTI and ATC each submitted a bid.

We found out ATC had no local investors. Looking at their application, ATC proposed to give twenty percent of the company to non-profit organizations that would be named later—if they were the successful applicant. ATC didn't contact any of the non-profit organizations in the application but they still included the statement within their application. On closer scrutiny, some of the non-profit organizations ATC proposed to give shares to were organizations that did not even actually exist at that time of the application submission. This portion of the proposed ownership for the franchise was never challenged by the DOT. Why would a powerful national corporation such as ATC want to give twenty percent of its company away?

———◆———

Councilman Lindsay called us into his office. "Now that the application packages are in, the bare-knuckle fighting will start," he said as he folded his hands and swiveled slightly in his chair. We'd been told by others as well that the political pressure would start in earnest.

"I'm already receiving calls," Councilman Lindsay said. "But I wanted to keep the pressure off you while you were finishing your applications."

He was receiving calls from other councilmen and the mayor's office regarding trying to force us to merge with their friends.

"Yes, I've gotten more than a few calls," Councilman Lindsay said. "If there's a dollar, they find it. They don't care whose it is."

"We want this to get back to an honest bidding process," I said. We believed that once standards were established and implemented for all the franchise applications on a consistent basis, we would have a chance to obtain a franchise area based on the quality of our application.

"Don't know if that's possible but I'm willing to help you try," Lindsay said.

In our experience, and to the City of Los Angeles' shame, it usually worked another way. At every turn, the process lacked fairness, intelligence, honesty, and democratic principles.

We would soon find out that no standards were applied on any basis of consistency. The rules and standards for the applications for franchise areas were altered based on political motives—and little else.

On May 15, 1980, Councilman Lindsay told us Danny Bakewell wanted a meeting with us in Lindsay's office. Lindsay reiterated Bakewell was a protégé of Mayor Bradley, making him a very powerful person in South Central Los Angeles. As we knew and further research confirmed, Bakewell had numerous financial interests in South Central Los Angeles as well as the surrounding minority-dominated cities, such as Compton. The *Los Angeles Times* would later call Bakewell the "Godfather of South Central."

Carl and I arrived at the May 15 meeting to see Danny Bakewell, Channing Johnson, and Bob Davidson waiting for us. This created an immediate problem because of Carl's intense dislike for Johnson. The history concerning Johnson trying to strong-arm Carl and the late Edgar Charles in the cable television application process affected us deeply, especially Carl. Edgar had tried to "trust" the councilmen and bidding system since 1970 and Carl felt Johnson and Councilman Farrell had betrayed Edgar's trust as well as all of the citizens of South Central.

Danny Bakewell immediately took charge of the discussion and, in a most unusual move from our previous encounters and meetings, Johnson said very little.

"Seems like Johnson knows he's not the top dog in this situation," Carl whispered,

"...and he's got to give the lead over to Bakewell."

This was, after all, Councilman Lindsay's office, and Johnson had managed to alienate Lindsay, who was still very vocal about Johnson and Councilman Farrell's bypassing him during the 1979 division of the South Central franchise.

We discovered others disliked Johnson as well. We'd heard comments from Bob Gay, Councilman Lindsay's chief deputy. Having worked with Channing Johnson in city hall, Bob Gay said Johnson was a "singularly disliked person."

In expressing his own dislike for Johnson, Gay said, "If I was the Sparkletts' water delivery man and Johnson was dying of thirst in the desert, I would pour the bottles into the sand before I would sell it to him." We knew how Gay felt.

Gay also relayed comments from Bakewell regarding Johnson. Bakewell described Johnson as "an arrogant little prick."

In addition to a poor reputation, Johnson had other problems.

As we told the city council, Johnson had been actively and forcefully involved with the cable franchise licenses. In this ongoing illegal environment of rule-making and breaking in dealing with Los Angeles City Hall and its departments, we were prepared legally and vocally to be very active in every arena to make sure all rules were kept in strict obedience to the law.

Channing Johnson was supposedly subject to the one-year conflict-of-interest rule. This rule prohibited a former employee of the City of Los Angeles to be actively associated with a company for any contractor license in which a city employee (as he was) was involved during his employment with the City of Los Angeles. An investigation by the LAPD was referred to the district attorney of Los Angeles County where the case died.

———

Bakewell, a very light-skinned, medium-height, stocky man with wavy dark hair, talked about his achievements for several minutes. Based upon his activities in South Central and the way he spoke in the meeting, it became clear he was powerful and wanted everyone to know it.

The meeting turned out to be nothing more than general talk about cable television and the South Central neighborhood. After we left, Carl said grimly, "Well, we've met the new member of the opposition."

———

Bakewell arranged another meeting to be held on May 27, 1980, at the Biltmore Hotel in downtown Los Angeles. In addition to Carl and I, Perry Parks volunteered to attend the meeting with us. Our sources said Bakewell had now taken charge because Johnson, for the time being, at least, seemed concerned about the one-year conflict-of-interest stricture concerning his employment in Councilman Farrell's office, and therefore agreed to avoid any appearance of a conflict of interest with his participation at this point in the franchising process.

But only to a point, it seemed. Such conflicts did not appear to overly concern Johnson. Johnson's mother, Jeffalyn Johnson, was a shareholder of CTI, according to documents submitted to the City of Los Angeles.

We'd still have to keep a close eye on the players and the rules.

Bakewell began the discussion. "I want to tell everyone about the necessary participation of the "Mayor's Group" in our future discussions," Bakewell started. *What?* We had been involved in the cable television franchising process with the City of Los Angeles for more than eighteen months and had never heard about any "Mayor's Group." Who exactly were they?

The "Mayor's Group" consisted of three people. The first person was Dr. Hiawatha Harris, a local psychiatrist influential in the South Central neighborhood, who they identified as a close personal friend of Mayor Tom Bradley. The second person was James Reese, a Los Angeles Superior Court judge. The third person was Bob Carter, who was identified as a salesperson for a media company.

Carl and I started doing our research on these three men, who were calling themselves the "Mayor's Group." Dr. Hiawatha Harris *was* a close personal friend of Mayor Bradley's, according to the *Los Angeles Times*. We continued to research James Reese and Bob Carter.

The "Mayor's Group" was identified as personal friends of the mayor who wanted to be included in any franchise awarded in South Central. Included in the franchise? *Our* franchise group?

Carl and I were angered again. Throwing around the term "Mayor's Group" so carelessly...and with such authority. Now we definitely knew people were openly trading on Bradley's name and those people felt free to poach into our South Central franchise application as well. Didn't they know that brazenly raising the unethical and illegal interference to the mayoral level would be disgusting to us, rather than a welcome prospect? Johnson, Laidley, Bakewell...and now the Mayor Bradley contingent? All these powerful black men looking to take advantage of a situation rather than looking out for the needs and rights of the citizens of South Central?

At the time, their arrogance and seeming proof of Mayor Bradley's culpability seemed beyond words—leaving us speechless.

———◆———

At the next meeting, in June 1980, Bakewell made CTI's position abundantly clear to us. "Deal's simple. You get a third and CTI gets two-thirds," Bakewell said, with an arrogance that became his verbal trademark—as irritating as Channing Johnson but with more power to back up his threats.

Again, with their proposal, we and Six Star took *all the risk* and provided *all the financing* and they had *all the control* in the company. They must have thought that we were fools.

So the people we knew who were now directly involved with CTI were: Johnson, Laidley, Bakewell, Harris, Reese, and Carter, with several other minor shareholders including Johnson's mother.

"What about Wilkins and his company, SYNCOM?" I asked.

"You don't need to know about people, you need to know about this deal," Bakewell barked.

Bakewell's tone when he got angry and wanted to assert his authority would be described by Carl as that of street thugs, like the ones we had dealt with as youths in our family neighborhood in New York City. We couldn't help laughing at such low-grade behavior in city hall.

Carl, Mr. Parks, and I sat passively as Danny aggressively attempted to persuade us that the only opportunity to participate in cable television was to follow his lead and do as he said.

"You've got no power or input into the terms of the deal, except for Lindsay as a courtesy to a councilman," Bakewell said gratingly.

As the meeting began to wrap up, Carl was becoming visibly annoyed with Bakewell's attitude of superiority. "I thought we came in to negotiate, not be dictated to."

Bakewell slammed his hand on the table and said, "That's the deal, take it or leave it."

From our perspective, Bakewell's proposal that our company receive only one-third of the franchise did not seem like a reasonable starting point for negotiations. We declined the offer.

———◆———

When we told Councilman Lindsay we declined the offer, he reassured us of his commitment by saying, "I'm still with you on this but I've told you before that I've only got just so much influence and a mayor trumps a councilman *almost every time*."

There were extensive internal discussions regarding making any concessions to Bakewell and Johnson's group. My position was that we could maintain control of the company with a fifty-percent interest.

Since we always felt Bakewell and Johnson's goal was merely a financial gain on the transaction, I felt strongly that we could eventually acquire additional shares from their shareholders looking to make a quick profit. The biggest danger of joining Bakewell and his group under their conditions was if they had anything *above* fifty-percent control of the company, they could make quick and reckless side deals that might lead to unknown legal problems for us as minority shareholders in the franchise and/or derail our programming plans.

In our formal counteroffer to Bakewell's group, we offered fifty percent of the company to CTI. Considering we had all the financing and technical expertise, we thought our offer of fifty percent was a very generous one. Six Star and Skulsky had made it clear that they would *not continue* in any joint venture unless we owned at least fifty-percent interest in the company. Although we and Six Star preferred having at least fifty-one-percent interest in this venture for control reasons, Six Star understood our political predicament.

Carl and Al Watson were against making any concessions to Bakewell's group because they felt being involved with people of such low integrity was contrary to our company's ethical standards.

Mr. Parks, on the other hand, was in favor of the fifty-percent offer because he felt we should make every effort to try to bring cable television into South Central as soon as possible.

My position, in conjunction with Mr. Parks, was ultimately accepted by the rest of our board of directors (Virgil Roberts, one of our legal counsel; John Mack, president of the Los Angeles Urban League; and Ernest Shell, vice president of the Golden State Mutual Life Insurance Company) because they felt we had to be cognizant of the political power of our adversaries.

The fact Johnson and his cronies attempted to cheat Carl in the initial phases of the transaction was important, but we could not let these instances blind us to the fact that we still needed political support to complete this transaction. "So we'll keep our guns on the table and watch their every move," Al said.

———————

Later in the summer, as our first meeting with the "Mayor's Group" unfolded, Dr. Harris identified himself as the person who would speak on behalf of the group. Harris also claimed to have messages and threats against the fifty-percent counteroffer of our group from Mayor Bradley, regarding our unwillingness to cede control of our company to Mayor Bradley's friends, including Harris and Bakewell.

Judge Reese withdrew his involvement with the Mayor's Group shortly after the franchise applications were filed. Reese said, "There are too many potential conflict-of-interest factors here for me. I don't want to get myself in any potentially embarrassing situations." Bob Carter seemed to have little real influence, always saying he was a friend of Danny Bakewell when pressed to say anything.

Another meeting was held at the Biltmore on June 3, 1980. Once again, the meeting was attended by Bakewell, Johnson, Harris, Carl, Mr. Parks, and me. This meeting started as the last meeting had ended—a stubborn insistence from everyone in the CTI group demanding to control two-thirds of any agreement.

We would not be controlled by Channing Johnson at the time of the first offer and we weren't going to be controlled now. Johnson and Bakewell were becoming more insistent—accept their offer immediately or risk being excluded from the process.

The meeting ended as most meetings with the CTI group ended. Channing Johnson was talking again now and, as always, threatening to exclude our company from the franchise unless we immediately agreed to their terms.

Our final June meeting in 1980 brought out the big guns—at Mayor Bradley's office.

We had been summoned to the meeting by a call from the office of Councilman Lindsay, informing us that the mayor had convened a meeting of the black applicants for the South Central Los Angeles franchise. That meeting was to take place three hours from the time of the phone call.

At his mayoral office conference table, ten men, all hastily invited, waited for "His Honor." Three members of our organization attended—Carl, me, and Virgil Roberts, one of our attorneys at this phase of the process. This last-minute invitation had only one item on the agenda—summoning CTI and us as the two minority bidding groups for the South Central Los Angeles cable franchise.

The tall black man walked into the conference room with a smirk on his face. His blue pinstriped Brooks Brothers suit matched well with his polished, manicured nails and a facial-treated glowing face. After all, this man was Tom Bradley, Mayor of the City of Los Angeles, and he played the role grandly. We looked at a man who was at the height of his power and expected to run for the office of Governor of California.

Bradley shook hands with eight of the ten sitting participants, even spending a minute speaking privately into the ear of Danny Bakewell.

The mayor did not reach across the table to shake hands with Carl or me. Bradley merely nodded in non-directional acknowledgement, indicating Carl and I were being given a "throw-off," or a less-than-cordial greeting. Carl and I were in the mayoral doghouse, so to speak.

We'd heard he'd sneeringly dubbed us "the Galloway boys" as we began the increasingly difficult fight through the cable television application process. We'd found out that our *not agreeing* to back down to political pressure, especially from the black politicians, was a crime in black Los Angeles...and the mayor's office.

If Bradley intended to intimidate or offend us in our first face-to-face meeting since Carl and I started our cable television franchise attempt, the tactic didn't work. Once my brother and I got a look at him, we could not help but smirk to ourselves at this officious setting and the behavior of all involved. We wanted to respect the office but maintain our character and values in this business effort and in the South Central community we felt we represented. If these men assembled here didn't like our behavior, we thought the "throw-off" was a complement to our character and upbringing.

In those ten minutes, Bradley managed to undo all the favorable publicity and claims of his grand reputation we'd been told about him...and what a shining example he was for our race for the past twenty years. We learned fairly early in the meeting that Bradley was not there to assist us in negotiating a cable television deal. Rather, he wanted to demonstrate the political connection the competing bidding group had with him.

As I watched Bradley, I couldn't help but think he saw himself as some sort of royalty— black royalty, perhaps. Untouchable, like the popular kid in high school, he acted entitled with a swaggering cockiness, seemingly assured of his velvety place in the world.

A Brooks Brothers suit might impress others, but I felt differently. From the time I left college and started work with an international accounting firm, I'd seen a vast collection of well-dressed, manicured men. From my perspective, it was the man who made the suit, not the suit who made the man. The Tom Bradley who attended the meeting was merely a caricature of the Tom Bradley the press had portrayed—the "emperor" needed a new attitude to match his clothes.

What a gaping disappointment it was for us, as two black men, to learn this seemingly admired man who'd been talked about so kindly in the press did not exist. In his place paraded a man with an inflated ego.

My interaction with Bradley led me to believe that any politician could easily place themselves in a different class from the rest of society—a "political class." They made a cozy "status" home for themselves somewhere between the middle and upper class or, perhaps, in the upper class. *Was their biggest goal when they got to the "political class" just to stay there as long as possible? Would politicians do anything to protect their control over their constituents? As indicated in our experience, had they begun to believe their own lies about what they were doing for the public?*

Our concern for the citizens of South Central and the cost to taxpayers appeared to be a minor concern to these guardians of the public trust. This was especially troublesome in Black America where politicians seemed to be the only link to mainstream America. They have fallen victim to the power and prestige of the "political class" at the cost of their constituents and would withhold the economic opportunities for even the poorest communities for their own benefit.

After ten minutes, Bradley ordered us to leave and continue our negotiations. As he made his way back toward the door, my brother passed me a note with one word on it in big block letters—"BOZO."

———◆———

The mayor ordered that further negotiations *must start immediately.* We were ushered to a conference room one floor below Bradley's office, at the office of the Commissioner of Public Works. Mayor Bradley's deputy, William Elkins, convened the meeting.

Elkins tried to straighten up from his naturally hunched position to look bigger as he relayed Bradley's sentiments to us, but the effort did not work. Elkins put it, quite simply, in a much less regal way, "The mayor has spoken and all you niggers had better get together."

His warning was so obviously directed at my brother and me that our mouths gaped open. We had been through a lot in this process and this seemed like the last straw for Carl. I had to grab my brother to keep him from rising and verbally assaulting Elkins.

This meeting, forced by Mayor Bradley's edict, lasted for three hours. CTI (the Bakewell/Johnson group) continued to press for controlling interest of whatever entity would be awarded a franchise for South Central. The arrogance and rudeness displayed by our competitors completely validated our opinion *never to consider* taking a minority position in any organization they were running.

The meeting ended as most meetings ended, with the same mantra of curses and threats from Bakewell and Johnson, promising we would be *completely excluded* from the cable television industry in South Central unless we acquiesced to their demands.

As we left the office in Public Works, Carl made one final comment to Elkins. He stood less than a foot from Elkins's face and said, "You don't know me well enough to call me nigger." Because Carl had a justifiably earned reputation for having a short fuse, I was afraid he might say something more. Carl didn't, but secretly I had hoped he would.

To say this was a time of painful realization of the moral bankruptcy of those in power was an understatement.

———◆———

After the second meeting ended, Councilman Farrell called Councilman Lindsay at his home. He pleaded with Lindsay to force us to accept the offer CTI had made to us. Lindsay responded, "Farrell, you shouldn't be involved in this anyway, and you're playing with fire because your poking into this matter is probably a violation of the law." He closed the conversation by telling Farrell, "Neither you or your group can force UCS to accept any deal they do not want to accept."

———◆———

After hearing and basing our lives on trying to uphold the values incorporated in our families' and friends' heritage stories of slavery, such immoral attitudes at the highest levels of government by black officials and businessmen were deplorable...and seeing them so easily subverted in modern-day politics and business was too painful for words.

Let's be clear. We were not naïve black men. We knew from personal experience some instances of racial scrapes and lack of racial harmony, and we thoroughly understood the prejudices of whites and police in our youth, despite our beliefs and the advances of civil rights in the United States.

We wanted to succeed personally and corporately in the American economic system, but we were experiencing another form of slavery in our midst—the slavery of political corruption. The worst part was the concrete realization that this was happening at the hands of fellow black citizens.

At the very core, both white and black elected officials and their friends were subverting an established, equitable process in the free market system for power and financial gain.

At times, watching and experiencing how easily the black elected officials could delay and subvert the system against their own people and neighborhoods and those who so desperately needed the opportunities, jobs, and technology, left us feeling only pain and despair.

———◆———

Most people not involved in our dilemma seemed to think things were going well in Los Angeles city government or chose to look the other way.

Back in 1980, Mayor Bradley's expected run for governor of California was the talk of the South Central neighborhood—a black man as governor. The entire city, state of California, and now the nation was becoming enamored with Mayor Bradley, who we knew to be power-hungry and corrupt.

Mayor Bradley assumed national prominence and some polls indicated he would win the gubernatorial election. Bradley had rich, influential backers that included major entertainment, real estate, and industrial business interests. There was even "heady" talk of Bradley being considered for the vice presidential slot on the 1982 Democratic presidential ticket.

We became "those Galloway boys" to those within the hallowed halls of the City of Los Angeles. And we had three missions: to gain the three cable franchises we had applied for, to expose the grossly illegal and unfair application process in cable television, and to unmask the corrupt politicians behind it all.

Chapter Four

The Shakedown

So what we were going to do as a company?

We knew we faced more than an uphill battle to get people to listen to our story since many thought things were going so well in Los Angeles and Mayor Bradley was such a good mayor.

"It's surprising how a little sunshine and a little economic prosperity can cloud people's minds about what is right," Mr. Parks lamented. "Have to look at it all, no matter how painful it is."

"We need to stand for what we think is right and let the chips fall where they may," Mr. Watson said.

———◆———

On July 3, 1980, a meeting was held with Councilman David Cunningham at his offices in City Hall. Immediately upon our arrival at his office, Cunningham became quite aggressive about the proposed merger of our company and CTI. "From my perspective, I'm dissatisfied the negotiations have not reached a satisfactory conclusion between you and CTI."

We explained to Cunningham the gravity of giving up two-thirds of our company while retaining *all the risk and no control*. "No one from Johnson on up ever negotiates. They just tell us things and threaten us," Carl asserted. "It's unfair and unprofessional. Don't get me started."

All Cunningham could say in reply, attempting to circumvent the principal issue, was, "You know they don't like Six Star as your partner." *Another veiled comment about racism?*

Cunningham went on to say, although he voted for Six Star's franchise for the Hollywood-Wilshire franchise area, that he was upset with not knowing what he was voting on. Cunningham stated it was only *after* the bids for the South Central area were released did he become aware of cable television and its possible financial importance. So Councilman Lindsay was right. Cunningham was miffed he'd blown the opportunity to cash in on cable in his district before now.

We looked at each other after his comment and thought Cunningham knew plenty about cable television and was lying. Furthermore, Cunningham felt he had not been paid the proper amount of contributions and other types of remuneration given the size and value of the Hollywood-Wilshire franchise award. We could not figure out how Cunningham's previous dealings with Six Star should bias anything to do with our terms to bring cable television to South Central. Six Star's building record and neighborhood performance were well thought of in Los Angeles and in the industry.

In a vindictive and unprofessional manner, Cunningham indicated he was mad at Six Star for their "error" and he now wanted to try to get even in this situation by opposing *our* joint venture with Six Star for the South Central franchise. Six Star's "error," as far as we could understand, was failing to throw large sums of money at Cunningham. So our association with Six Star was his method of political payback for a perceived political slight—with no thought or feeling for the needs of the neighborhood?

Cunningham proposed we put pressure on Six Star to give our group a piece of the already-awarded Six Star franchise in the Hollywood-Wilshire area. According to Cunningham, if Six Star gave our group, UCS, twenty percent of the lucrative Hollywood-Wilshire franchise, Bakewell and Johnson would be able to get sixty-six percent of the South Central franchise. "Everyone will be happy...and I'll back your deal."

Cunningham's proposal asked us to *turn against Six Star* and attempt to *extort* a part of the Six Star Hollywood-Wilshire franchise to curry Cunningham's backing. Both counts were illegal and an amoral backstabbing. Mr. Parks, Carl, and I firmly and immediately rejected both of Cunningham's "suggestions," and we told him so in no uncertain terms.

"I've never gone back on my word to anyone, Cunningham," Mr. Parks said incredulously.

When we rejected the idea, Cunningham's obese frame seemed to shake as he glared at us through his large, square, rose-colored glasses. Cunningham yelled that "under no conditions" would he allow our joint venture to obtain a franchise until his conditions were met and Six Star was no longer a partner in the joint venture. Cunningham reiterated that our group would have to give up a controlling interest to the Bakewell/Johnson group in order to have any opportunity to participate in the South Central franchise.

Mr. Parks asked Cunningham, "I've been around a long time. Why do you and the rest of the council always force all black companies to merge together instead of compete?"

Cunningham replied, "Never mind talking about other black companies, Perry. You're here for your company and getting the cable franchise." He stared at Mr. Parks. "CTI *doesn't have* the money. You might. But what they *do have* is being friends of the mayor and myself, who need and deserve consideration."

Mr. Parks would later explain he was insulted Cunningham would assume we were the kind of people who would go back on a word and attempt to extort our own partners. "I call the kind of thing Cunningham is suggesting immoral. No doubt in my mind about it. Shaming the good people who voted for him as well." Like Mayor Bradley, Councilman Cunningham was only interested in money and status.

For us, the price of consideration at City Hall was two-thirds of our company.

———————

On July 3, 1980, less than ninety days after the submission of the original cable television applications for South Central and the two "new" franchise areas, DOT sent letters to all the applicants asking for a clarification of the information on the applications that had been submitted. There had never been such a request in the history of Los Angeles cable franchise licensing before.

DOT claimed it took an additional ninety days for them to know this new information was required. So...how had they awarded twelve franchises already without this clarification?

In answering questions regarding this highly unusual post-bid request, DOT told us the information they had originally requested in February was not enough to provide adequate review measures for the bids. But...the information that they asked for had already been submitted by our company with the original application. Once again the application process was being changed.

We heard through several internal City Hall sources that the applications of CTI and BVT were of very poor quality and that neither CTI nor BVT had complied with the information requested in the original applications.

If that information was accurate, and we had no reason to think it was not, the CTI and BVT applications, just as any other bidding application before the City of Los Angeles, should have been thrown out and not allowed to proceed in the bidding process.

This unprecedented DOT request for additional information would allow those with substandard applications to continue in the bidding process, review the other competitors' applications, and resubmit their applications based on the review of their competitors' applications with new, edited information to correct their applications.

In the private sector, permitting something like this to happen—allowing competitors to gain private information in the course of obtaining new business—would be akin to corporate espionage.

It was also quite clear the competing bidders for the South Central franchise were less than able and less aware of what information needed to be submitted. Councilman Cunningham had indicated as much about their financial package when he was yelling at us in his office. The only reason for this delay, then, was the illegal and unethical efforts on the part of the city, through DOT, to prolong the process in favor of CTI and BVT.

The DOT process subterfuge allowed CTI in its South Central application and BVT in its Boyle Heights application more time... and allowed them to "cheat" by seeing all our application documents—in what was supposed to be a closed, confidential bidding process.

We felt DOT, as a Los Angeles regulatory department, acted in an illegal and under-handed fashion. For example, DOT General Manager Don Howery chose the day before the Fourth of July holiday to request these "additional information" changes in the application process *without* any further approval or discussion from the BTC (Board of Transportation Commissioners) or the Los Angeles City Council. This unprecedented change of procedure from the other twelve previous cable franchise application processes happened on a day when these changes would be less noted.

In addition, the surprise request of giving all bidders forty-five days to amend their applications was problematic. Since we had three pending applications to amend during the forty-five day schedule, the time constraint put us under tremendous pressure.

"I can't believe it," Carl fumed. "This will tear me away from the family and they're already seeing less and less of me with my medical schedule. Go get Al, Mr. P., and Councilman Lindsay on the phone to see what we can do."

"I'll take care of it from this end," I assured him and headed for the phone.

———◆———

On July 29, 1980, a meeting was held at the offices of Councilman Lindsay. Danny Bakewell and Bishop H.H. Brookins were in attendance on behalf of CTI.

Bishop Brookins's name had never been mentioned in any of our conversations concerning CTI, he had never been at any of the meetings, nor had his name ever appeared on any of the applications, documents, or legal filings of CTI. Yet, at this meeting, Bishop Brookins was introduced as a shareholder of CTI.

In our previous dealings with CTI and BVT, we had never questioned CTI's or BVT's access to political power or influence. They would tell us, it seemed, in every other sentence, what prestige and power they had because of their political connections. As we listened to their constant diatribe, we indicated a continuing reluctance to give them such a high price for their politics. *But now were they influencing prominent church and cultural leaders to join their roster?*

We knew Bishop Brookins was a prominent citizen in South Central, a leader of one of the largest AME congregations in the country, and that he held a position in the AME national office. *Was Bishop Brookins's attendance at the meeting evidence of AME's support and political power within the South Central neighborhood?* We would see.

Councilman Lindsay made it clear that we would have to deal with Bakewell and Brookins because of their access to the mayor's office. "The bishop will be welcome to any and all meetings we have...as if you were welcoming me." Councilman Lindsay looked sternly at Carl and me as he made it clear we needed to graciously accept Bishop Brookins's new involvement.

"Channing Johnson won't be here today," Councilman Lindsay said. Lindsay believed we could make more progress without Johnson being in attendance, given Carl's intense dislike of Johnson because of his actions in the South Central franchising process thus far.

"First off, Danny, don't come in here and try to force my guys to take only a third of things," Councilman Lindsay said. Bakewell, from the beginning of his attendance at the meetings, had tried to pressure us and get Councilman Lindsay to force us to take a one- third interest in the application.

Bakewell stated, "You exclude the Mayor's Group and it's a *direct insult to Mayor Tom Bradley*." He looked at Carl and me. "You want to do that?"

We marveled at Bakewell's arrogance because the Mayor's Group was down to only two people, Harris and Carter, and our sources indicated that even with all their bluster during these needless meetings, CTI still had no financing package, little knowledge of the industry, and they had not submitted a strong franchise application. *But would they continue to gain ground in the process through nefarious means orchestrated in the changes in the application process?*

We thought the only possible purpose of this meeting, once again, revolved around their display, for our benefit, of their influence in the South Central community and with Mayor Tom Bradley, and bluster about their power.

Nothing was accomplished. We refused to budge from our offer of the equal fifty-fifty split we had proposed as an alternative to their attempts to control the company. We were willing to talk about the South Central programming needs and our plans for programming for the South Central franchise but we didn't give them any more information concerning the evolving cable industry.

Bakewell and the CTI representatives didn't want to talk about programming—just money and their share of the business. "We get two-thirds of it or you'll get nothing." The same old mantra we'd heard from a few different people at the table.

We entered the meeting with the knowledge that if we gave away two-thirds of the company, there was no need to negotiate anything else. The group with a two-thirds majority could dictate all additional terms of the merger.

The only thing we *did* gain from the meeting was that Councilman Lindsay, for the first time, witnessed the strong-arm tactics being attempted by Bakewell.

———◆———

After the meeting, Lindsay told us that he could not guarantee a victory for our company but he was willing to go in whatever direction we chose. He noted our competitors never mentioned anything about the effect of cable television on the citizens of South Central and the neighborhood. As always, neither Bakewell nor the other CTI representatives ever mentioned programming or anything else concerning the neighborhood when they met with us, even when we tried to broaden the conversation and discuss our programming ideas. *Were they ever interested in any aspect other than the deal?*

———◆———

On August 4, 1980, we were summoned to a meeting with CTI, held at Bishop Brookins's offices at his AME church on Crenshaw Boulevard located in the South Central neighborhood.

Carl refused to attend the meeting because he, like Councilman Lindsay at the previous meeting in his office, felt it would be counterproductive to have both he and Johnson in the same room.

I asked my friend, a fellow businessman whom I'd known from college, Gene Forte, who was also in the investment banking business, to join me so we could have an independent evaluation of proposals being submitted by our competitors.

Channing Johnson, Dr. Hiawatha Harris, Bishop Brookins, and Danny Bakewell attended for CTI. Dr. Harris's name now appeared on the new submission allowed by the DOT.

Dr. Harris was quite vocal at the meeting. According to Harris, the Mayor's Group required one-third of the franchise, even though they had not submitted an application. In telling us about his history and interest in cable television, Harris indicated he had been contacted about but had not joined with the ATC (American Television and Cable Corporation) bid that had been submitted at the same time as ours in April 1980, but their offer to him was unclear.

"ATC tried to get me in line for their deal," Harris said. According to Harris, he was approached during what he thought was about one week prior to the submission of applications for the South Central franchise to put together a group of potential minority investors to provide a minority presence for the ATC application. "Didn't have enough time to arrange the money. ATC started too late."

Secondly, Harris claimed he did not become part of the ATC application because both Bakewell and Johnson promised to give him a place in their company, CTI. *How did this become our business?*

"So this is a just another street hustle for you and Danny and Johnson?" Mr. Parks asked. "The neighborhood's supposed to listen to you?"

"You just need to accept *the fact* that we're the real politically connected people here...and we've got the political access key," Harris continued.

We held firm to our fifty-fifty strategy but offered an alternative solution to the distribution, which we outlined as the negotiations continued. We'd planned for this contingency, marveling at the ever-changing number of people saying they were involved in CTI. *How many more people were going to claim they had rightful ownership in CTI?*

Johnson said he'd talked to Councilman Farrell and they'd agreed that nothing would go forward in the bidding process if we did not reach an agreement—their agreement.

We, on the other hand, would *not* put our company and ourselves in a business position with less than an equal controlling interest, not with our reputations and livelihoods threatened by the whims of these already-proven unethical people.

We offered the counterproposal in which each company with an active application would receive a fifty-percent interest in a joint venture formed by our company and CTI. We would then make available equity positions for persons involved in the Mayor's Group.

The meeting ended badly when Johnson, once again, became quite vociferous with his standard blustering barrage of threats after hearing our proposal. He yelled that if we did not consent to their demands, we would be left with our pants hanging down and nothing to show for it.

We agreed to meet again in the first week of August after CTI had a chance to consider our counterproposal and see if we could find common ground.

———•———

In the meantime, we were called into Councilman Lindsay's office. "Now, don't go flying off the handle till I've had my say. There's a counterproposal to your idea that's been offered to you." A counterproposal idea by CTI? I didn't like the sound of that.

Councilman Lindsay started by saying, "Carl and you are offered a *really* low price on some downtown real estate, near Ninth Street and Hope Street, which will give you an immediate equity of over two million dollars, if you are willing to give control of *your* company to another bidding group."

This wasn't a counterproposal. This was a bribe. Was financial compensation in another *totally different industry* supposed to be a prize for us—awarded for accepting a reduced interest in the cable television enterprise? We told Lindsay that we would not accept.

"Why would you refuse to accept *guaranteed* real estate money?" Councilman Lindsay wondered aloud.

Our answer was simple and clear: what had brought us into this industry in the first place was the opportunity to make a substantial impact on the development of our race within Los Angeles and, maybe, the United States.

Councilman Lindsay shook his head and told us, "Your goals are commendable, but if I were you, I'd take the guaranteed money."

"Does this offer mean you're withdrawing you support?" Carl asked.

"Knew you might think that, but, no, you still have my support. I'll keep going with you all the way down the line," Lindsay replied. "But it's going to be a rough, bloody fight."

We'd be offered real estate in exchange for a controlling interest in the cable franchise *two more times* before the franchises were awarded.

We turned the offers down each of the three times.

———◆———

Harris continued his standard mantra. "Unless you do what Tom wants, you're disrespecting Mayor Tom Bradley."

Carl had had enough. "When the mayor starts wearing a royal crown, like the king you're making him out to be, then we might let Mayor Bradley dictate our business decisions."

We could only think Dr. Harris was under the fantastic misapprehension that when Mayor Bradley spoke, the mayor's words were really the law of the City of Los Angeles. The vehemence and irrationality of his and his partners' statements made us wonder about Dr. Harris's business acumen, his understanding of the legislative process in the City of Los Angeles, and, more precisely, confirmed our questions concerning his personal character and that of his fellow members of CTI.

———◆———

On August 15, 1980, the "additional information" allowed by the Department of Transportation for the three franchises was submitted by our company, UCS, and in the applications of CTI and BVT.

DOT would take *almost a year* to evaluate this information before making its recommendation to the BTC concerning their choice to receive a franchise. This long delay seemed contrived and purposeful.

———◆———

On November 3, 1980, another meeting was held with CTI at the offices of the Golden State Mutual Life Insurance Company. One of our directors, Ernest Shell, a senior vice president at Golden State, the largest black-owned life insurance company in the United States, thought the competing groups should make one more effort to combine the two minority companies.

Shell was concerned that this great opportunity for minority cable franchise ownership might be lost if we could not join forces to present a united front. "Although your Universal group could provide all financing and technical expertise...we have to be cognizant of the *political realities*."

Shell had a long history with helping the South Central community. In his late sixties, he was very concerned about the future of the South Central citizens and keenly attuned to the different needs of the minority community he had served his entire professional life.

Among these, Shell recognized the importance cable television held for South Central specifically and Black America in general. "You know the importance of economic development within the South Central area is critical to all aspects of life from giving educational opportunities to affecting and reducing crime by providing jobs and information." Shell could not understand how anyone could see things any differently.

"We, as a community, are losing out." Shell shook his head. "I keep telling everyone in the neighborhood and down at City Hall that money *leaves* our community every day because the jobs and services we need aren't planted here. They go elsewhere and the tax base and everything else goes with it."

Shell was talking about needing businesses, large and small, to come into South Central so the monies businesses received and paid in things like salaries and supplies would stay in the South Central neighborhood to provide jobs, a better standard of living, opportunities, and gain government monies for better infrastructure decisions concerning schools, parks, and services for the South Central citizens.

"The net outflow of funds from minority areas means the community cannot provide the employment necessary to maintain full employment at the levels experienced by the general population." Shell shook his head again. "How can we expect people to learn to be law-abiding citizens when they feel they can only support themselves and their families by breaking the law. I haven't got any more jobs to give to them...and the churches in the area are trying the best they can as well."

Shell saw cable television as a chance for the citizens of South Central to gain self-determination through media ownership and the educational opportunities and insights niche programming could bring. "We can get good jobs as well as good programming from your plan. Money needs to be retained within the South Central community. Self-determination is the essence of the American culture."

We bluntly asked Shell if he thought it was in our best interest to accept a one-third position in a combined company. Shell was reluctant to answer. He had friends in both companies, but also understood our reluctance to relinquish control to a company in which Channing Johnson wielded substantial influence. "But don't forget, a cable company in South Central could produce up to 1,000 jobs in an impoverished area where the unemployment rate was close to twenty percent. In my estimation, this cable company could be the largest financial investment within South Central *for the next ten years*."

———◆———

In December 1980, Shell called and said that he could no longer be involved in cable television. "I'm ill...and can't give it the time it needs." We reluctantly accepted his resignation. Like Mr. Parks, Shell had always stated he was too old for the money to be made in this venture to matter to him. His primary interest in being involved was to see that the technology was brought into South Central like the rest of the United States.

———◆———

It was now May 1981. More than one year had passed since the original applications had been submitted for evaluation by the DOT, months after the resubmissions were filed as well, and the pressure from City Hall for our company to merge with the CTI group continued.

Our group believed, and the history from 1979 indicated, that unnecessary stalling and delays were now part of the modus operandi of the city and DOT when it came to awarding a cable television franchise for South Central Los Angeles—and not in our favor.

We wanted action *immediately* and felt we'd waited long enough. In our estimation, DOT was not equipped to handle making decisions regarding cable television franchises and they were always open to political pressure to subvert the process.

At our urging, in May 1981, Councilman Lindsay called Don Howery, General Manager, of DOT, complaining about the unacceptable and ongoing delays in evaluating the bids. Howery responded that DOT "did not have sufficient information" to analyze the bids. *Did not have sufficient information?*

Councilman Lindsay reportedly screamed at Howery because Howery's response seemed ridiculous. "Didn't your department evaluate franchises before 1979?"

Councilman Lindsay asked Howery how this was possible with the additional knowledge that DOT had already asked for the information not once but *twice*. "You delayed the usual application process once. Then you received the bids in April 1980. And then you open the process again to allow for changes when there's *never been* a process to allow for changes. Now you change things and want *a second set of additional information* to clarify anything you think you failed to ask for in the original bids on August 15. A year's about gone by...and now you say you need *more information*! What's going on down there?"

As a senior member of the City Council, Councilman Lindsay said he would *start an investigation* if the DOT and Mr. Howery continued to unduly delay the process. At the end of the conversation, Howery told Lindsay, "We'll issue the reports starting in the first week of June."

Without a doubt, our franchise group, UCS, believed DOT would have delayed the process further if Councilman Lindsay hadn't pressured them to issue reports. The glaring lack of independence shown by DOT since 1979 would soon become abundantly apparent in the evaluations of 1981.

Prior to the rise of cable television, DOT's primary responsibilities were the oversight of traffic lights, the regulation of the taxicab industry, and taking care of parking meters in the City of Los Angeles.

"Collection of nickels, dimes, and quarters clearly gives DOT the ability to understand the complexities of establishing and regulating cable television," Carl would frequently fume. "But they sure are nickel-and-diming us!"

How could the City of Los Angeles, a mecca for media and television, allow cable television franchise decisions to be made in DOT? Did they want it that way?

It was our view that some politicians in the City of Los Angeles *purposely wanted* the procedure to be handled this way. DOT's complete incompetence benefited the politicians because they could use it as a defense. Our sources indicated that the politicians routinely threatened DOT and any other department that didn't agree with them, making menacing comments about the makeup, number of jobs, employee hiring, salaries, and promotions they could influence in the Los Angeles City Council and the mayor's office. The people who worked in City Hall knew it. Representatives of both the mayor's office and the city councilmen could go down to the DOT and threaten and harangue their employees. "Stay in line, or else!"

The various politicians' threats about paychecks, benefits, and retirement packages of these DOT employees gave them "fear power" over employee decisions and, more specifically, power over the cable television industry decisions in the City of Los Angeles.

In our case, this practice of government interference attempting to control all media within a given geographic area clearly violated the Constitution of the United States and our constitutional rights. "You'll have to consider this if you go to court," our lawyer, Harold Farrow said.

"We already had a thick folder identifying all the illegal and unethical behavior you've experienced in the process," Ted Eagans agreed. "This is all so illegal and inappropriate on so many levels, Clint. At the very least, you've got a court case here based on constitutional grounds for the affect on your rights and failure of the city government to protect the South Central community's right for free speech and information by their callous and uncaring actions."

Another weakness of the system was that the manager of the DOT was an appointed position. Mayor Bradley could ask for the resignation of the manager of DOT at any time, if the mayor was dissatisfied. On one level, this was a concern to us because an appointee might already agree with and admire the policies of the administration that appointed him or her. That was one drawback. On another level, the end-of-paycheck and possible swift unemployment issue loomed if the presiding mayor became upset or displeased. Might appointed managers in City Hall try very hard to keep the mayor and his friends satisfied at the expense of business interests and the community?

The process and all the evaluations were supposed to be based on objective and independent analysis. The concepts of objectivity and independence were now compromised and the future ability of DOT to have independence and objectivity were certainly in doubt as well.

We also saw this as a business problem. We felt the DOT situation illustrated how elected officials might wield their power to the detriment of free enterprise and not serve the community and its constituents.

Chapter Five

Bureaucratic Shuffle – Busting the Evaluations

As the evaluations were issued, our fears were realized. The evaluations were so obviously biased that to repeat all the inaccuracies and lies contained within them would be boring and redundant.

Instead, I will focus on the dramatic differences between the evaluation of the Boyle Heights franchise and the evaluation of the South Central franchise—between our company, UCS, and the competing companies of CTI and BVT.

For our presentation here, I will also limit our discussion to a comparison of a few areas for each franchise, with special emphasis on the financing aspects of the franchise. These discrepancies were so egregious that the entire appearance of independence of DOT was totally destroyed. The evaluations in their entirety are available on the internet at our website, www. cablecomestosouthcentral.com, so anyone can look at them and decide for themselves.

———◆———

There were five sections in the original bidding package. Then, in DOT's second request, there were the five sections and several added sections asking additional information. Out of all of these, DOT devised a three-category, thirteen-section evaluation process to score and evaluate each bidding package.

What we saw and experienced was a "slicing and dicing" of information that enhanced the CTI and BVT application packages and downgraded and denigrated our company, UCS.

———◆———

FIVE-POINT SYSTEM:

Scoring and performance of the bidding packages now revolved around the section-by-section "evaluation process" and awarding of five points for each of the thirteen sections.

The company to get the Boyle Heights or South Central license had to get the most points overall—the highest responsible bidder.

According to DOT scoring methods, each of the thirteen sections was granted equal weight in determining the highest responsible bidder. For some inexplicable reason, the ability to finance a franchise bore the same weight as the selection of local programming in determining a responsible bidder.

We objected to the DOT premise when we discovered financial criteria were not given more points in the process. We'd already seen how defaults had deprived other franchise neighborhoods as witnessed by BVT's yet-undeveloped Los Angeles County franchise. South Central and the other two remaining franchises deserved immediate build-outs, broadcast capability, and programming.

If a company had no financial ability to perform the building of the franchise for the community, then none of the other things the company offered could be provided to the community either.

Additionally, in the evaluation process, past performance bore the same weight as the number of government access channels each company indicated on the application. So, a company that performed poorly in past business and franchise efforts might still be able to be the "most responsible bidder," as this information was overshadowed by high points in other categories. According to DOT and their system of evaluation, oranges were apples and apples were oranges.

We were concerned about the point system because a concrete, reliable standard for awarding points was never clearly delineated in the evaluation process. Subjective, unquantifiable decisions riddled the process. This left DOT in a position to continually alter the standards by which franchise applications were evaluated.

APPLICATION EVALUATION:

The evaluation standard was shameful in this part of the Los Angeles city government bureaucratic shuffle. We will only point out a few of DOT's most glaring inconsistencies in the evaluation process for the franchise areas.

The first section of the application was called "Biddable Items." In this section, eight categories outlined what each company might offer in terms of public benefits for each franchise.

The eight "Biddable Items" categories were:
Number of Public Access Channels
Number and Location of Public Access Studios
Public Access Studio Equipment
Number of Government Access Channels
Local Programming
System Capacity
Schedule of Construction
Other Consideration of Public Benefit

Most of the categories in this section of the application were straightforward numbers filled in by the applicant for the license.

For example, in the "Schedule of Construction" section the applicant would say, "*One year* for completion of entire system with construction commencing *three months* after award of the franchise license." There should have been little subjective interpretation of the categories. Unfortunately, the "Biddable Items" section became *very* subjective despite the fact that it was supposed to be a numerical comparison between offers.

The eighth and final category, "Other Consideration of Public Benefit," was clearly a place for subjective input by the evaluator. The use of such a nebulous term could not provide any objective criteria for this category. There was no definition of criteria for this category. The points were awarded without *any* information being submitted by the applicants.

———◆———

The second section of the application was called "Capacity to Perform." This section covered the financial and technical abilities of the applicant to successfully perform as a business under its franchise contract with the City of Los Angeles

The three categories in the "Capacity to Perform" section were:

Ability to Finance
Past Performance
Personnel

We felt these sections were the most critical sections in determining each company's ability to be a responsible bidder—a financially and industry-aware company. The company's ability to be a responsible bidder indicated that it had the strength and immediate competence to finance and operate the system license.

———◆———

The third section was called "The Technical Proposal," which described the cable system and community services and system safeguards. The two categories in the "Technical Proposal" section were:

System Design

Service Procedures

This section covered the basic design and construction build-out of the franchise and related service procedures to assure continuous service for the customers, maintenance, troubleshooting issues, and procedures for rectifying emergency or system failure problems.

In our view, once again, the subjective nature of the categories would lead to the award of points based upon inaccurate information and would inappropriately favor our competitors.

Again, please refer to a point-by-point comparison of the evaluation at www.cablecomestosouthcentral.com for the complete evaluation.

———— ◆ ————

The Boyle Heights franchise was the first franchise evaluated.

As stated before, even though Boyle Heights was not financially viable, our business decision to bid for the Boyle Heights franchise was based on the fact we felt it was better to have a business base and license in the cable industry than attempting to compete without any franchise license and be completely outside of the industry. Also, if we were successful in getting the Boyle Heights franchise, we intended to launch competing systems in surrounding areas in Los Angeles County to create a viable cable business.

Our group also felt the Boyle Heights franchise area evaluation report might give us important insights into how the city might establish evaluation "ground rules" and indicate guidelines and clear standards for all future franchise reports and evaluations.

We were disappointed. After studying the Boyle Heights evaluation, we identified the evaluation process was rigged. We soon learned the evaluation process was unique for each franchise area.

On looking at the scoring, we saw a trend indicating that the number of rating points awarded depended upon the desired outcome by the DOT. Unfortunately, the desired outcome seemed heavily dependent on which of the councilmen or mayor's assistants screamed the loudest at Don Howery, and not on impartial grading or evaluation standards.

———◆———

On June 1, 1981, DOT issued their recommendation to receive the Boyle Heights franchise. BVT, Esparza's company, was recommended for the Boyle Heights franchise as the "highest responsible bidder."

This was despite the fact their financial rating was three points out of a maximum five points. This meant BVT could only demonstrate the ability to provide sixty percent of the financing necessary to construct the franchise area. The concept of a responsible bidder would dictate that the bidder have at least the minimum amount of money to do what he had applied to do.

Conversely, our company received five points out of the maximum five points allowed. Despite our financial ability we would not be allowed to construct the franchise in an area where the only other applicant had failed to meet even the minimum standard of financing to build out the entire franchise. *As a citizen, would you want a company to gain a franchise to build only sixty percent of the system?*

As we stated before, at the outset, our group, UCS, and other new prospective franchisees for Boyle Heights, were handicapped in two ways: (1) the politicians and bureaucracy were part of the hustle, and (2) this financially non-viable franchise area was intentionally and uniquely designed by those same politicians and bureaucrats exclusively for the benefit of BVT.

We thought, and the scoring of the applications indicated, that the decision to award the Boyle Heights franchise had been made *before* the applications had even been submitted based upon the division of the franchise for the benefit of BVT.

As if carving out this financially non-viable new franchise area of Boyle Heights was not bad enough, seeing how the DOT manipulated the "objective" city application process in favor of BVT showed the application evaluation was not credible. The term "highest responsible bidder" was supposed to ensure the integrity of the bidding process, selecting the company that could perform and offered the most inducements to the city. The selection of BVT was anything but objective.

———•———

In the second section of the bidding package, in "Capacity to Perform", DOT wanted to gauge the bidding companies' ability to build out the franchise. "Past Performance" was one of three items in that section.

What was BVT's past performance? BVT had not even started building their other franchise. Was that *the acceptable behavior* of a "highly responsible bidder" in the case of the people still waiting for service from BVT?

BVT had agreed to finish construction of the East Los Angeles County franchise by April 1979 as a condition of receiving the franchise. As of July 1981, over two years after being awarded their Los Angeles County franchise, BVT had not begun construction of the franchise because they were unable to meet the condition of posting sufficient capital for the construction costs. BVT had no operational franchises and had failed to construct the only franchise that it had already been awarded. How could a company with this track record be in the bidding process at all, let alone get points for being a highly responsible bidder?

The County of Los Angeles was culpable in this as well. They continually granted extensions to BVT to construct the franchise. In written statements, the county granted these extensions of time because, in their words, BVT had "community identity," a term the county failed to define in their reports and one DOT used in its report with no definition as well. *Could this be a political euphemism?*

DOT gave BVT the highest rating available in the past performance category, despite the fact that BVT failed to perform on the only existing franchise they had already been awarded. This was the same five-point rating as our joint venture partners at Six Star, who were successful cable franchise owners and had built out their systems with little or no problems—on-time and in-place.

How do you compare total failure of performance by BVT (which had no operating cable television franchises) with the stellar track record of Six Star in building and operating twelve existing franchise systems as well as providing quality cable service to their existing franchise customers?

Yet our joint venture received the same rating as BVT. To DOT, no experience was the same as extensive successful experience.

———◆———

By utilizing the DOT evaluation of the Boyle Heights franchise area, we attempted to track the evaluation process and standards in other categories. None were consistent and each gave false impressions of the various franchise groups.

Biddable Items

The concept of "biddable items" indicated how each company determined to provide the most in-home cable channel access services to the public. For system capacity, our bid was 108 channels total capacity and all other competitors' offered 54 channels total capacity. Industry research, and looking at what had and continued to happen in the cable television industry, clearly showed that by the time the system was built, the amount of content would have expanded and additional capacity would be necessary.

We determined our customer's future needs based upon analysts' reports issued by Smith Barney, the international investment firm, where I was employed at the time. The report indicated cable television was rapidly expanding and exceeding the capacity of the older systems. Therefore, we used the most current projected programming growth industry information to decide that more capacity would be needed for our customers in the near future and we needed to plan accordingly. Systems of fifty-four channels would be inadequate.

Instead of receiving additional points for our higher bid, the DOT gave us both the same number of points. Giving the same number of points to BVT and UCS when our 108-channel capacity offer was twice the size and information capacity of our competitor?

DOT claimed that we had not disclosed a need for having more than fifty-four channels. Therefore, DOT unilaterally decreased our bid when the application had specified that the only criteria in evaluating the applications was the number submitted in the original application, and not an explanation of that number.

To the City of Los Angeles, 108 was equal to 54. That was the new political math. It is no wonder they have a hard time balancing their budget.

———•———

The most heinous concern was that DOT felt free to illegally make alterations of our application and alter their scores based on the changes they made—a mockery of any system of objective application evaluation. DOT displayed a clear, illegal, and outlandish violation of the law and previous DOT processes in evaluations.

We were outraged, as usual.

A process that used different criteria for the same evaluation process, depending upon who is submitting the information, is tainted, corrupt, and distinctly unreliable in identifying anything in the best interest of the citizens of Los Angeles.

Capacity to Perform

Any franchise applicant needed to demonstrate a strong financial ability to be awarded any city franchise. Each party needed to demonstrate the ability to operate and survive in challenging economic circumstances so citizens could be assured of uninterrupted services.

We submitted a strong presentation in the "Ability to Finance" section with the backing of our joint venture partner, Six Star. Throughout the process, the other franchise bidders' weakest points remained their inability to obtain strong financial backing to include in their bids. As we stated previously, our sources and several councilmen had told us these facts.

———•———

To provide a bit of context for our outrage about the extra time, benefits, and the enhanced evaluation given to BVT, we have to go back to 1980. DOT had asked for more information and had given all applicants time to resubmit their applications.

Al Watson called in July 1980. "I've got some more bad news—seems the time given to request additional information has given BVT an opportunity to find a partner for the Boyle Heights franchise."

BVT attempted to add a financial partner, Colony Communications, Inc., and alter the BVT application for the Boyle Heights franchise during the "request for additional information" time given by DOT. BVT stated in their revised application that they had sold a fifty-percent interest to Colony Communications, Inc., a Providence, Rhode Island-based company whose primary business was publishing newspapers. Their major newspaper was the *Providence Journal*.

We filed a protest with the Los Angeles City Attorney, stating that this business transaction constituted the forming of a "new" company and that the original bid should be considered null and void. In a rare difference with DOT, the city attorney said the merger did constitute a new bid and should be disallowed.

After the merger of BVT with Colony was prohibited by the city attorney, BVT was once again without financing to construct the franchise.

After BVT's merger attempt was rebuffed, they submitted the financial statement of a sole proprietor business to DOT to substantiate their ability to finance the construction of the Boyle Heights franchise. This new financial information was being submitted more than one year after the DOT had given BVT a second opportunity to submit new financial information in August 1980. BVT asked the DOT to keep the financial information secret during this public process.

Since financial statements and financial ability were part of the evaluation, all information was supposed to be available for review for independent scrutiny as a matter of public record. This was how the integrity of a public process was supposed to be protected from fraud and misstatements. *Why did BVT want to keep their finances secret?*

In an unprecedented change from past cable television franchise application procedures, DOT complied and denied the public review and scrutiny of the financial statements during the application process.

For the Boyle Heights franchise, according to DOT, in looking at an applicant's submitted financial statements, the officials said their position was that they were not asking the applicant to prove financial capability at this time.

It was yet another new change in rules and regulations—the franchise applicants didn't have to prove financial capability. How could the rights for service and that interests of the community be protected if no financial capability review was done?

What the change *did* do was allow BVT to stay in the application process—and eventually win the Boyle Heights bid.

———

We protested many times during this period, before the reevaluations of BVT's financing were released. As we asserted in our complaints to DOT, our franchise group, UCS, was at a disadvantage because we could not contest information that was supposed to be part of the public process—but was kept secret.

The DOT, on every occasion, refused to release for review the financial statements used by BVT for the Boyle Heights franchise to substantiate their financial ability. The basis for the DOT refusal was that the person who had submitted the financial statements had requested that they not be made public. The public process was completely changed, just for asking, when you had friends at City Hall.

The effect of the refusal of the DOT for public review meant we would have to rely on the integrity of DOT to tell us whether the financial statements for BVT were sufficient to assure the building of the Boyle Heights franchise. In our estimation, DOT had been unreliable since our first dealings with them in 1979. Of the many things we had learned after more than two years of dealing with

DOT, saying "integrity" and "DOT" in the same sentence did not reflect reality.

Immediately after the refusal by DOT to allow access to what previously had been public information, we filed a written protest with the Los Angeles City Attorney, asserting that potential franchisee financial information was required to be open to the public.

The city attorney issued a written opinion regarding the DOT refusal of information submitted by a bidder—in favor of withholding public information.

The city attorney's opinion said that any bidder in a public bidding process could request that their financial information be shielded from public scrutiny. The determining factor was whether the bidder wanted his financial information to be made public during a public process. How could a process be both public and secret to make a determination of what was best for the citizens of any community?

We argued that these events were completely contrary to the long-held public bidding rules—thus forming a "new" public application process precedent. The concept defied both basic logic and the law. The public bidding process was now composed of secret information—another essential political oxymoron.

———————

We later discovered BVT's secret shareholder was H. Frank Dominguez. Dominguez was a real estate developer from San Bernardino, California. His financial statements were used in this attempt to support the financial ability of BVT to build the Boyle Heights franchise. At the time of their submission to DOT, Dominguez's financial statements showed a negative net worth. A negative net worth means a person is near or actually bankrupt. Mr. Dominguez's secret financial statements indicated he had more liabilities than assets or, as Mr. Watson put it, "More bills on his desk than dollars in his bank accounts."

As a CPA, I was trained and licensed in the evaluation of financial statements as well as giving opinions regarding the accuracy and integrity of financial statements. Given the opportunity, I could have clearly pointed out the defect in relying on financial statements with a negative net worth, which made the applicant more of a candidate for bankruptcy court rather than being a viable cable franchise backer expected to provide millions of dollars in financing to BVT.

The public versus private documents and negative net worth arguments notwithstanding, we had other concerns with the DOT financial process. Again, unlike other City of Los Angeles financial procedures, the financial statements submitted by the franchise applicants were not audited by any accredited accounting firm to check for financial stability, accuracy, and capability within the applications.

Another flaw we uncovered in the procedures was that DOT employees could make their recommendations and not be called to testify, under oath, to explain their actions, criteria, or written recommendations. So our company could not, if we felt we had been unjustly denied the franchise, ask any DOT employees to testify at the Los Angeles City Council or at any of the hearings. DOT was immune from having to support its recommendations and free to make any recommendations that they chose, regardless of justification or sensibility. DOT could make the most nonsensical decisions, make preposterous recommendations for franchises, and not be held accountable.

So in the political setup to help BVT's cable application, DOT helped BVT in three ways. First, DOT said that final financial ability could be provided after the award of the franchise, thereby allowing BVT to continue in the process merely by demonstrating the ability to provide only 60% of the financing necessary to construct the franchise. Second, BVT could continue in the bidding process even when BVT tried to merge with another company and this merger was negated by the Los Angeles City Attorney's office. And finally, BVT could base their financial ability on the "secret," unaudited, negative-net-worth financial statements of a "secret" shareholder.

The new company, now called "BVT of Boyle Heights," emerged from this process and they did not even have to resubmit their company's cable franchise application.

———◆———

As our company's protests and inquiries to the City of Los Angeles and the city attorney escalated, the deeply flawed evaluation of the financial statements in question deteriorated to totally secret meetings and decision making by DOT by the end of the process.

All information concerning BVT's financing was based upon statements by members of the DOT who were the only ones allowed to examine and give points in the bidding process, but were not required to be under oath concerning their actions.

———◆———

It was six years after the franchise had been awarded before our group, during our subsequent litigation, was able to get copies and examine the complete financial statements DOT had relied upon in the evaluation process.

———◆———

System Design

Although we also proposed to build a system that was better than our competitors, we received a lower point rating based on the fact DOT said they "liked" the other system better. They gave no reason nor did they define what they liked better about the other system.

As we waited in the hearing room for the meeting of the BTC I pointed out that the city had defined our bids as a contractual obligation between the city and the bidders, once submitted. "This is a contractual obligation they're tampering with," I fumed. "They're breaking the law."

During the hearing regarding the Boyle Heights franchise results, we asked John Haggerty, a deputy city attorney, to clarify whether our bid was evaluated "as written" or whether DOT had altered our bid. We also asked the city attorney for an opinion relative to the legality of DOT making changes to our bids. The city attorney refused to answer either question.

But as the city attorney had previously indicated in his statements, applicants were bound by the numbers contained in their original applications. Why wouldn't the city attorney answer our questions now?

For the first time, the city attorney allowed the DOT to alter applications, which was contrary to the application process and to the previous rulings of the city attorney's office. The city attorney seemed more like the politicians all the time—not allowing testimony under oath, not requiring public financial documentation, and now giving DOT permission to change bids.

Our application was changed by DOT because DOT was allowed to alter numerical bids to something other than what was contained in our original application. If we were bound by the original numbers submitted in our original application, how could we receive credit for a lesser number?

In subsequent testimony and applications, the city attorney refused to discuss his previous rulings and refused to issue a ruling regarding what had been submitted in our application.

In each subsequent evaluation, DOT changed the evaluation criteria for each franchise area. We knew the extent of the changes because we had bid in all three franchise areas and the discrepancies became abundantly clear.

Every time the criteria were changed by the DOT, it always worked to our detriment—and to the advantage of BVT and CTI. The evaluation process was not even close to being objective.

———◆———

In July 1980, we received a phone call from Paul Skulsky.

"I've hung in there as long as I can with you guys. A damned shame things got so tangled for you. It's a great deal if you get it. But I've gotten a great offer to merge Six Star with a large financial partner." My heart sank as I pondered the possibility of losing our partner.

"Don't worry. Our new partners are ready to put their intentions in writing to go on with the South Central franchise application, all three applications, to be precise, if they should fall back into the bidding process. Don't want to leave you in the lurch," Paul stated.

"We'll tell the city and give it to you in writing when all the documents for the merger of the company are ready. We'd have to anyway as a part of our legal obligation for the all our franchise licenses, including the dozen or so we have in Los Angeles," Paul continued. "That's when we'll also inform them *in person* and *in writing* that we fully intend to honor our franchise application commitments to UCS."

"Mind if we check with all the attorneys?" I asked.

"Not at all," Paul replied. "We'll meet with you so you can get to know the new partners. I've told them you're an impressive team."

In the next few months, the lawyers indicated that everything was taken care of and the credit rating and a strong financial package remained in place for our franchise application. We notified DOT and submitted all the paperwork.

———————

While completing the ownership change for Six Star in our applications, we had to object to the awarding of Boyle Heights to BVT.

"Hopefully we'll get our chance to tell our story when the hearings come up," I said. "BVT can't get away with this."

The hearings at the BTC included numerous delays to allow BVT to find the financial backing that was absent in their original application. The hearings at the BTC consisted of five different hearings stretching from August to December—five months to give BVT more opportunities to change their original application.

The hearings were supposed to be the city's legislative part of the government process. The process was supposed to allow the BTC and the Industry and Economic Development Committee (IEDC), the subcommittee involved, and a one-day council calendar hearing for the full city council, to learn about and debate the aspects of the proposals, applications, etc., concerning cable television in the Council chambers. *Would our efforts to expose the inequities of the application work or would the political games continue on this level?*

The DOT recommendation of BVT getting the Boyle Heights franchise began the hearing process, which consisted of three phases. The first hearing would be before the Board of Transportation Commissioners (BTC), a commission appointed by the mayor. The BTC would evaluate the reports and recommendations they were given by DOT concerning the pending applications.

After the hearing at the BTC, the commissioners could agree with the DOT or change the recommendation of the highest responsible bidder for the franchise.

The BTC recommendation would then be sent to the IEDC for a hearing before a committee consisting of three of the fifteen Los Angeles City Council members.

After the hearing at the IEDC, there was to be a hearing at the full Los Angeles City Council meeting for a final vote by the full council on the Boyle Heights franchise award.

"We're not going to make any headway with the DOT, so we've got to make our case clear to the commissions and city council during the hearings," Mr. Watson said.

"This might be rough because you know the BTC has no experience in the area of cable television," Carl said. "They've just basically rubber-stamped everything sent to them from DOT after the politicians have gotten through with it."

"Do they know anything about cable television?" Mr. Parks asked. Carl shook his head.

Carl was right. The BTC was supposed to be a five-member "citizens commission" to look out for the best interests of the public in Los Angeles, mostly with concerns about traffic and taxicabs in the City of Los Angeles.

Lack of knowledge wasn't our only concern. Getting a fair hearing from the BTC was going to be problematic. "You need to watch out for them," Al Watson said. "If they get appointed, some stay on the commission bandwagon for years to keep their power, prestige, and information. It's another political game."

We found out the members of the BTC were appointed by Mayor Bradley and composed primarily of those who had made large contributions or had hosted fundraisers for Mayor Bradley's mayoral and gubernatorial campaigns.

The chairman of the BTC was Robert Chick, who served on various citizen commissions then, and for the next two decades. According to a 1991 *Los Angeles Business Journal* article, Robert Chick was, "in short, a veteran of Los Angeles' system of citizen commissions and a direct beneficiary of Mayor Tom Bradley's 18-year tenure."

Norman Emerson, another member of the BTC, would also go on to have a career as a government bureaucrat on various state and local commissions and boards. He and Chick, the most senior members on the BTC, were both fundraisers for Mayor Bradley's gubernatorial race.

When we started the process, we thought we might be able to get an objective and lawful hearing from the BTC and the IEDC assigned to the cable franchise system. Now we knew to expect problems with the IEDC, and we got them. We were presented with a merry-go-round of meaningless hearings, evasions, and blustering with little substance or merit.

Our history with the BTC and IEDC always proved to be problematic, much like dealing with the DOT. Our protests and problems were submitted to both boards and were basically ignored or sent to the city attorney or other departments to be lost, mishandled, or denied.

During the entire application process, BTC never objected to the long delays in awarding the franchises, the BVT financing debacle when they should have been thrown out of the process when the city attorney ruled their merger with Colony Communications was inappropriate, or when a secret bidder and equally secret financial statements were allowed in a previously open and public process.

We were stonewalled in every encounter. I was told by two of the five BTC members, Robert Chick and Eileen Woodson, that they had been directed by Mayor Bradley to make sure our company did not receive any recommendations for a cable television license regardless of the location. They were very straightforward and honest about the situation and expressed their regrets about having to do what Mayor Bradley wanted—but they did as they were told.

Despite the glaring discrepancies within the evaluation performed by DOT, BTC supported the DOT recommendation of BVT for the franchise in Boyle Heights. BTC refused to allow discussion of the discrepancies that existed within the DOT report.

As Carl and Mr. Watson predicted, the BTC recommendation was merely an acceptance of the DOT recommendation issued regarding Boyle Heights and BVT. It was a rubber stamp, just as we had feared.

———————

The next hearing would be held before the IEDC, which was composed of three members of the Los Angeles City Council, who would review the recommendation of the BTC and make their recommendation to the city council. Our dealings with the IEDC did not improve our confidence in City Hall.

Art Snyder, who represented the predominantly Hispanic East Los Angeles section, was the chairman of the committee because of his seniority on the council. Joan Flores, a relatively new member of the city council and a former deputy to John Gibson, the former councilman who represented the Wilmington-San Pedro area, was the second member. When we first met with Joan Flores she was still a deputy to Councilman Gibson. Pat Russell, who represented the Venice area and had been on the city council for approximately eight years, was the third member.

Chairman Snyder continually, and sometimes publicly, indicated his dislike for Six Star and for our company as well. In 1979, even before applications had been submitted for South Central-Harbor or the subsequent three franchise areas, Snyder had written a very negative letter, calling Carl and Edgar Charles a "minority front" for Six Star, alleging both Carl and Charles were only a part of the application process because they were black.

Secondly, BVT cable operator owner, Moctesuma Esparza, was a Snyder supporter and Snyder had supported the division of the franchise for the benefit of Esparza with his vote on the city council.

Thirdly, Snyder was in a very vulnerable political situation. "You know he's got to listen to his Hispanic contributors because his constituency is seventy-five percent Hispanic," Al Watson informed us.

"Snyder won't go against Mayor Bradley and don't think for a minute he's going to alienate Esparza. Snyder doesn't have a drop of Hispanic blood in his body and his whole district is Hispanic. He needs all the help he can to keep his council seat. Got the picture?" Councilman Lindsay added.

Our optimism faded as the abuses under Snyder's chairmanship mounted. The hearings at the IEDC did not go well, and were a continuing sideshow.

"We've got to face Snyder again," was all I said when it came to the days we'd attend the IEDC hearings.

Councilman Snyder, as the chairman, effectively prevented anyone from asking questions. Snyder refused to allow questions to be asked directly to DOT and its representatives regarding their evaluation report. Our questions would go unanswered and the additional members of the DOT only deferred to Snyder as chairman of the committee.

Since DOT had written the application evaluation reports, we sought to get an explanation regarding the inconsistencies in their evaluations. The procedures and rules DOT specified were not being followed by their employees. They continually changed them. As was clearly indicated above, the rating process changed for each franchise and these changes always favored the political allies of the councilmen and the mayor.

In one meeting after another, Councilman Snyder would not allow our company to ask questions directly of the DOT General Manager, Don Howery. Instead, we were supposed to address our questions to Snyder and the IEDC and they would ask DOT the questions. We did not get any answers to our questions. Snyder rephrased half the answers and made mistaken assumptions on many others, which effectively misdirected the thrust of the needed information. The remainder of our questions were simply not answered at all because Snyder did not ask them. *Were DOT employees not competent enough to understand the questions asked by the bidders?*

When we protested this procedure and the continual lack of answers to our submitted questions, Councilman Snyder would always say, "If you're not satisfied, you can bring these issues to the floor when the full city council was in session. It will be put on the calendar and DOT will inform you when the meetings will be held."

Finally, the IEDC approved the BVT bid for the Boyle Heights franchise and the hearings moved on to the full Los Angeles City Council. That neither the BTC or the IEDC faced the shortcomings of DOT's flawed and secret financial evaluation was just further evidence that the end result was developed before the materials were reviewed.

We researched Councilman Snyder's assertions about the scheduling and timing of calendar issues before the city council. He was correct. DOT was responsible for notifying each applicant in advance of the dates and times for the hearings before the Los Angeles City Council. The agenda of the city council was changed each day and the final decision to hear a particular issue was subject to the priorities determined by the council.

Here we suffered from more political deceit that deteriorated into more lies. DOT used its power of notification to prevent our ability to present our case in front the full Los Angeles City Council.

For the Boyle Heights franchise hearings before the Los Angeles City Council, DOT refused to tell us when hearings were going to be held, although they had the current contact information for everyone in our company, including our board members. We called several times but were always told that no date had been set for the hearing.

DOT sent a letter postmarked on a Friday afternoon informing us about a city council hearing on the following Monday morning. We received the letter on Monday afternoon, hours after the meeting was held.

At the hearing before the full Los Angeles City Council, Councilman Lindsay asked Howery if we had been notified. Howery told the council members we had been notified and had chosen not to attend the hearings.

Don Howery deliberately lied to the council despite the fact we had made it abundantly clear that we intended to present our complaints about DOT and their deceptions before the full city council. DOT and Mr. Howery showed that they would go to any lengths to keep their rigged evaluations and mask the political manipulations and maneuverings from being discovered by the full city council and the public.

Carl sent a telegram, on the same day as the award, to Mayor Tom Bradley and asked him to investigate our allegations that we had been prohibited from testifying before the full city council. At this time, Carl was actually more concerned about developing a future court record because he realized that he could expect no assistance or justice from the office of Mayor Bradley.

The mayor wrote back and told us that he had already signed the franchise ordinance that awarded the franchise to "BVT of Boyle Heights" even though "BVT" was the original applicant. His letter also stated that he had signed the ordinance on the same day that it had been passed by the city council—an almost unheard-of event in Los Angeles city government. The mayor acknowledged that BVT of Boyle Heights had received the franchise despite the fact that BVT had been the original applicant. He attempted to explain the discrepancy by saying that the two companies were essentially the same. Companies with different names are not the same companies regardless of how close the names seem.

So Boyle Heights was awarded to BVT of Boyle Heights on January 18, 1982. For the franchise there had been only two bidders, BVT and us.

The Boyle Heights franchise would not be built for more than five years nor would they ever file the financial documentation necessary to finalize the award of franchise according to the city law. They were allowed to hold the rights of the citizens of Boyle Heights in abeyance for more than five years before they decided how they could make some money off of defaulting on the franchise.

In January 1988, H. Frank Dominguez filed for protection of the U.S. Bankruptcy Court. Dominguez had never provided any financing for the Boyle Heights franchise when he filed his bankruptcy petition.

Chapter six

What Color Is Your Money?

Our company had seen that the motivation behind the lies, decisions, and deceptions were solely political and greed-based.

We needed Councilman Lindsay, as our ally, to step in more strongly, counter these bidding abuses, and gain support from other of his fellow council members not aligned with Farrell, Cunningham, or Snyder. We also needed ties with the media to tell the affected neighborhoods and the public about these abuses. We knew we were dealing in millions, and Councilman Lindsay was dealing in billions in his redevelopment of downtown Los Angeles. *Would he be able to give us the help we needed?*

As we'd discovered, delays helped the friends of certain Los Angeles City Council members and Mayor Bradley find ways to strengthen their bids, and when those tactics failed, to have the politicians and DOT change the bid procedures to fit their predetermined decisions.

"The delays might be a good thing." Councilman Lindsay put his hands up at our groans. "Because if we can *prove* to the other councilmen that BVT hasn't built out their county franchise or done any work to get a staff together to build Boyle Heights, we might have a chance to change some minds." Gil went on to say, "We can also show the whole council the DOT reports don't make any sense at all."

Gil had told us on more than one occasion that he knew the reports were rigged, "But I didn't really have time to delve into the situation until it came to South Central."

"I'm not much of a betting man on these things, Gil. But I think we're headed for court," Al Watson replied. No one said anything more in reply.

———— ◆ ————

The hearings at the BTC and IEDC and the fights for information from the DOT didn't occur in a vacuum. At the same time, political pressure concerning the South Central franchise from the mayor's office, councilmen, and political "friends" became unrelenting.

For example, on June 24, 1981, at a meeting held in the office of Councilman Lindsay, CTI continued their efforts to force us to merge with their company.

William Elkins, special deputy to Mayor Tom Bradley, said the mayor had determined that if we did not merge with CTI with sixty-six percent of the company going to CTI and thirty-three percent going to our company, CTI would attempt to arrange a merger with American Telecommunications Corporation (ATC). Our company refused the merger and the terms.

"Guess they've changed their tune about a minority-owned company being an option," All Watson said sourly.

"Remember when Councilman Snyder wrote that letter saying Edgar and I were a 'black front' for Six Star in 1979?" Carl added.

"Wonder if they're abandoning the neighborhood for a dona-tion to Bradley's governorship campaign chest?" Mr. Parks remarked in reply.

"Is there any doubt?" I asked sarcastically.

We'd made our decision to say "no" to CTI, so we'd just have to wait and see.

———————

Things were no better at DOT. DOT still had no capability for analyzing anything in the cable television industry because they had no experienced personnel within that area. Even after all the problems concerning evaluating the Boyle Heights franchise, including questions regarding years of delays in the process, our sources indicated DOT still had not hired or trained personnel in the department to adequately evaluate the cable television industry. So, the city would continue to use the incompetence of DOT as shield for their unrestrained malfeasance and corruption.

The South Central recommendations were coming up soon.

———————

DOT notified the bidders its office would issue its recommendations for the South Central franchise on August 13, 1981, at the next BTC meeting—a notice to us that South Central bids would finally be evaluated and would soon become a bigger part of the BTC meeting conversations.

The report was officially titled "Evaluation and Recommendation of Highest Responsible Bidder for the Cable Television Franchise for South Central Los Angeles."

The hearing process with BTC and IEDC for the South Central franchise began in the middle of August 1981. There were three bidders: our company, Universal Cable Systems (UCS); Community Telecommunications, Inc. (CTI); and American Telecommunications Corporation (ATC).

At this August 13, 1981, meeting, DOT issued its report recommending ATC as the highest responsible bidder for the South Central cable television franchise. CTI finished second in the evaluation process and, to no one's surprise, UCS finished third, or last.

CTI was able to finish ahead of UCS despite the fact DOT said CTI could only demonstrate the ability to fund sixty percent of the cost to construct the franchise. DOT had taken great liberty with the term "highest responsible bidder" in the past, with the Boyle Heights franchise award, and would do so again for the for the South Central franchise.

We thought an applicant who could not finance an entire cable television franchise could not be considered responsible. Therefore that applicant had to be eliminated from consideration as the highest responsible bidder. The wording clearly indicated that only those bidders who were in fact "responsible" could vie for the designation as the highest responsible bidder.

The inaccuracies, distortions, and outright lies in DOT's evaluation are too many to describe in full in this text. Therefore, I shall provide samples from each of the sections for which we were being evaluated.

Biddable items

One area where the DOT was able to make a purely subjective evaluation was in the area of local programming. The DOT in its own report states that "all bidders propose more or less equivalent numbers and types of local programming." In the ratings, however, ATC was given five points while we were only given three points. DOT was making a subjective evaluation as to the content of our programming meeting their unknown and unexplained criteria as opposed to the needs of the community.

In the area of system capacity, the DOT, once again, gave our competitors more credit for offering 112 channels of capacity versus the 116 channels that were offered by our company. Since the category was strictly a numerical comparison, we were unable to determine how a lower number could get a higher rating.

Technical proposal

The section identified as system design was once again used in a subjective manner to reduce the rating for UCS. The DOT report said that it preferred the design of ATC to the design that we had provided. The DOT had also stated that the systems were virtually equivalent.

DOT gave our competitors five points and gave us four points for essentially the same cable television system. The evaluation continued to be random and without tangible support for the rating points issued.

Ability to Finance

The DOT evaluation gave UCS the highest financial rating available during the process. That rating of five points meant that according to DOT, we had the ability to provide 100% of the financing for the construction of the cable television system for which we were seeking a license. From our standpoint, the ability to provide the financing for the project represented the "responsible" part of the "highest responsible bidder."

Because we did have the ability to finance the cable television system we were seeking to construct, DOT would have to find other areas in an attempt to portray us as unsuitable to develop the South Central franchise.

———————

At this same August 13, 1981, BTC meeting, our group wanted to ask questions in the first public hearing regarding the South Central bidding process. The meeting was cut short after Donald Howery announced CTI and ATC had proposed to merge their bids into a new joint venture, saying they had been in merger talks since June 1981. CTI was talking to our group about merging on June 24, 1981, in Councilman Lindsay's office!

Fortunately, even with those new allies for CTI, our efforts to publicize the inequities in the bidding process for the Boyle Heights franchise were starting to pay off. People and media were beginning to question the whole cable television franchise application process after the Boyle Heights award.

With increased public scrutiny, applicants would be forced to show their true ability to build and finance their proposed cable television companies. Since this was not possible for CTI, a merger was the only solution. The BTC, at the request of the

DOT, announced that they would delay any hearings in order to give CTI and ATC time to attempt to form a merger. Once again, the principles of government favoring Los Angeles city government insiders continued to be allowed without question.

We had just been through the same process with BVT and the Boyle Heights franchise. The city attorney had previously ruled that any mergers during the application phase were illegal and would not be allowed. Clearly, ATC and CTI's proposed merger fell under the same guidelines covered in the Boyle Heights ruling. The matter of mergers had already been decided during the Boyle Heights hearings. Hadn't they?

Secondly, our group had been told in countless meetings and conversations that Councilmen Farrell and Cunningham wanted a cable television company that was minority-owned and Six Star did not meet the criteria. Now, ATC, which was not minority-owned, was welcomed as a merger applicant. Now that their political cronies, Bakewell and Johnson, were aligned with ATC, a "white partner" was acceptable? How could the black Los Angeles City Councilman Farrell defend this?

Councilman Lindsay often said, "Bakewell's ties to the mayor are critical in Bradley's run for governor of California a year from this November." So Bakewell's involvement made everything and anything acceptable?

"No doubt," Mr. Watson huffed.

Lindsay continued, "No one wants to get on Bradley's bad side if they expect to have a political career or get more favors after his expected election for governor."

This was true. Tom Bradley was in the midst of beginning his official run for governor in the state of California. According to the *Los Angeles Times*, Tom Bradley was now the most powerful Democrat in the state of California.

So, CTI now supposedly had the financing of ATC and the political backing of Bradley, Farrell, and Cunningham.

———————

One month later on September 24, 1981, another hearing was held by the BTC regarding the South Central franchise. The five members were Robert Chick, the chairman, and board members Aileen Woodson, Nathan Terry, Norman Emerson, and Blanche Orban.

At the hearing, CTI and ATC announced that they intended to enter into an agreement whereby if either party received the franchise, they would form a merger. This was what they called a "Participation Agreement." They sought to avoid the use of the term merger since that had already been rejected by the office of the city attorney in the Boyle Heights process.

In the city's franchise-award history, creating mergers prior to the award of a franchise had always been denied. We were incredulous that these merger talks were allowed to continue despite the previous rulings in Boyle Heights regarding mergers during the franchising process.

Because of the changes in documentation and procedures, and the misrepresentations continually being put forth by DOT, Carl asked that the proceedings be held under oath. The city attorney was very familiar with our complaints regarding DOT's behavior and evaluations. John Haggerty, a deputy city attorney, screamed across the room, "This is a legislative process and not required to be under oath." The heated response of the deputy city attorney was puzzling. Why was he so concerned about people being put under oath?

In a surprise move, Chairman Chick asked the city attorney, "What would be necessary to reject all applications for the South Central application process and start the franchising process again?"

This move was especially troubling since two of the three applicants, ATC and us, had demonstrated that we had 100% of the financial ability required to construct the franchise. ATC was the largest cable television company in the United States at the time—a fact evidenced in the DOT report recommending ATC as the highest responsible bidder in August 1981.

The City Attorney said he did not know what would be necessary but the city council had wide discretion to reject all applications if they found them insufficient for their purposes. This was just legal gibberish for "we can do anything we want."

No such talk regarding the rejection of all applications had occurred for any of the other franchises on which we had bid. We had already sunk hundreds of thousands of dollars into this process. Would this eliminate the existing applicants under the guise that a new bidding process would bring more and better applications? Was this a move by BTC to eliminate our company from any future bidding processes?

According to our records and the actions of Los Angeles city agencies, from that day forward, the ongoing goal of the city attorney working in conjunction with Councilmen Snyder and Cunningham, would be to reject all applications and to eliminate all black applicants from the application process. This represented a total reversal of their previous position that they would seek a minority-owned company for the franchise, which they had stated would be in the best interests of South Central.

So it seemed like our political adversaries were now running on two strong but different tracks, to get CTI the franchise or to ignore the minority ownership and community participation proposed in the Community Antennae Television Master Plan altogether.

Was it one or the other, or could there be some other unknown strategy?

We did what we could within the city government system. After the September 24, 1981, BTC hearing, we protested the merger attempt of CTI and ATC on the basis of the city attorney's previous ruling. The process had already been delayed for months based upon CTI's attempt to find financing.

We also wanted to get this information on the public record at every possible meeting to document the bizarre explanations and interpretation of numbers given in the DOT evaluations. Being cheated in numbers and explanations, in most every area of the bid, was especially infuriating to me as a CPA.

We now knew beyond a shadow of a doubt that South Central needed an independent media voice and the citizens of Los

Angeles needed to know what was going on in City Hall. We notified the District Attorney of the County of Los Angeles about the improprieties in the bidding process. We also notified the Attorney General of the State of California and the Attorney General of the United States. We were being railroaded and our civil rights were being violated in the light of day.

We pointed out the many ways the South Central cable television franchise had been segregated by the City of Los Angeles to the detriment of the neighborhood, which was unable to receive the benefits of the new technology because of the ever-changing bidding process. The response from all parties was the same.

Our company had to complete the legislative and administrative processes before we could raise the issue of improper behavior or malfeasance by the local government. Did it matter that the Los Angeles County District Attorney, the Attorney General of California, and the United States Attorney General were all members of the Democratic Party? Sadly, we now knew most of our efforts would involve keeping records for the court fight to come.

We felt from the previous political efforts to help the CTI and BVT companies that the process was now delayed by BTC an additional two and a half months in order to facilitate attempts by both to attain financing.

"I'll try to find out if they're *really* trying to cut out minority owners in favor of ATC," Al Watson said, "and I'll let you know."

On October 30, 1981, ATC and CTI submitted their "Participation Agreement" to the BTC for consideration. On that same date BTC asked the city attorney for an opinion regarding the proposed merger or "participation" of ATC and CTI. The two companies had identified four ways they could be awarded the franchise and still merge companies. All methods involved the participation to the exclusion of the only remaining bidder for the franchise—our group, UCS. The BTC, under Chairman Chick adjourned this meeting by asking the city attorney to give them an opinion at that future meeting about the "Participation Agreement" proposed by CTI and ATC.

Why would it take so long for the BTC to ask for a legal opinion on the same subject since it had been considered in the Boyle Heights franchise area months earlier? Another political move? This was certainly not an indication of a high level of integrity exhibited by the BTC.

———◆———

On November 9, 1981, the city attorney, James Hahn, issued the opinion regarding the proposed merger of CTI and ATC. It obviously did not take much time to determine whether the proposed activities by CTI and ATC were legal.

In summary, the city attorney said any merger would represent an illegal bid enhancement and was therefore prohibited by city law. Once again, CTI was forced to stand on its own merits, a problem since CTI had no independent financial or technical ability in the cable television industry.

CTI's financial rating of three of the five maximum points indicated that they could hopefully raise sixty percent of the financing. This represented the ability to provide sixty percent of the financing necessary to construct the franchise application area.

———◆———

On November 10, 1981, the BTC held a hearing to review the opinion of the city attorney and determine future action regarding the South Central franchise.

At this hearing, ATC formally withdrew its application for the South Central franchise. Once again the BTC delayed any hearings regarding the South Central franchise in order to consider the implications of ATC's withdrawal from the franchising process.

The evaluations had already been presented. If the former procedures regarding franchise applications were followed, ATC's withdrawal from the process should have had no effect on the existing evaluations that had already been completed and submitted.

At the same hearing, Norman Emerson, a commissioner of the BTC, asked about the term, "minority participation encouraged," as referenced in the published notice by the city for the submission of applications for the South Central franchise.

Once again, it appeared to us that the more nebulous and subjective term, "encouraged," gave the appearance minorities would participate in the process, rather than the original edict that minorities would have *majority* holdings in the cable television franchise. Was this another hint to ignore the Community Antenna Television Master Plan created by the City of Los Angeles?

We did not seek nor did we receive any benefit for being black citizens in this process. If anything, the opposite is true. At every point, we, as a black cable television company, had been discouraged from participation. There was no consideration of the Community Antenna Television Master Plan at any point in this process.

The city attorney responded to Emerson that the term "minority participation encouraged" was too general to provide any guidance to any effective use during the evaluation process. This was completely contrary to the intentions of the Community Antenna Television Master Plan and all public pronouncements identified by Mayor Bradley and Los Angeles city councilmen since the 1970s.

The city attorney went on to say that "minority participation had *not been identified* as a factor" during the evaluation process. Therefore, it would be inappropriate and illegal to add minority participation as a factor after the submission of applications—again, another far cry from the meetings and political maneuvering we witnessed in our effort to that time.

Aileen Woodson and Robert Chick questioned the city attorney about allowing minority participation to become a factor in their evaluation, even though it had not been considered by DOT. *Were they hoping to use the concept of minority participation to allow more time for under-qualified or friends to continue in the process?*

Emerson continued to express his feelings by saying, "It is important that the South Central franchise have a *dominant minority company* in the bids for both financial and management capabilities to assure that the system is a credible system."

Emerson and Woodson pointed out that the city had a master plan for cable television that called for minority ownership of the South Central franchise in order to properly serve the community. Developing such a master plan was one of the great reasons given in 1975 for refusing to allow the development of the South Central franchise, stopping at least two black companies (and numerous applications) from being addressed, and developing cable television franchises earlier, including the ones from Edgar Charles and Ted Eagans.

The city attorney said the master plan did not have any effect upon the evaluation at hand because no reference had been made to that report in the original notice of sale for the applications. According to the city attorney, the master plan for cable television, which had been developed by the City of Los Angeles, would have no meaning in the actual development of cable television within the City of Los Angeles. *What?* A plan was ordered, written, referred to, and acted on as policy for many years...and now it had no meaning?

When is a master plan really a master plan? If their master plan was not really being followed as a master plan, it was just another piece of bureaucratic junk, created at taxpayer expense for no reason.

There also was no legal basis to ignore these and previous applications by the city, which chose to place a moratorium on the development of South Central, at the request of Tom Bradley, while other areas in the city were being developed.

The long-touted Community Antennae Television Master Plan for the City of Los Angeles and the importance of minority ownership was now being conveniently forgotten and excluded from consideration in the franchising process.

———

ATC had effectively withdrawn from major new opportunities in the Los Angeles market. Why would the largest cable television company in the United States withdraw from the number-two television market in the United States?

Gayle Greer, a vice president for ATC said, "ATC is supportive of minority ownership in areas where the minority is the dominant population." Publicly, the importance of minority participation in media that could benefit the lives of the people in South Central was not lost upon the nation's largest cable company. Ms. Greer, as a black woman, understood the importance of media for, and within, the black community. Privately, however, might her reasons have been different? Was ATC, as we were, tired of all the strong personalities and opinions of CTI and the strong-arm tactics of City Hall? Had CTI demanded majority interest in the South Central franchise as they had with us?

After ATC withdrew its application, our company was the only remaining applicant retaining the maximum financial rating. This would not bode well for CTI. Political connections could only get them so far. The public hearings were coming and people in the neighborhood and media were catching on to the truth about the political intrigues and changes going on with the cable television franchise application process.

Now that ATC had withdrawn, the only bidders remaining were our company and CTI. For the first time in this go-around, two minority-controlled companies were vying for a major urban cable television franchise.

———◆———

We tried to press our advantage. Our company *did have* the support of the community and we could effectively operate a cable television system that would be of benefit to the South Central community. We invited more citizens of South Central to come and see the public meetings and hearings.

When people from South Central saw the process—and how different the process was from their expectations—they were shocked.

We should have been encouraged since we were clearly the stronger of the two remaining bidders. But both Mrs. Woodson and Mr. Chick had told us that they had already been directed by

Mayor Tom Bradley to come back with a recommendation that would leave us as *least-desirable* candidate for the franchise. If the process was predetermined, it was not an independent process.

From our perspective, the most important part of the evaluation process, and the one area the DOT could not deny or refute, was that we consistently retained the strongest financial rating—five points. This was a key rating that should be used to determine who was the "highest responsible bidder."

Councilman Lindsay said he was "very proud of our financial performance" because it meant he could talk to other council members and indicate our ability as black businessmen. "Councilman Lindsay talking us up is a good thing, but Snyder's stonewalling so we can't get answers from DOT. Seems like they're eating away at things, as I see it," Al Watson said.

At the BTC hearing of December 10, 1981, Chairman Don Howery repeated DOT's position that the intent of the financing ordinance meant bidders only needed to demonstrate the ability to finance. The final financing would be arranged after the council had voted on a successful applicant.

While we had financial commitments from our joint venture partner, the final documentation would only be accomplished after the award of the franchise. The final financing arrangements would involve substantial payments for loan fees and legal expenses.

The city attorney, however, now contradicted Howery by concluding that financing should be finalized before awarding of the franchise. Again, the two previous franchises that had been awarded within the previous ninety days had not received any such requirement, yet the city attorney wanted to impose this financing change only for the South Central franchise.

Historically, final financial commitments involving tens of millions of dollars required stiff fee payments. The fees were paid to banks and investment bankers to protect the banks against any failure to complete the specified financing arrangements. This payment of increased fees would increase the cost of the bidding process and reduce the number of applicants who could afford to bid for the franchise. Additionally, if applicants paid the funds to acquire such financing and did not receive the franchise, applicants would have to pay the underwriting fee in the area of several hundred thousand dollars—even though they did not obtain the franchise.

With this departmental conflict, the precedent established in the two prior franchise awards, which we had also applied for, were now being arbitrarily ignored.

Chairman Howery insisted that perspective bidders were not required to have firm commitments of funds because generally a fee was paid for such commitments. He pointed out the difficulty of trying to comply with rules that were continually being changed by various departments and members of the City Council.

The BTC attempted another angle to thwart the process—trying to reopen the bidding process. Despite our financial ability, the city would now take the new strategic course, introduced by Chairman Chick at the September 24, 1981, BTC meeting, to seek ways to throw out all existing applications and open the way for new applicants to bid for the franchise.

Chairman Chick began making inquiries of the city attorney. Despite the fact that the largest cable television company in the country, ATC, had submitted an application, Chick was seeking a way to refuse to award a license to build in South Central. *Why?*

Chairman Chick asked John Haggerty, a deputy city attorney, for an opinion, which would allow for the reopening of franchises for additional bidding. If the power plays we had already observed were true, we felt Haggerty had been directed to arrive at the conclusion that it was acceptable to deny all applications, and Haggerty would give the opinion being sought by Chick.

At the meeting on December 10, 1981, Deputy City Attorney John Haggerty told Chick, "The city may reject bids if there are no adequate and responsible bids presented." But neither Haggerty nor the BTC had defined what the term "adequate and responsible" meant. Without definition there is no way to comply with such a broad and nebulous term. Was that the BTC's intention?

The BTC would try other tactics as well. They would ask for clarifications and more opinions to use such things as "the length of time to build the franchise" and the meaning of "minority participation" to create delays in the franchising process once again.

Delays, delays, and more delays. Delays dating back to when Edgar Charles and other black entrepreneurs had been unjustly denied access to the application process. The effect of that error meant South Central had been deprived of the benefits of cable television for more than ten years.

———•———

On December 21, 1981, DOT issued a revised Evaluation and Recommendation for the South Central Cable Television Franchise. The DOT report recommended CTI as the highest responsible bidder to build the South Central franchise. The evaluation was issued "theoretically" because ATC had withdrawn from the franchising process. *Why was another DOT evaluation necessary?*

CTI had a rating of three out of the maximum five points awarded for financial ability. We were reminded that the awarding of the Boyle Heights franchise to an applicant with a financial rating of three points had been recently completed by the City of Los Angeles, thereby establishing a bidding precedence.

In their "new" and "theoretical" evaluation, DOT changed our financial rating from five to two. DOT did not provide an actual reason for this change except a nebulous statement that they "did not believe the commitment which has been provided by joint venture partners, who had added additional investors, was the same." The same company now supporting us was the same as provided to the DOT in August 1980. Our perfect financial rating was based upon this same relationship. After all the various changes of partners, secret financial statements, and negative rulings from the city attorney's office concerning CTI and BVT, DOT had the audacity to lower our rock-solid financial rating?

How could they justify such blatant political maneuvering? The key was that DOT did not have to justify or testify about anything because the city attorney said DOT employers didn't have to justify their writings or recommendations.

This process made no sense to us. Were they referring to the Six Star merger from sixteen months before this report? The city had been supportive of the merger prior to this time.

According to DOT, the contractual relationship in our company had changed despite the fact that no evidence was ever submitted to indicate any contractual commitment change. Nothing had changed in the contractual relationship and contractual commitment since the original evaluations were done from Six Star—only the new additional owners of Six Star had changed. The new company had more capital than the old company.

The change in our financial rating seems to have been the purpose of this new evaluation. The only actual revision in this new evaluation was the reduction of our financial rating by sixty percent, with no explanation. We might add that this was the only change to financial rating points during the entire process for the three separate franchise processes in which our company participated. As part of the South Central evaluation, DOT recommended that CTI be awarded the South Central franchise. What a coincidence.

These DOT assertions directly contradicted the statements of the chairman of the board of Six Star Nielsen Cablevision, our joint venture partner. Bill W. Nielsen, from Six Star, notified the city, both in writing and in testimony before the council and the various subcommittees, that Six Star continued to stand by their contractual obligation that justified the initial rating from the DOT of five points.

Time and time again we'd seen the people, board members, investors, mergers, and financial backers change for BVT and CTI, but DOT had never changed any of their rating scores because of it.

The attempt by DOT, now aided by the city attorney, to unilaterally declare a change to the contract was ludicrous. They allowed financial records to remain secret for BVT. They allowed both BVT and CTI to indicate they would only build out sixty per-cent of the franchise while we were contractually and financially able to build out one hundred percent. They allowed BVT and CTI numerous delays to find financing. Now they were saying that sixty percent was better than one hundred percent.

There was never any indication that an actual review had been done on this issue. Although the new investors and Six Star had been legally in place for more than a year by this time, the entire issue was raised only after ATC had withdrawn its application.

The city was not a party to our joint venture agreement. The joint venture contract was merely acquired by the new owner-ship group in transactions that occur every day in standard busi-ness practice. The city changed the ownership for Six Star's Hollywood-Wilshire franchise without any concern—making Six Star the largest cable franchise owner in the City of Los Angeles. DOT seemed to only have a problem with Six Star when it came to the South Central franchise.

During the sixteen months since the change of ownership of Six Star, neither DOT nor BTC requested any information from us regarding our joint venture. Why had DOT come up with another impediment that didn't exist when BVT of Boyle Heights changed financing packages and their corporate make up?

BVT's change of partners and financing for Boyle Heights never caused DOT to make any adjustment of their less-than-satisfactory financial rating, which continued to be assessed at three points.

So DOT could secretly, without informing the other bidders, change information in the bids and ratings at their whim—all fully and unequivocally a clear violation of the law and the application process.

So, the change of ownership went smoothly for the Hollywood-Wilshire franchise but in their efforts to serve the South Central citizens they were not so judicious. Was the problem with us and not Six Star? Was the reason perhaps more heinous and sinister?

The citizens of the Hollywood-Wilshire franchise would have access to cable television for almost a decade before South Central would get cable television. The Hollywood- Wilshire franchise was contiguous in many locations to the South Central cable television franchise. A mere block away, new technology would be available, while on the other side of the street, in South Central, the citizenry would have to wait a decade for the new technology to reach them.

———•———

At the December 21 BTC hearing, conversations continued, pushed by BTC members, about methods and reasons to abort the franchising process and to start over again. Since financing was not an issue at this point, BTC was looking for excuses but could not come up with any logical reasons.

Robert Chick continued to lay the groundwork for throwing out the existing applications for the South Central franchise. According to Chick, "We are not sure we can approve any bidder individually." But they had done just that in the award of the Boyle Heights franchise and other cable television franchises in awarding cable franchise bids historically.

———•———

Now all that was needed for the CTI franchise license approval was getting through the IEDC and a majority vote of the Los Angeles City Council.

"Get yourself, ready," Ted Eagans said. "This whole mess needs to land up in court so people can look at what a travesty our city government has become."

"You mean our mayor and the city council aren't the most upstanding representatives of their constituents and their community," Al Watson said, using droll humor to ease his anger.

———•———

In the eighteen months the city had held the applications, two other concerns emerged regarding financial ability matters. The rapidly evolving cable television industry now routinely used other financing methods for their building and business needs. Previously, obtaining commercial bank financing was the industry standard for getting the necessary loans for building and starting a cable franchise. This was also the only way the city allowed cable franchises to be financed in the bidding process.

However, the current cable television financing industry standard now used investment banking instead of commercial banks to arrange for debt financing. These alternative financial institutions invested in the more risky growth industries, which at that time included cable television, computer software, alternative energy, and wireless communications.

"We need to look at investment banking alternatives. Six Star is using non-banking sources almost exclusively now and we need to get up to speed," I said. "Commercial banks will make us pay too much for the money we need…and that will cut into our programming budgets."

"Is Six Star using them in their other franchises in Los Angeles?" Al Watson asked.

"Nielson said they are," I replied.

"Sounds good to me, if the City of Los Angeles will allow them," Mr. Parks said. "The deals are as solid as a commercial bank?"

"My company deals in cable television financing all the time now and the terms are better than any commercial bank," Skulsky said.

It was clear that the restrictions, imposed by the City of Los Angeles, upon the use of standard financing procedures were intended to severely restrict our ability to provide the funding to build the South Central franchise.

"But they're going to make us stick with banks, even though these other deals seem safer and less costly through investment banking options?" Carl asked.

"For the time being," was all I could say.

"How is this a problem?" Mr. Parks asked.

"It's mostly because of all the application delays caused by DOT," I replied.

As I explained to Mr. Parks, we were now being limited to commercial bank financing despite the fact that obtaining bank financing with a seven-year franchise was not feasible. Repaying a multi-million-dollar commercial bank loan in seven years was very improbable.

This was a second financing problem. Since the city wouldn't allow any non-bank funding for the South Central franchise, time wasn't on our side for getting commercial bank financing or for paying off the loans in this delay-shortened time period.

Without explanation, the city council had also recently decided that all existing cable franchises, including the South Central franchise, were due to expire in 1989. This approach was clearly contrary to the standards being used within the cable television history at that point in time.

When the franchising process started for the South Central-Harbor franchise, the franchise length the city would allow was slightly less than ten years. After all the changes, delays, and the city's split of the franchise into three franchises, the time left for the South Central franchise was now seven years...and becoming shorter every day.

Our financial projections indicated that even with the most favorable building schedule and the most favorable subscriber payment structure, we could not repay the millions of dollars we needed for a standard commercial bank debt contract. No one could—not without a huge cash repayment at the end of the seven years.

Fifteen different cable franchise areas would have been issued at different times by the city. The city now sought to have all franchises expire on the same day in 1989. Why? The city just said it wanted to renew all franchises at once.

"Sure has Six Star scrabbling, but they'll be OK with investment banking refinancing for their other franchises," I said. "All the franchises are."

Al Watson looked at me, wanting to understand the situation. "It's being allowed by the city for them? Investment banking financing. For previous franchises?" I nodded.

"But not for us?" Mr. Parks asked.

"Not for the South Central bid," I replied. "Commercial bank financing *only*."

We knew this was just another thinly veiled attempt to kill our bid.

———◆———

The IEDC, at the hearings in April 1982, specified investment banking commitments were not acceptable in the application process, regardless of the quality of the investment banking firm, even though these types of investment instruments had become industry standards. The statement was made specifically by Art Snyder, chairman of the IEDC.

The statement was not based on any part of the actual franchising application rules in the cable franchising ordinance. There was no discussion of acceptable types of financing within the ordinance. The decision on what was acceptable financing was left up to the employees and commissioners of DOT, BTC, and IEDC. It seemed that differing standards were never written but only based on the feelings, emotions, and political whims of these three parties.

In the recent past, for the Boyle Heights cable franchise, the standard for acceptable financing for DOT and IEDC was a secret personal financial statement. The use of secret information in the financial evaluation process was not discussed within the franchise ordinance or at any time within the documentation provided by DOT, BTC, or IEDC.

But now the city would require a firm commercial bank financing commitment, despite the fact that this was contrary to the original franchise application instructions given by DOT manager Don Howery. During the Boyle Heights hearings, Howery had specified in testimony before the BTC, the IEDC, and the Los Angeles City Council, that firm financing commitments were not expected prior to the award of the franchise.

Things shifted again without explanation during the South Central franchise process, where full financial commitments were required prior to any franchise being awarded. Haggerty, from the city attorney's office, had given them their ammunition with his contrary opinion. This singular and discriminatory restriction by the City of Los Angeles against the use of investment banking commitments and the legal assurances of extremely wealthy individuals negated our ability to acquire capital in the open market.

Our sources indicated that officials in DOT, IEDC, BTC, and the Los Angeles City Council were fully aware that traditional commercial banking sources would not finance any franchise in term of less than nine years. Councilman Lindsay, in his many conversations with the councilmen, bureaucrats, and appointees, scolded officials and members of DOT, IEDC, BTC, and Los Angeles City Council. "You know how much time and how many times I talked about my pride in your financial package. Now they've changed things and I'm trying to get alternative banking sources approved for you," Councilman Lindsay stated.

There was no method of financing that would appease the city now that it had created a new approach to deny all existing applications for the South Central franchise.

We had played the game and watched while our time, our rating points, our joint venture partner, and our financing methods were being besieged.

———◆———

In January 1982, Larry Goldblatt, a music producer and a friend of Carl's, arranged a conference with Robert Nederlander, the Broadway theatre owner and producer. Larry was inquiring whether Nederlander had an interest in investing in the cable television industry. He said he did not, but he put us in touch with Hal Brown, president of Gannett Outdoor Advertising (which was originally known as Pacific Outdoor Advertising), a division of the Gannett media conglomerate.

Brown, on behalf of Gannett, retained and paid for the due diligence work for the services of Daniels and Associates, to evaluate the investment potential of the South Central franchise. At that time, Daniels and Associates was the leading investment banking company in the cable television industry and had placed billions of dollars worth of cable television financing over the past ten years.

Daniels and Associates reported back to Brown, saying the South Central franchise was very viable and could eventually represent an excellent investment. Brian Deevy, a senior vice president with Daniels and Associates assigned to our project, was favorably impressed. When he did a site visit, he discovered the well-maintained, middle-class homes that dominated the franchise community.

To his surprise, Deevy found that South Central represented one of the largest remaining franchise areas in the United States that had not been developed for cable television in any way.

Even with his very favorable preliminary report, Brown later informed us that Gannett could not work with us to pursue the franchise at this time because of the "intense political pressure" in our franchising process.

Even if Gannett couldn't help finance our franchise, Daniels said they would continue to work with us. Daniels let us retain their services for half their usual rate because they were so impressed by potential of the South Central franchise.

Daniels also did the preliminary work necessary to determine financing viability of our project. They were able to give us a financing commitment to arrange the debt financing on our behalf.

Daniels issued a letter to the City of Los Angeles stating that they had agreed to handle placement of our debt financing on a contractual basis. In their letter, Daniels informed the city that they had never failed to provide financing to any company to which they had provided a commitment.

We were hopeful that adding the financial presence of Daniels and Associates to the substantial equity commitments we had already presented to the city would eliminate any concerns regarding our ability to finance. Once again, we were wrong. What was good enough for the rest of the cable industry and business community was not good enough for the city of Los Angeles and the poorest community within it.

DOT and Councilman Art Snyder, chairman of the IEDC, announced that Daniels and Associates' letter of commitment was unacceptable because Daniels had not stated a specific lender that would provide funds for debt financing. This requirement by

Chairman Snyder was outrageous. It was not standard practice (or customary) in the investment banking industry to specify potential lenders prior to the franchise being awarded. The appropriate lender would be determined based on the amount of financing required and other factors within the financial projections—after the franchise size, needs, and business plan were evaluated.

The city had already said that there was a twenty-day period after the franchise award to provide firm financing; plenty of time for us to make the appropriate funds available and provide the city with final documentation. The city had already given BVT of Boyle Heights more than five months to arrange their financing package in clear violation of the cable franchising ordinance.

Even Councilman Snyder had to acknowledge Daniels and Associates was a leading investment banking firm and concede that Daniels had never failed to provide financing for any of its commitments. But Councilman Snyder stood behind a legal opinion given by Ed Perez of the city attorney's office. It was Perez's contention that information provided by Daniels and Associates was inadequate because it did not specify a particular financing institution in this matter.

A deputy city attorney, obviously ignorant of standard practice in the investment banking industry, was telling a company that had successfully raised billions of dollars for the U.S. cable television industry that it was was inadequate.

The representatives of Daniels and Associates were incredulous. "You told them we have billions of dollars in investments in well over a dozen cities and we've never had any financing problems, right?" We told the people at Daniels we had.

"You've told them these people and companies have impeccable credit ratings?" We told them we had. "This Perez guy from the city attorney is a moron," they concluded.

What could we say? The entire process had become moronic.

"This is the only deal in the City of Los Angeles that can't use investment bankers. Are they playing you?" they asked. All we could do was agree with the Daniels' representatives. Investment banking financing was only inadequate in this instance and only in this South Central franchise.

"Before this, Howery of the DOT said there didn't need to be any final financing commitments before the awarding of the bid, now we're only allowed commercial bank financing," we informed the Daniels' people.

"Then, they must be out to kill this deal and prevent a good investment opportunity," they asserted.

All my assertions as a CPA with experience in accounting and investment firms were disregarded. I should have saved my breath but I wanted anyone who would listen to know of the political mishandling of these three cable television franchises. I continually stressed that the arrangements with Daniels had been done in a timely and efficient fashion, and that the insistence that financing should be arranged subsequent to the award of a license was now being changed by the city and the DOT with no explanation. I also made clear that these were not firm rules and could be changed depending upon the franchise and the desires of the DOT and Snyder—and all the changes were directly intended to disallow our company's bidding package.

The rejection of the commitment from Daniels was simply another step in support of the city's position that no matter what we did we would not be allowed to build a cable television system in South Central. Nowhere in the material provided by the city were investment bankers prohibited from providing financing for the system. Investment bankers were the standard method of financing cable television systems in the United States. To be denied the access to the primary financing method is to be unlawfully denied access to the market.

Councilman Lindsay called Don Howery, chairman of the DOT, and told him he was a "low-down dirty dog" for cheating in the process. Councilman Lindsay said Howery defended himself by saying in a flippant remark, "Why bother me? Call your friend in the mayor's office."

The rejection of Daniels and Associates and their impeccable financing ability by the city effectively locked us out of the capital marketplace by prohibiting our use of the investment banking industry.

After denying us the ability to use Daniels to gain investment banking capital, Art Snyder, the head of the IEDC, said if we could arrange the $25 million debt financing in seven days, it would still be considered. We saw Snyder snicker at the suggestion as he sat at his seat on the hearing dais. We controlled our emotions, which were hanging by a thread.

"We're not going to give up," Mr. Watson thundered in the car after the meeting. "Just to see us wipe that smile off of Snyder's face is worth working on this every hour for all seven days!"

———◆———

We got on the phones and started calling all our contacts for help. Carl called Dr. Herbert Avery for advice. Carl and Dr. Avery had been friends for years and Carl knew the distinguished OB/GYN spoke to many people involved in city and South Central politics.

"Whatever you do, don't ask me to talk to Johnny Cochran. I'm on the outs with him right now," Dr. Avery said.

"What's the trouble?" Carl asked.

Johnny Cochran had represented Dr. Avery in a lawsuit against the City of Los Angeles regarding police brutality and the use of the chokehold in a traffic stop involving Los Angeles police. Although Dr. Avery won, he was upset with Cochran regarding the handling of the case and the potential distribution of the funds after winning the case.

"Things aren't going well?" Carl was concerned.

"It's not only Johnny who's giving me trouble, the dam U.S. District Court judge where I'm assigned is a problem, too! She's stonewalling everything and acting just like a lapdog for the city. The second thing is, I *certainly* don't like how Johnny's handling my lawsuit! Doesn't object too much about the process. No justice in it at all!" Dr. Avery fumed.

"Who's the judge," Carl asked.

"It's Consuelo Marshall," Dr. Avery replied. "She's going slower than molasses and doesn't seem to understand there's a plaintiff in the courtroom. She's only talking to and ruling for the city."

Carl listened and then explained he was calling about further financial commitments regarding the South Central franchise. "We need $25 million and we've only got a few days."

"Wish I had that kind of money," Dr. Avery replied. "But I know someone who does." Dr. Avery said he knew Mohammed Khashoggi, the son of international businessman and the world's richest man, Adnan Khashoggi. "I'll give him a call and see if he can give us some help."

Khashoggi's representatives agreed to meet with us.

Our plan was simple. We presented the financial projections generated by Daniels and Associates. Because they were one of the largest investment banking firms in the cable television industry, their projections and opinions were well known and highly respected throughout the industry. They were also highly respected by one of the world's richest men who had used Daniels and Associates' services before.

Khashoggi's American accountants took the financial projections, flew to London on less than twenty-four hours notice and got a firm commitment from the billionaire for our cable franchise financing.

Khashoggi's company agreed to give us the $25 million. We presented a new commitment letter from Khashoggi for the $25 million to the city and Councilman Snyder within five days.

The city spent two days verifying the authenticity of the Khashoggi letter commitment to our company. After the commitment was verified by the city attorney, Ed Perez, we were informed by the city attorney's office that the commitment would not be acceptable because they claimed it had been approved after four days, an artificial deadline they had set for themselves but never transmitted to the bidding parties.

Seven days were no longer seven days. Seven days were now four days. Once again, math in Los Angeles was different. The newly imposed deadline was less than the seven days they had granted in the meeting. It was now four days, and the four days had expired without notice, explanation, or recourse.

The rules were ever-changing and mercurial. Time allowances were stretched for political cronies and shortened for adversaries of City Hall. The twenty-day period for submitting a financing plan had already turned into 120 days (and would continue for five years) for the Boyle Heights franchise with their political connection to Councilmen Snyder, Farrell, and Cunningham and the office of Mayor Tom Bradley.

Ed Perez asked me later how we had gained access to one of the richest men in the world. In response, I simply looked him in the eye and laughed out loud and walked away. If he wasn't going to give me an answer about why the seven days had been rescinded, thereby exposing their flagrant disregard for our company, I certainly didn't have time to answer his question.

———◆———

Councilman Lindsay said he had underestimated how low city officials were willing to sink to prevent our company from getting the franchise. Councilman Lindsay would subsequently always ask Carl in future conversations, "Are you sure you didn't do something else to these people?"

Carl truthfully replied with a smile, "No."

———◆———

We were being pushed out of the South Central bidding process by every and any means possible. Each report, meeting, and decision always arrived at the conclusion that our company, UCS, was the lesser of the two possible choices for a cable television franchise for South Central. The fact that our competitors had no experience and no operating capital did not dissuade the DOT from recommending them for the cable television franchise. The city was willing to accept individual financing provided by an individual for the Boyle Heights franchise, but was not willing to accept financing that was guaranteed by the richest man in the world.

There was another problem. "You're not going to believe this," Carl fumed as I answered the phone. "We said we're locating our head end 800 feet outside of the Los Angeles City limits where Six Star has its facility. Right?" The "head end" Carl was talking about was the facility that receives satellite signals to retransmit through the cable system.

Six Star built and used this head end for their adjacent Hollywood-Wilshire franchise and intended to increase the size of the facility if we won the South Central franchise—800 feet outside the city limits.

"Did you know in BVT's winning Boyle Heights application, BVT's locating their head end in Dominguez Hills—eight miles outside the City of Los Angeles!" Carl said.

"Yes," I replied.

"Well, now they're making noises about being 800 feet outside the Los Angeles City limits for our South Central head end," Carl yelled into the phone.

DOT wanted to reduce our rating because we are not within the city limits. They wanted to give us a lower rating than bidders that had not even specified where their head end would be located.

This was more clear proof that Los Angeles city officials could do whatever they wanted and change the ratings in any way they wanted. The location of the head end was not even discussed in any other franchise area except for South Central.

DOT could not explain why the location of this facility would matter since the satellites sending the information were located hundreds of miles above the earth. Once again, DOT had proved itself to be neither objective nor independent in this matter. Their clear lack of knowledge of the industry was abundantly apparent with the discussion of the head end.

The same head end, which served many Los Angeles cable company interests, would be used for years by the subsequent cable franchise company who would build out the South Central system, American Cable Systems, and by other subsequent operators, with no protest from the city.

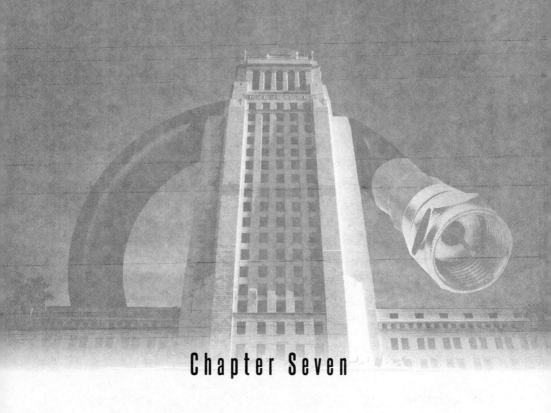

Chapter Seven

The Final Squeeze

Mr. Parks came in looking very somber. I knew something was wrong. "John Mack's resigning." I closed my eyes. We'd been hoping John Mack's influence at the Urban League, as well a member of our board of directors, might push back against all the changes in the application process.

"What did he say?" I asked.

"Said he was asked to choose…and he chose to protect his other community programs," Mr. Parks replied. "I know I said to take it easy on him…and not to ask him to react too soon to help us. Now we've lost him."

Community leaders had attended all the hearings including the BTC hearings but Mr. Mack had influence we wanted and needed through the Urban League and his many contacts. "We'll just keep going," I sighed. "Since Mack can't help us now, let's think of other ways to get DOT to open up about their written report."

John Mack would go on to join the city's bureaucracy as one of the Los Angeles City police commissioners. He would also go on to receive a lucrative airport concession contract from the Los Angeles Airport Commission, another city commission of bureaucrats appointed by the mayor.

John Mack, president of the Los Angeles Urban League, had been one of our directors until he resigned in 1982. Even though he had attempted to put pressure on us to merge with CTI under their highly unfavorable terms and resigned from our board of directors, we would have welcomed his presence in the gallery to see exactly how we were treated.

We redoubled our efforts to get community support. After we informed a number of community leaders about the situation and the politically motivated new rules and changes specifically in the South Central application process,which did not apply to the Boyle Heights franchise, they became irate.

"I'm going to get every one I can to the May 19th IEDC meeting," Mr. Parks said. "Everybody's got to hear from the people in the neighborhood."

On May 19, 1982, IEDC held a hearing regarding the South Central cable television franchise. Our strategy, as before, was to publicize the changes in the application procedure, so more community activists could see how corrupt the application process had become.

All the public seats were taken and others were standing, including ministers and civil rights leaders who came to voice their concerns regarding the changing South Central application process.

One noted member of the gallery coming to help us was Dr. Rev. E.V. Hill, whose church was in the South Central area. He wanted to speak at the IEDC hearing. Dr. Hill knew the power of cable television and went on to operate one of the most successful television ministries utilizing cable television.

Looking around the room at all the attendees, the absence of both the NAACP and the Urban League representatives was conspicuous because of the importance of the issue.

Councilman Snyder seemed undeterred by the larger-than-usual gallery. He again indicated that he favored rejecting all applications and starting the bidding process over.

By this action, Councilman Snyder, with the majority of the BTC members, would change the law that had only been in effect for ninety days—again. Imagine trying to run a business, identifying where you were in an academic process toward graduation, or planning for your life if everything meaningful changed every ninety days. You can then sympathize with our situation.

According to Councilman Snyder, "a bid put forth in 1980 is not an acceptable bid in 1982." But looking at what had happened since 1980, Snyder had voted in favor of the Boyle Heights franchise, which had been submitted in January 1980 when our application had been submitted. We had been the only other applicants for the Boyle Heights franchise. The system and equipment offered were the exact same as we had offered in the application under consideration.

In February 1982, Snyder supported the application of Colony Communications for the Wilmington-San Pedro franchise. The application was filed in 1980 at the same time as our South Central franchise application. We were the only other applicants for the franchise. The same information put forth in 1980 was acceptable for evaluation in 1982 for the Boyle Heights and Wilmington franchises for Chairman Snyder—but not for the South Central franchise.

The key reason now used to reject all applications was that no bidder had demonstrated financial ability to construct the franchise—an utter falsehood. We contend, and showed, that the rules were changed multiples time so no one could finance a franchise.

Now that all applications were from black-controlled companies, it seemed Snyder was even more anxious to reject all bids for the South Central area. The new requirement, effective only for South Central, as announced by Snyder, was "full cash upfront." Although other members of the IEDC were less inclined to reject all applications and start the process over, Snyder was adamant.

———

People attending the meeting wanted answers regarding their community's cable television system franchise, the outrageous and constantly changing financial requirements, and why Councilman Snyder and the IEDC worked in conjunction with the city attorney to continually change the rules and standards of the application process. Different franchises had different rules. This was not objectivity or equal protection under the law—and those attending wanted to know why.

As before, using his authority over testimony and questions regarding IEDC staff decisions, actions, and recommendations, Chairman Snyder refused our questions as well as those from the community members in attendance.

As the chairman of the IEDC, Councilman Snyder hid behind his power and continued to refuse to allow our company to ask any direct questions to DOT. During the hearing, we were asked by Councilwoman Joan Flores if we believed we were getting a fair hearing during this process. I responded to her, "Of course not, you can see what's going on here."

To our shock and dismay, when the questioning from the neighborhood representatives started, instead of answering questions, Councilman Snyder accused the disgruntled community activists and civil rights leaders of acting as if they were "savages from Africa." His offensive comments inflamed the members of the community in attendance. The police had to be called to the hearing room to restore order.

While the police remained in the room, Snyder called for an immediate vote. The IEDC recommended the award of the franchise to CTI in support of the DOT evaluation and the BTC recommendation. The recommendation passed by a two-to-one vote with Flores and Councilwoman Pat Russell voting for CTI. Snyder was the dissenting vote because he was in favor of rejecting all applications.

We felt Councilman Snyder knowingly harassed the gallery and used inflammatory language to stop debate and push the resolution through his committee. He hadn't gotten rid of CTI yet but he still had time. He thought he'd gotten rid of us.

———

"The City Council vote on the South Central franchise is scheduled for May 21," I told Carl as I hung up the phone. "I called Mr. P. and told him to get as many people there as possible."

"How's Councilman Lindsay doing?" Carl asked. I looked at the writing pad on the desk. "He's short a vote...but he doesn't think that CTI can get the votes either."

It seemed Danny Bakewell had angered some people on the Los Angeles City Council when he attempted to obtain some city-owned real estate with no money down in 1978.

"So Bakewell got caught with his hands in the councilmen's cookie jar?" Mr. Watson asked. "If it's like what Councilman Lindsay said a few years ago, and I'm sure it still is, that boy's going to have to pay big for his misstep and lack of manners."

"What do the lawyers say?" Carl looked over my shoulder.

"Besides estimating the costs of getting and evaluating all the documents from the city, DOT, BTC, and IEDC, it will cost us about $50,000 minimum if we go to court," I replied.

Carl grimaced and rubbed the back of his neck. "Daddy's house cost half of that."

"That was when I was what...three years old?" I cracked a smile. "This is the age of cable television."

"Guess I can tell you bad news now that you're smiling," Carl replied. "It doesn't hurt so bad after a smile."

"What?" I said, alarmed it might be something to do with him or his wife and children.

"Don't look so sad," Carl began. "It's not me, Esperanza, or the kids."

"What, then?" I asked, relieved, but unsatisfied. "Is it Daddy or Mother Dear?"

Carl shook his head. "Al Watson says someone big is sniffing around the franchise."

"Who?" I asked.

"Al doesn't know yet, but you know he'll keep digging till he finds out. Al says he'll let us know as soon as he does."

Two doses of bad news. Someone new was interested in the South Central franchise but we had no information on who it was and I had to figure out how to pay for the first installment of $50,000 in legal costs for what might cost hundreds of thousands of dollars if we went to court.

———

On May 19, 1982, the same day as the IEDC hearing and two days before the city council meeting to vote on the South Central cable franchise, Carl received a phone call, at his private number at home, from Burt Pines, a former Los Angeles City Attorney from 1973 to 1981 and someone we had met in 1979 as we were beginning to develop our interest in cable franchising.

When we first met Pines, he was working on the cable television corruption case but now Pines was in private practice. In our early research, when we were first interested in cable television franchises, we talked to Pines regarding a City Hall scandal concerning city employees. Pines, as a city attorney at that time, was in charge of the original complaints when allegations of city employees working special deals with cable companies or going to work for cable companies surfaced.

At first, Carl didn't remember who Pines was and he was alarmed because only a handful of people had this private number. "How did you get my private number?" Carl asked. During the whole fiasco of trying to keep his practice going, dealing with the fallout from the *60 Minutes* debacle and giving me his assessments and guidance on the cable television applications, he'd kept his private home telephone number available to only a few people.

Pines brushed off Carl's question. "I've got a deal for you and your brother." Pines told Carl he was representing Kaufman and Broad (KB). KB was the parent company of KB Homes, one of the largest homebuilders and real estate developers in the United States and traded on the New York Stock Exchange. "They've got no interest in cable television yet or any media outlets, but this opportunity has come to light," Pines said. This "opportunity" was the South Central franchise, he explained.

Eli Broad, one of the namesakes of KB, was known as a powerful influence in California political circles. Broad, one of richest men in the United States, was also a major fundraiser for the "Bradley for Governor Committee," which was going full bore at this time.

Pines told Carl that his clients at KB were interested in helping us with our case at City Hall. When Carl asked Pines how his clients planned on helping us, Pines sidestepped the question and said it would be in our best interest if his client spoke with Carl directly. Pines arranged for a meeting between Carl and his clients from KB on the evening of the next day at Pines's law office in Century City.

The full Los Angeles City Council was scheduled to hold the final hearings and vote on the South Central franchise award in two days.

———◆———

On the next evening, May 20, 1982, Carl met with Bill Schainker, a vice president of KB, at Pines's offices in Century City. Schainker explained they had good working relationships with many members of the City Council.

"We're on friendly terms with Councilman Cunningham and, as you know, he is having a very difficult time considering voting for a minority-controlled cable company for the South Central franchise," Schainker said.

Schainker recapped, with great detail and specificity, our involvement in the South Central cable franchise. Carl was taken aback. Schainker seemed so straightforward and knowledgeable about what was going on in the South Central franchise.

"If you give us fifty-one-percent ownership of the cable television company, we would be in a position to guarantee a successful vote for the franchise for you at the City Council at the hearing on May twenty-first," Schainker offered. "I need an answer tonight."

Carl responded by telling Schainker and Pines, we had negotiated previously with other bidders for the franchise and would be willing to explore a potential arrangement that needed to include a perfect split down the middle: their ownership of fifty percent of the company and our ownership of fifty percent of the company—the same merger offer we'd given CTI in all our meetings with them.

The meeting ended when Schainker and Pines made it clear they would not negotiate their position regarding ownership or the controlling interest of the company.

Carl called me and Councilman Lindsay to discuss the offer by KB, and told us about the meeting. Lindsay asked Carl if he had called me, since Lindsay had said he perceived me as being the "reasonable one," and Carl simply responded the truth. "No, I didn't have to," because Carl knew that my decision would be whatever he decided. Lindsay thought Carl and I should have discussed it prior to a final decision being made but Lindsay understood the family dynamics.

"I don't know, son. Eli Broad can make Bradley do things that I can't even dream of getting out of him," Lindsay told us.

"Tell you one thing. Dave Cunningham is in Eli Broad's pocket, so if you want to have the satisfaction of seeing Cunningham vote for your company, you'll get it if you take the deal." We could hear the high laugh of delight coming from Lindsay's home. "It would almost be worth it!"

The addition of KB into an already complicated, barely navigable equation did not bode well for us. Still, we remained loyal to our principles. The same rules that applied to Bakewell and Johnson's offer applied to KB. KB were just a much bigger fish in the same pond.

Now that KB had expressed their interest in obtaining the South Central franchise, the recent motives of numerous elected officials became more clear, specifically the actions of Councilman Cunningham and Councilman Snyder in their vehement opposition to black ownership of the South Central franchise. They knew KB and/or some other big corporations were being courted…and these politicians wanted to be on the right side with their hands out to get a share by showing they were loyal to the "big fish." *Was corporate influence over the elected leadership within the black community greater than the influence of the black community itself?*

We did not delude ourselves that all of a sudden things were going to change at City Hall. We would push our plan until the final votes came in at the city council. We were realistic because Gil Lindsay had already told us that he doubted that he had enough votes to get approval for our application. Although we were accepting of the fact that we would not win city council approval, we saw this as one more battle in our war.

"So what are we going to do if we don't get the franchise," I asked Carl, knowing we'd anticipated that our next approach to obtaining the right to build our franchise would have to come through litigation. We already knew that it would make no sense for us to continue wasting our time and money pursuing a license to operate in such an obviously tainted process as existed in the city.

"We're going to sue," Carl said quietly and without hesitation. "I've still got my hands full with my case for *60 Minutes* so I'm asking you to agree with me and run this litigation, if it comes to that."

"Run a franchise or run litigation," I repeated. With a small smile, I said, "I'd rather run a franchise."

The day came for the Los Angeles City Council vote. Now that we had reached the full city council level, we did not expect to alter anyone's mind.

Trying to unravel the mess of the application evaluation process was just as daunting a task. We would be given a total of ten minutes to summarize the events of three years. Would we actually get a chance to speak, or be called "savages from Africa" and have to be restrained by police?

How and where would we start? Explaining the years-long process of altering the standards of evaluation to a point where the objectives and standards were unrecognizable with stipulations seemed mind numbing.

Standards were no more than whims during the cable television application process. Since the rules seemed to change every day, there was no real way to comply with the ever-shifting, impossible standards that meant no one would receive a franchise. Every bidder had failed the process, but only in South Central.

As Carl and I walked the final block from the parking lot we reflected upon our numerous visits to City Hall over the last three years. Hundreds of meetings with elected officials and bureaucrats had left a bad taste in our mouths. This would be our final visit to City Hall, in all probability, and we at least found solace in that. There was a musty smell of a decaying structure as we entered the building, which we, of course, attributed to the occupants rather than the aging building itself. We held a faint hope that the injustice of this process would be corrected by the full city council.

As we approached the final street to the entrance to City Hall, we noticed for the first time an engraved quotation of the south wall of the building. "He who violates his oath of office profanes the divinity of faith itself" - Cicero. The quotation from the Roman philosopher, who lived before Christ, seemed prescient as we went to face the day's fate.

———◆———

The councilpersons sat on the dais. The cable franchise agenda item on the calendar came up quickly. They started the discussion. Most of the councilpersons were distracted by other things; a majority were not even in their seats. It was clear the decision had already been made without the benefit of any testimony at this hearing.

This same government was telling us two different things on the subject of financing. Councilman Snyder was saying we would not be given a twenty-day period to produce final documentation while the city attorney was saying the DOT general manager had indicated that the rules provided we would be allowed twenty days to provide firm financing for the project—just another example of the total lack of objective standards in the evaluation process. But now, these two city employees would give conflicting testimony on the same day before the full city council after years of hearings concerning the continuing barrage of changes.

Councilwoman Russell asked Ed Perez of the city attorney's office to repeat what he had said. Perhaps, Councilman Russell wanted to show that the testimony by the city attorney's office directly contradicted Councilman Snyder, chairman of the IEDC, when Snyder said, "All the money is required to be provided *prior to* the award of the franchise."

Under Snyder's tenure at IEDC, more than two years and many delays in the processing of those bids were caused by the city itself and not by the bidders. All the time, Councilman Snyder and Councilman Cunningham continued to push for a rejection of all the applications for South Central.

With Chairman Snyder and the IEDC's "new" standards, all cable franchise applications would have to be rejected by the city to allow the process to start over again for the benefit of someone else. Now we knew the "someone else" was Kaufman and Broad.

Councilwoman Russell vehemently objected to the dual standards that were now being applied to South Central. She explained to the council the award of the Boyle Heights franchise within the past five months and how that application had been submitted within two days of the South Central application. She openly wondered why, all of a sudden, the evaluation process had changed after issuing the previous two franchises.

Russell, also a member of the IEDC, identified one example for the full city council of the inconsistent rules and requirements applied to the South Central franchise, stating that Councilman Snyder had no justification for his beliefs that existing applicants would not be able to perform. Russell had voted for the IEDC report, which recommended CTI to receive the franchise.

Councilwoman Russell went on to say, "In the past two franchises we have addressed the financing issue by allowing for the financing *after the award* of the franchise." She looked down at her papers. "This position was confirmed by Ed Perez, a deputy city attorney, when he stated, 'The bidder is given twenty days to provide firm financing.'" Confirmation of the testimony by the city attorney of the existing policy directly contradicted the testimony of Councilman Snyder, the chairman of the IEDC. If they could not agree with the law that was on the floor of the Los Angeles City Council how could we possibly comply with their unreasonable request that consistently changed?

The bids had been accepted by the BTC and a recommendation made by the IEDC. There was no finding by the BTC of the bids not being in good and proper order. "These companies have been trying to respond to unclear requests and unclear standards used by both the Department of Transportation and the office of the city attorney," Councilwoman Russell continued.

Russell went on to say that both bidders "are responsible and able to develop the franchise" based upon her participation in the hearing process as a member of the IEDC and in contradiction to Councilman Snyder's statements. "There is a twenty-day period that allows for financing. The same thing was done for Buena Vista in Boyle Heights."

DOT's general manager, Don Howery, had also previously testified, at the BTC and IEDC, that it was not the position of the city to require applicants to get binding financial obligations prior to the award of the franchise. However, Howery did not volunteer this information when it came to the South Central franchise hearing. Russell made sure that Howery admitted to that fact in front of the entire city council.

The statement made by Councilwoman Russell, supported our contention that BVT had been given preferential treatment during the Boyle Heights evaluations. Although we, as the only other bidder for the same franchise, had received the highest financial rating of five, we were not awarded the cable license for Boyle Heights.

The twenty-day period became important in South Central because we had shown the ability to finance a cable franchise on three separate occasions, which was the stated standard according to Councilwoman Russell and the general manager of DOT, Don Howery. We had received an original maximum rating of five points for ability to finance the cable television franchise. We had presented additional financial commitments from Daniels and Associates, the leading cable television investment banking firm in the United States, and obtained full financial backing from one of the richest men in the world.

For South Central, the city deemed all our methods of financing as unacceptable in relation to obtaining the South Central cable television franchise. Yet in Boyle Heights they could accept a personal financial statement from some "secret" person with a negative net worth.

Councilman Robert Farrell spoke next. He pointed out that certain franchises had still not provided financial commitments to the city even though they had been awarded a cable franchise license months previously. "There are franchises that were awarded and have not put up any money yet."

Was the entire issue of financial ability merely a subterfuge to avoid awarding the franchise to one of the bidders for South Central? Our evidence clearly shows it was. Different franchises had different rules—different days, different laws.

As the debate continued, Councilmen Snyder and Cunningham were both adamant about rejecting all existing bids and opening up the bidding process again for new applicants. According to Councilman Snyder, choosing between the UCS and CTI was like choosing "between strychnine and arsenic."

Councilwoman Russell shot back, identifying the vitriol of the comment, "No other franchisee has received the scrutiny of South Central. All franchises would have been rejected if they had to go through the process like South Central." It was clear to Councilwoman Russell that the rules had somehow changed mid-stream.

In support of his attempts to reject all existing applications, Councilman Snyder stated, "Let's, for the first time, go out for a properly defined process with what we have learned." So no other cable television franchise had a properly defined process?

We had been subjected to the process being defined, re-defined, and changed a dozen times. We knew we were worthy of getting the South Central franchise award.

Councilman Lindsay fumed about his futile discussions with DOT personnel, "The staff does not know how it can improve the process. You are not going to get any better than you've got."

Councilman Lindsay asked Councilman Snyder why the same systems approved in the last five months, for other franchises, were no longer acceptable when it came to South Central. Snyder did not reply.

Perhaps Snyder didn't answer because it would hurt his attempts to get new business. We discovered that, in 1982, during the time Councilman Snyder was chairman of the IEDC, Snyder sent personal solicitations to cable television companies in the City of Los Angeles offering to represent the same companies as a private attorney. In what we thought was unethical conduct, Snyder solicited business from the cable companies he was supposed to be regulating. Once again, in Los Angeles City Hall there is no such thing as conflict of interest.

To fill in the silence, Councilman Cunningham started speaking and said he demanded excellence for a franchise in South Central. Cunningham was all of a sudden concerned about the excellence of the cable television franchise for South Central when he had delayed that same franchise for years.

Cunningham acknowledged, "One of the financial difficulties is the fact that there will be a short franchise window that is difficult to finance before a renewal." We'd tried to introduce rock-solid investment bank financing and then secure backing from an impeccable individual's banking source when the franchising time shrunk from the normal ten years to only seven years. Repayment of a commercial bank loan would take nine years, according our projections.

Councilman Joel Wachs, after hearing the testimony, said he felt all the bidders were capable. "We are not at a point to expect perfection." He said he felt deceived by both the IEDC report and by the DOT report that had been sent forward to the council.

With thirteen of the fifteen members of the Los Angeles City Council in attendance, the first vote on the council floor was on a recommendation issued by the IEDC for CTI to receive the franchise. The vote was 9-4 against the IEDC recommendation for CTI. Johnson and Bakewell were thwarted in their attempt to get the franchise.

Channing Johnson had bitten off more than he could chew. While he had the ability to divide the franchise and segregate the black community, he failed to anticipate that he would actually have to put together a capable business plan and the financing required to develop the franchise—even after months and months of politically motivated delays to help his franchise's cause.

Johnson was always so adamant that "the Galloway boys" should get nothing. His arrogance and greed had come back to haunt him. In this instance, he got nothing as well.

The council took the next vote on the motion of Councilman Lindsay for the UCS bid to receive the franchise. The vote was 7-6 against awarding the franchise to our company. The swing vote to defeat the award was that of Councilman David Cunningham.

Councilman Lindsay charged that Councilman Cunningham was already in the pocket of KB, who had now made it known they wanted the South Central franchise. Councilman Cunningham cast the swing vote and all minority-controlled applications for South Central were rejected.

Councilman Lindsay was clearly disgusted with Cunningham as he screamed, "You didn't ask that requirement of the others," referring to the franchise that had been awarded to BVT within the last five months for Boyle Heights without any concern for "excellence." Lindsay shook his head in disgust at the other black councilman. "Dave, I'm surprised. You're killing your own people."

Even if we had received seven votes it would not have mattered. Councilman Lindsay told us after the vote that Mayor Bradley would veto any legislation in order to help KB. "That's what I've heard and I've got no reason to doubt it." In order to override the mayor's veto it would require ten votes and Councilman Lindsay sadly made this clear to us by saying, "I can't promise I can deliver an override if we win."

Gil told us honestly. "Our only hope would have been that if we had gotten the votes, the Mayor might have been afraid to veto a black company in South Central when he is running for governor of the State of California."

Everyone was aware that rejection of the existing applications would delay cable television in South Central for a minimum of two years and probably substantially more. Sadly, the council's actions would delay the technological advantages to South Central for at least another five years. The changes in community programming and targeted education that could have been brought to South Central would never come to fruition because the City of Los Angeles would prohibit a black-owned company from ever receiving a franchise to operate in South Central.

The city also made it clear now that under no circumstances would they award the franchise for South Central Los Angeles to a black-controlled group. Ironically, the major opponents of minority ownership in the City of Los Angeles were elected black officials, with the exception of Councilman Lindsay.

In other words, the city was intentionally deceiving the public and South Central when they encouraged minorities to spend years of time and hundreds of thousands of dollars in this process the city clearly and continually rigged.

Councilman Cunningham, a black councilman, cast the deciding vote in our 7-6 loss. He appeared steadfast in his refusal to support a black franchise under any circumstances. The fact that Cunningham's district had only a minimal interest in the franchise area did not dissuade him from attempting (once again) to prevent South Central from gaining access to the new approaches that were transforming technology and communications.

Cunningham also played a powerful role in dividing up the large South Central franchise in 1979 so that all of the now smaller franchises, which had previously been the South Central-Harbor franchise, were essentially segregated by race.

Councilman Cunningham would subsequently become a major supporter of the KB franchise application, which was submitted in December 1982, just as Councilman Lindsay predicted in his statements on the day our UCS bid was rejected.

Somehow the "excellence" Cunningham demanded from the black franchise applicants was completely forgotten when it came to KB. They had no operations in the cable television industry. They would not gain any experience in South Central. Kaufman and Broad would never put an inch of cable line on the poles or provide any programming for the South Central neighborhood. They did, however, make millions of dollars.

Chapter Eight

Friends In High Places

Now that the City of Los Angeles had eliminated all potential black applicants from the South Central franchise process, they were ready to move forward at a break-neck bureaucratic pace in comparison to our experience with the South Central franchise area.

On July 22, 1982, less than sixty days after disposing of the two applications, DOT issued its recommendation for a new notice of sale for the South Central franchise area.

In the same sixty-day time period, the city hired an out-side cable television consultant, based in Arlington, Virginia, to replace DOT in the evaluation of cable television applications. Since there was only one cable television application remaining, they evaluated only one cable television franchise out of the total fifteen franchises—the South Central franchise. In violation of the proscribed bidding process, the cable television consultant was hired without a competitive bidding process—giving the appearance of independence but, yet again, not following rules or procedures set up by the City of Los Angeles.

According to the city, the new consultant was able to make substantial changes to the bidding process that would only affect the South Central franchise area. Lots of changes were made. All of the evaluation standards for biddable items, an important part of the bidding process since the inception of cable franchising bids for the city, were eliminated for the new application process in South Central. The biddable items section of the application had comprised more than sixty percent of the rating points just a few months previously. "The Community Antenna Television Master Plan" was gone for good.

Among the other items to be eliminated from evaluation were the number and location of public access studios as well as other benefits that were offered to the city by all other applicants as required by the notice of sale.

We thought this change was counterproductive in South Central because we felt these items were important for a minority community to gain proper representation of neighborhood ideas and views, to provide for education opportunities and jobs in South Central, and to foster interaction and airing of divergent opinions to other groups and government officials.

———◆———

This new bidding process, for South Central only, ended up having only one bidder, Kaufman and Broad—with no major cable companies submitting applications.

———◆———

"You're not going to believe it and it's a bitter pill to swallow but I've heard that Bakewell and Channing are shareholders in the KB deal," Al Watson fumed.

"It doesn't surprise me," I replied wearily. "If we look further there might be some other familiar names we've been arguing with over the years."

"I'd heard Mayor Bradley protected people and gave out sweetheart deals but this is brazen, even for him," Mr. Parks said sadly. "When is he ever going to protect the South Central neighborhood?" The city could move quickly when big contributors like Eli Broad were involved. It took less than ninety days to find and hire a consultant to replace the DOT. In that same time they had managed to change the entire bidding process.

———◆———

The city attempted to justify their alteration of the bidding process in several flat, procedural words: "The attached draft of the Notice of Sale contains several changes relative to the previously used bidding process."

The city effectively gutted all the previous standards, required as absolutely necessary in the application process just months before, including the biddable items area, which was the principal section used by the DOT to effectively eliminate all black applicants during the previous South Central bidding process.

How did the city attorney justify the elimination of the biddable items that had been required of fourteen of the fifteen franchise areas? Was this alteration really for the benefit of the citizens of South Central? Not at all.

The franchising proposal issued by DOT went on to say, "The City Attorney now indicates that this exclusion is not in conflict with Franchise Procedure Ordinance 58200" despite the fact that the same ordinance required these biddable items.

———◆———

The city, and most definitely Mayor Bradley's office, were swiftly moving in another direction. No city council, BTC, or IEDC hearings were held and no questions were asked about the implementation of these changes despite our protests and continued community concern. It appeared that the city felt no justification was necessary in dealing with the South Central community and they went ahead with their political plans without any consideration for South Central.

———◆———

We subsequently learned, through the discovery process in the court case we filed, that Kaufman and Broad met with Mayor Bradley at the mayor's office in August 1982, to discuss the award of the South Central cable television franchise even though there was no "Notice of Sale" pending for the franchise. The mayor's official appointment schedule indicated that Eli Broad was the representative of KB at the meeting. The headline on the mayor's schedule read, "South Central Cable Television Franchise."

In addition to Eli Broad, Sam Williams, a prominent black lawyer who was a past president of the California Bar Association and was appointed by Mayor Bradley as the president of the Board of Police Commissioners, attended the meeting. Williams, a man whom the *Los Angeles Times* described as a close advisor to Mayor Bradley, would be hired by KB to represent them in their quest to win the South Central franchise.

The fourth person who was in attendance was Bruce Corwin, the man who was the Treasurer for Tom Bradley's gubernatorial campaign fund.

———◆———

After we lost the franchise and long before we knew about the meeting between Mayor Bradley and Kaufman and Broad, Councilman Lindsay said he'd thought of talking to Sam Williams for us. "I'd talk to Williams for you but I'd be wasting my breath. He's Mayor Bradley's go-to man for advice. Bradley's not happy with either of you, so neither is Williams."

Why would a personal friend of the mayor, Williams, and Corwin, his campaign finance treasurer and a large contributor to his campaign, attend such a meeting? This is not a recipe for honest government.

In less than one hundred days, the City of Los Angeles started the franchise application process again. It showed how quickly it could move in contrast to how slowly it moved in the original South Central cable franchising effort. What happened to the extensive evaluation Councilmen Snyder and Cunningham said they wanted on May 21, 1982?

On December 7, 1982, less than seven months after the rejection of all applications from black-owned companies, KB submitted their application for the South Central franchise. Theirs was the only application submitted—for a ten-year license to operate the South Central franchise. We had only been allowed to apply for a seven-year license, which cascaded into our "Ability to Finance" fiasco and our bid's demise.

It did not appear that financing should be an issue for Kaufman and Broad. They were a New York Stock Exchange-traded company, which meant they were industry leaders with extensive financing capabilities.

If chosen, KB could utilize investment banking financing, with the "blessing" of the "new" process, which had previously been excluded from the financing process.

What had taken more than two years during our franchise process, now only took a few months for Kaufman and Broad with the benefit of a much easier process.

On September 13, 1983, the Los Angeles City Council approved the award of the South Central cable television franchise to Kaufman and Broad.

But something strange happened. On November 8, 1983, Kaufman and Broad officially accepted the franchise and the award. We had several questions. Why did it take KB so long to accept the award? What happened to the twenty-day period for presentation of financing that the DOT and BTC had harangued us about? Was KB technically in default of the franchise? Once again the rules proved to be only a pretense.

The unrealistic financing demands and deadlines that plagued us disappeared for Kaufman and Board. The IEDC and Chairman Snyder's "cash up front" requirement in our application process meant to disable our franchise application was abandoned during the application process for Kaufman and Broad. As stated in Section 2.3 of the new ordinance, "The grantee shall, within twenty days after said data publication, provide initial documentation of the availability of $46 million to construct, equip, and operate the proposed cable television system until the system becomes self-supporting. Final documentation which *irrevocably commits* $46 million must be in a form acceptable to the Department and City Attorney. The franchise shall not become effective until the department has certified that the documentation has been submitted and is acceptable. Failure to timely file such acceptable documentation may be grounds for termination of the franchise process."

The city had reversed itself yet again. For KB, the twenty-day period to provide suitable financing for the South Central franchise was disregarded and never enforced. Only after the award of the franchise did they have to commit funds. So the city would wait for KB but they wouldn't wait for us.

Curiously, in KB's November letter to DOT, KB stated, "...we also recognized that the franchise does not become effective until your department has certified that the documentation has been submitted and is in a form acceptable to your department and the City Attorney." So the commitment of funds required by KB only started ticking after the city did its work to certify the documentation with the DOT and the city attorney. How civil—or was this something more?

Since the franchise was awarded to Kaufman and Broad, the ordinance said KB was supposed to submit documentation that irrevocably committed funds for the building of the franchise.

Such financing was supposed to be supervised and approved by the DOT and the city attorney. Right?

———◆———

The South Central neighborhood waited...and waited...and waited for KB to begin construction. Two years after the award to KB, in 1985, the South Central franchise had not become effective because they had failed to provide firm financial commitments. Kaufman and Broad never submitted final financial documentation or provided the final financing to begin the construction phase of the franchise. Never!

The city council claimed the reason for rejecting all black applicants in 1982 was because they did not "like our financing."

Community pressure and outrage forced the issue. The community wanted those tens of millions of dollars spent in their South Central neighborhood. They wanted the jobs that would be created in South Central for the building, broadcast, billing, and servicing of the cable franchise. They wanted to know how the city was going to improve their lives without the ability to provide jobs or capital formation in their own community.

———◆———

In May 1985, the city council held a hearing regarding the status of the South Central franchise area, which had been awarded to Kaufman and Broad in 1983 and had not submitted financial commitments as required by the ordinance, to make the franchise award final. There was continuing speculation that KB did not intend to build the franchise at all.

Councilman Farrell spoke at this city council hearing, saying it was important to have minority representation within this franchise area regardless of who owned the franchise—a far cry from his previous opinion. He indicated a consensus had been reached by the black elected officials, including Mayor Tom Bradley, as to which black people would get an interest in the franchise if Kaufman and Broad decided not to finance and build the South Central cable television franchise.

Councilwoman Joan Flores, now the chairperson of the IEDC, accused Councilman Farrell of cutting a backroom deal to facilitate the minority shareholders (Bakewell and Johnson) who had been with KB. Councilwoman Flores challenged Councilman Farrell. "How could you have already selected participants for this transaction since KB as yet has not informed the city they will not build the South Central franchise?"

———◆———

Later in 1985, KB indeed did decide they were not going to build the franchise and notified the city. More money, time, and opportunities lost by the city for the citizens of the South Central neighborhood.

Kaufman and Broad would later claim they could not finance the franchise because of our pending litigation against the city concerning the franchising process. In short, Kaufman and Broad were falsely perpetuating the story their company could not proceed as long as we were pursuing the ability to exercise our constitutional rights. How preposterous to think a couple of middle-class, regular guys who had been raised in Jamaica, New York, could cause a multinational company to change their plans.

KB's contention that they were unable to finance the construction of the franchise was absurd. A letter dated November 3, 1983, from Security Pacific National Bank was presented to the city by KB. The letter to the City of Los Angeles acknowledged a $90 million revolving line of credit for KB. The letter went on to say, "Currently, the entire $90 million from this agreement is unused. Please be advised that Kaufman and Broad, Inc., is a major multinational corporation with assets over $1 billion and has other credit facilities available to it and its subsidiaries in addition to those mentioned above.

"We are aware of Kaufman and Broad's proposal to build the cable television franchise for South Central Los Angeles. There are no restrictions in our commitment to Kaufman and Broad which would prevent the company from funding the franchise construction costs out of the $90 million in unused credit." No restrictions!

This letter to the City of Los Angeles by Security Pacific National Bank was the basis for the financing ability, according to the city. Nowhere in this correspondence does the lender indicate any problems with existing conditions for the South Central franchise, legal or otherwise. They clearly stated there were no limitations on the use of funds.

The money was available to Kaufman and Broad, who had been fully aware that litigation would be pursued against the City of Los Angeles prior to their application for the South Central franchise. In August 1982, before Kaufman and Broad even submitted their application, Bill Schainker, the VP we had spoken to previously, called Harold Farrow, one of our attorneys, to ask about the intention of "those Galloway boys." Farrow told him we would not be bidding in the new process but we would be pursing the right to build a cable system—in Federal court.

Another reason why KB didn't build the franchise might not have been monetary at all. Perhaps it was the realization that they were ill-suited to enter the cable television business. Could they have been "parking" the franchise for the benefit of the local politicians? Was the dislike in City Hall for the "Galloway boys" or a minority-owned franchise in South Central so great that the franchise was kept "out-of-circulation" until the politicians could figure out what to do? Were there political benefits and favors KB could extract from helping City Hall by keeping the franchise?

Let's consider what transpired. No money was expended by KB, except for their time and legal fees, to win the South Central franchise. They were the only bidder for the franchise. KB never completed the final documentation or the final financing so they had not spent any money to build the franchise.

Did the city protest in any way the two years lost in this process? No. The city did not protest or fine KB for nonperformance at any time.

Since KB refused to perform under the contract to which it had agreed, why didn't the city simply terminate the contract and recommence the application process?

As public pressure mounted in light of the chronic delays, the City of Los Angeles created an entirely new bureaucratic department known as the Department of Telecommunications to deal with cable issues.

The newly created Department of Telecommunications and the IEDC were in charge of efforts to get the South Central franchise built. The members of the Department of Telecommunications Board were...appointed by Mayor Tom Bradley. Was there any reason to believe that this new department would get different results?

Our sources indicated that the city wanted to offer the franchise but avoid having another competitive bidding process. KB was not supposed to be able to sell an undeveloped franchise. Was this three-fold strategy of a new department, no competitive bidding, and a private selection of builder in place to protect KB's name and reputation, despite their default, and also to assure they could control the process and the company who "won" the South Central franchise?

We heard KB was interested in selling the South Central franchise and we were willing to buy it. We expressed our interest directly to the City of Los Angeles many times but received no response.

Contrary to the rulings of the city attorney, who previously had forbade the sale of undeveloped cable franchises, KB would be allowed to sell the completely undeveloped South Central franchise. Again, there was no protest from the city attorney or the Los Angeles City Council. How did a franchise that did not become effective as a business transfer to a third party without a protest from the city or the city attorney?

Once again, South Central was subject to singularly different rules regarding its cable television franchise.

———◆———

"They won't let us on the city council calendar, we can't get any appointments with councilmen, and Councilman Lindsay is sick in the hospital and his office won't give us an appointment either," Al Watson said.

"I've made three calls to the Department of Telecommunications and went down there once," I reported.

"Don't tell me," Mr. Parks said with a bleak smile. "They let you sit there for a long while."

"Yes," I replied. "I timed it with a need to go down there with other client paperwork so it wasn't a total waste of time."

"You've noted this all for our attorney?" Al Watson asked.

"Of course," was all I could say.

———

On December 17, 1985, the IEDC recommended the city issue a "Notice of a Request for Interest and Instructions to Respondents." The South Central area once again became the only franchise to have such a notice issued regarding the franchise—a step toward preventing competitive bidding for the South Central cable franchise.

In January 1986, a "Notice of a Request for Interest and Instructions to Respondents" was published by the city. The notice stated, "The provisions of procedure Ordinance Number 58200 and the Los Angeles Administrative Code are not applicable to this request for interest." Ordinance 58200 was the competitive bidding ordinance. No Ordinance 58200, no competitive public bidding.

Once again, South Central became the only franchise not awarded pursuant to ordinance number 58200. The unique treatment of South Central had continued for many years after the original segregation of the franchise in 1979.

There was absolutely no precedence in the City of Los Angeles cable television process for such a request of interest. The purpose of the request was to bypass the open-market system and derail any attempts for potential cable companies to bid for the franchise.

A secondary effect of this action protected the potential financial interest of those close to City Hall. No new bidding meant all the minority shareholders with KB would be protected and paid from the proceeds of the sale, even though they were part of a group that defaulted on their commitment to build the South

Central cable franchise. Bakewell and Johnson were a part of that group and their interests were protected. They would make money on non-performance and the South Central neighborhood would still have no cable television.

The December 17, 1985, IEDC report went on to say that "if interest is evidenced, the City will appropriately proceed toward a new franchise or multiple franchises for the South Central area of the City of Los Angeles." The notice of interest would allow a new company to receive a franchise without the pretense of competition.

Limiting an ordinance to fourteen of fifteen districts would appear to subvert the law. The city indicated by its public actions that it was less interested in free commerce or a free marketplace in the South Central district and effectively suspended the law in South Central in order to control the cable television franchise. Where was the outcry about black-on-black crime?

The law was infrequently consistent in this case; therefore, the law was neither served nor enforced in dealings with the city. Neither law nor order was evident in this case. Efforts to improve the neighborhood rule of law and provide economic and educational opportunities for South Central were consistently trampled. We only witnessed the rule of the powerful and those connected to the politically influential while anything and everything else was ignored.

The sale of the South Central franchise went seamlessly from Kaufman and Broad to American Cable Systems (ACS), in 1986, with the approval of the Los Angeles City Council and Mayor Tom Bradley. Once again, the major supporters of this unprecedented transfer of the undeveloped cable franchise were Councilmen David Cunningham and Robert Farrell. Their support also assured the participation of Danny Bakewell and Channing Johnson in the transferred franchise.

KB was allowed to sell the undeveloped franchise to ACS for millions of dollars. Ten million, we believe, to be exact.

Cable companies who owned "operational" Los Angeles-area cable franchises with constructed systems and actual customers made substantial profits when they were sold. But, in this case, KB's profit of millions of dollars was based upon deprivation: the deprivation of the rights of the citizens of South Central.

KB never built anything.

————

That wasn't all. In addition to selecting ACS to buy the South Central franchise in a process never made public, the City was proposing to assist American Cable Systems in the financing process by deferring sixty percent of franchise fees for the first five years of a fifteen-year franchise. Remember the seven-year franchise we were offered? How could anyone compete with a government-subsidized monopoly that was fundamentally unregulated?

American Cable Systems was able to completely bypass the standard application process (our application took two years while Kaufman and Broad's application took nine months). In less than four months, the city had published a request for interest (the only time such a request was issued) for the South Central franchise and had awarded a franchise to American Cable Systems without any public evaluation of their decision. No pretense of free markets or competition remained in this scenario.

We also found out from our sources, and later in public records, that American Cable Systems was required to accept the black group of political friends (the Bakewell/Johnson group) who had been part of the former KB franchise group. The city ordinance that transferred the South Central franchise to American Cable Systems showed Bakewell and Johnson, in addition to the non-profit organization the Brotherhood Crusade (previously run by Danny Bakewell), as part of the new ownership. More profit and opportunities for friends of Mayor Bradley!

173

———————

Several months after the transfer of the South Central franchise to American Cable Systems, Councilman Cunningham resigned from the city council before the end of his elected term. Cunningham immediately went to work for Cranston Securities. Cranston Securities had contracts with the City of Los Angeles to sell municipal bonds for the city. The president of Cranston Securities was Danny Bakewell.

———————

In the fall of 1986, the Los Angeles City Council approved the sale of the undeveloped South Central franchise from Kaufman and Broad to American Cable Systems. Since Kaufman and Broad had never done any construction of the franchise, the only thing that was being sold was the monopoly protection by the city.

By these actions, the city, in essence, subverted the free-market system three times. By getting rid of all competitive bids they systematically "exhausted" the free market bidding system and KB waltzed off with the South Central franchise. KB failed to perform, was never fined, and the city rewarded that illegal action by allowing KB to sell the undeveloped franchise without any competition at the expense of the South Central neighborhood and the Los Angeles taxpayer. No "cash up front," no fines, a large profit for KB from the sale of the franchise, and a city subsidy for American Cable Systems!

———————

On October 14, 1987, American Cable Systems requested the right to transfer the South Central franchise to Continental Cablevision as part of a merger of the companies. This would represent the third owner of the franchise within one year. So much for the city process providing cable franchise stability for the citizens of South Central.

Continental then sold the franchise to Comcast and Comcast sold it to AT&T. AT&T eventually sold it to Time Warner Cable.

There were a total of six separate sales of the South Central franchise in a twenty-year period.

These sales undoubtedly enriched numerous cable business companies and their owners, but once again these re-sales did nothing for the enrichment of the people of South Central. Unfortunately, economic and community development was not accomplished through continual sales and re-sales and the long-term construction plans and programming for South Central we envisioned never materialized.

As time would tell, conditions in the South Central neighborhood were deteriorating. Unemployment and crime continued to rise, while the high school graduation rate continued to decline. The area continued to have an increasing poverty rate. Could cable television, neighborhood programming, and well-run community access channels have stemmed the deterioration? We'll never know.

Another irony involved AT&T becoming an owner of the franchise. AT&T was able to avoid local governments completely and received its approval to operate in the cable programming industry directly from the federal government and the FCC—removing any city or community involvement by throwing it to a higher level of bureaucracy.

We'd hoped the FCC would intervene during our cable television applications problems with the City of Los Angeles. We had asked for such intervention when we wrote our letters about the South Central franchise fiasco to the Attorney General of the United States. Our legal counsel indicated the FCC had the legal ability to intervene during the time the City of Los Angeles was violating our constitutional rights.

At the time of the sale of the South Central franchise from Comcast to AT&T, the FCC was also aware of the report published by the Department of Commerce, detailing the irregularities in the award of cable television franchises—and our case in particular. While the FCC was now supportive of competition, it had turned a blind eye to the lack of competition in the early 1980s. The FCC did not take any action in order to promote competition when that competition was not done by former telephone monopolies such as AT&T and Verizon. The very same FCC did not care about our ability to compete but would assure that the former telephone companies would compete by overriding local laws governing the operations of cable television systems.

At the time, in the early 1980s when we were initially bidding for the cable television franchise, AT&T was barred by federal law from pursuing cable television franchises. Because of its monopoly power in the telephone market and unlimited access to telephone poles, the FCC had deemed entrance by telephone companies into the cable television industry to be anti-competitive.

AT&T, the large and powerful former telephone monopoly, was able to take advantage of their previous monopoly power to utilize the wiring and systems paid for by the telephone users and taxpayers during AT&T's monopolistic years. Now, their years of monopoly operation, through their former Bell Telephone systems, left AT&T with a large cash surplus and a national system of access to wiring and poles to compete with the existing cable monopoly.

At that time, as companies lobbied to maintain business power and a competitive edge, the political process enhanced these prospects through deregulation in one monopoly to allow competition in another government-created and -protected monopoly. In the regulation arena, AT&T had to break up its monopoly hold on telecommunications—it and other companies were now basking in deregulation and business in government monopoly opportunities like cable franchises. Did either the Democrats or Republicans care about the concepts of free speech or free markets anymore? Were campaign contributions on the federal level affecting their judgments and performance?

———◆———

Limiting competition in the cable television industry seemed to be the next move by the city to protect the cable company monopolies. To these ends, increasing the length of franchise licenses aided in entrenching media companies in Los Angeles. On July 31,

1985, Councilwoman Joan Flores made a motion on the floor of the Los Angeles City Council to place a charter amendment to modify the ordinance that governed cable television. The change would increase the term of a franchise from ten years to fifteen years. Just four years earlier, in 1981, Flores and the city council had wanted our company to have only a seven-year franchise.

The stated purpose of this charter amendment was to provide "capital investment to comply with such objectives [as] may prove economically viable over a fifteen-year franchise period." Therefore, the city could have the flexibility to determine the term of a replacement franchise in order to achieve the desired objectives. But the longer franchise term offered additional protection for the designated monopoly—they got a "gift" of five more years.

This charter amendment subsequently appeared on the June 1986 ballot and was approved in part because of the huge advertising campaigns funded from the substantial profits by the cable television systems that operated franchises within the City of Los Angeles. Unfortunately, this action also promoted moves toward such plans in other cities in the country under the mantra of, "Los Angeles approved it."

———

We couldn't let these shenanigans continue. It was time to take another stand.

In 1982, as the governor's election for the state of California began to run full throttle, Mayor Bradley's national prominence was enhanced because he was predicted to win. Many people, unfortunately, were falling over themselves to support his gubernatorial bid. As Bradley was sipping cocktails and toasting his upcoming glory, Carl and I were truly upset and trying to identify ways to prevent this travesty from happening.

This same black mayor who had been puppet-mastering this sham of a cable television application process on a local level was preparing to enter the governor's race for the state of California.

We believed then, as I believe now, that, with all battles, it's best to go down fighting. We devised our battle plan. Everyone whom we encountered during the six-month period prior to the election would be informed about Tom Bradley's coercion against financial investment in South Central. We'd make sure of that.

I had extensive contacts in the San Francisco Bay Area because I worked there for four years with a major international accounting firm before moving to Los Angeles. Between June and November of 1982, I made nine trips to the Bay Area to speak with numerous groups and individuals to express my opposition to the mayor's gubernatorial attempt.

I funded the activities with money I made selling my condominium in Playa Del Rey. By election time, November 1982, my brother and I had spent in excess of $50,000 of our own money in our efforts to derail Mayor Bradley's gubernatorial bid—without the benefit of any other people or political party.

Those who knew me knew I didn't want to be engaged in a political process, at any time, especially after all the public meetings, speeches, and talks I undertook in the cable television battle. But I felt we had to.

Many friends and associates told me I was wasting my time and money because, according to the election polls, the results were indisputable and Bradley would be the winner.

After several months of traveling to San Francisco and looking at the polls, I began to agree with them. One might say, with substantial evidence, that we weren't smart enough to know when to quit—but we didn't.

A fighter knows in his heart when he has done his best and given it his all. And there is a certain kind of peace in the knowledge of fighting clean, fighting to win, and accepting the outcome. I played sports all of my life. One of the most important things I learned during my competitive years in sports was that it's not whether you win or lose but how you play the game.

The San Francisco Bay Area is, by all indications, probably the most liberal area in all of California. People were shocked to see a black man spend his time and money to oppose the gubernatorial election of a black mayor from Los Angeles—if the stunned looks, gapping eyes, and tapping one another in incredulity I witnessed are any indications.

Up until the day of the election polls, Mayor Bradley had a four-point lead in the general elections. Exit polls also indicated Bradley would win the race.

On election night, I felt like a fool having spent three months and a princely sum of $50,000 in a losing effort. Imagine my surprise when I turned on the television to hear the announcer say the race for governor was too close to call after 15% of ballots had been counted.

The morning news brought the revelation of Mayor Tom Bradley's losing bid for governor by less than one half of a percentage point to George Deukmejian. Carl and I were elated!

Mayor Bradley and his supporters immediately began looking for reasons for the loss. Even though I had no scientific data on which to base my claim, I believe I knew the answer to the question. Based on the opinion of someone who spent $50,000 in addition to his own time and energy talking to people in an effort to defeat Mayor Bradley, the real truth was that Mayor Bradley failed to maintain his primary support base—the black citizens of California.

His television ads, noticeably devoid of any African-Americans, were not appreciated by the black population of Los Angeles. In fact, numerous, vociferous South Central residents were insulted by Bradley's neglect to include any black faces in statewide ads. Mayor Bradley took the black vote for granted, thinking black voters would back a candidate simply because he was black. He underestimated them. Enough stayed away from the polls to cost him the election.

The press coined the phrase the "Bradley effect," referring to voters who said they would vote for Bradley but did not actually cast their votes for him on election day. It was a lesson on the weakness of pre-voting polls having a substantially larger margin of error that estimated.

Another twist in the polling fallacy was the number of black voters who said they would vote for Tom Bradley and did not go to the polls because they assumed he would win based on the pre-election polls.

Thirdly, we certainly felt Bradley alienated a large portion of the black community with his failure to improve the conditions for the residents of South Central. In our estimation, Tom Bradley's actions regarding the award of the South Central cable television franchise might have played a part in alienating the average South Central citizen. In the fiasco, they'd been denied jobs, access to technology, and the ability to invest in their own community—by another black man.

We felt Bradley's tenure as the mayor of the City of Los Angeles saddled modern South Central with increasing poverty, crime, and the unforgettable 1992 riots. The largest race riots in the history of Los Angeles took place while he, a black mayor, was in office. Politicians like Bradley, after making their continual campaign promises to improve the neighborhood, failed to keep those promises. As Jonathan Swift said, "Power is no blessing in itself, except when it is used to protect the innocent." What a horrible legacy for an African-American mayor.

After the election, Johnnie Cochran told Dr. Avery, Carl's friend, that a substantial amount of the blame for the mayor's loss would be placed at the feet of "the Galloway boys." Cochran contended that we had made the City of Los Angeles look bad by going around creating suspicion about the mayor's involvement in the cable television franchising process. He felt we created a negative image of Bradley within the black communities of California. What a delusion!

Cochran emphatically told Dr. Avery that, in the future, "the Galloway boys" would never do any business in Los Angeles and that we had been blacklisted by all the black politicians and judges.

We were being vilified for exposing the corruption and its detrimental effects upon South Central that existed in City Hall. The emperor had no clothes—and the one named Bradley wasn't happy about it being discussed.

At that time, we had the great consolation in knowing that whatever role we played, Mayor Bradley did not achieve higher office, which made everything worth our time and money. We could work hard and make more money but we wouldn't have to withstand Bradley as our governor.

We felt the greatness of our country with the individual citizen telling the truth—like my brother and I did. Two average guys— black guys, at that—could have an impact in an election where millions of votes were cast. We felt proud that as individual citizens we could ultimately have some affect upon a statewide election in such a large state as California.

Mayor Bradley would run for governor again in 1986 and would lose by a substantial margin.

Mayor Bradley, Carl, and I each had something in common. We each desired something that we would never get. At least Carl and I could look at ourselves in the mirror and know we still had our integrity.

Chapter Nine

The Twenty-Percent Solution

The bad penny always returns, so they say. We saw the names of Danny Bakewell and Channing Johnson embedded in the KB cable television package soon after KB won the franchise. They were listed for twenty-percent ownership. It seemed that the interests of Bakewell and Johnson seemed to outweigh the needs and rights of the South Central community.

In recalling Bakewell's and Johnson's CTI negotiations with us, they demanded a sixty-six-percent interest. Our offer of fifty percent was rejected as being too small. They would now accept twenty percent from a company that was owned and run by white management, despite Johnson's earlier almost continual rant that there will be no white partners in this deal. It was amazing to see how their estimate of their own value diminished so quickly

The power of Bakewell and Johnson was worth sixty-six percent if you are black but only twenty percent if you were white. What does this say about the view of being black versus being white that was held by Bakewell and Johnson?

"I heard a business saying that's what's called a 'nuisance factor'," Al Watson offered when he heard about the KB deal. Bakewell and Johnson came to the table with no money and no cable television experience and wanted the lion's share of the deal, just because we were black. If they were white it would have been called racism. Should it be called anything else just because they were also black?

The threats that Bakewell and Johnson had used with us would not be effective with the likes of Kaufman and Broad. Eli Broad was one of the richest and most powerful Democrats in California. The power of Tom Bradley was made possible by large contributors like Kaufman and Broad, not by the rhetoric of Bakewell and Johnson. Rhetoric was the only thing they ever brought to the negotiating table during our discussions.

The paper trail we found is not kind to the Bakewell group. In a 1983 memo we uncovered during the litigation, from Channing Johnson to Mayor Bradley's special deputy, William Elkins, Johnson clearly outlined the dissatisfaction the Bakewell/Johnson group felt in their dealings with KB. At one point, Bakewell and Johnson thought they would be able to obtain a fifty-one-percent interest in the franchise. KB shot down the idea immediately.

Channing Johnson sought a seat on the board of directors of the company that had been awarded the franchise, but that was also immediately rejected by KB.

Johnson's memo to Elkins sought the intervention of Mayor Bradley's office in the negotiation process with KB. The continuing involvement by the mayor's special deputy, William Elkins, was clear evidence that the mayor was playing a part in the South Central franchise award and transfer. According to other documents we obtained, Mayor Bradley also provided support to KB when they sought to sell the franchise.

I was told later, by one of the participants at the KB offices during the original negotiations with the Bakewell/Johnson group, that Johnson had demanded a larger percentage. Eli Broad reacted negatively and called Councilman Lindsay. Broad bellowed into the phone, "You better get your boys under control."

The use of the term "boy" is a derogatory term from the perception of most blacks. A white man knowing this prohibition and using the term in referring to a black man was a purposeful and pointed attack on Johnson and Bakewell. Did either Bakewell or Johnson voice any objections to the use of the word when they stood to make a profit?

Broad was making sure everyone understood the controlling dynamics of the situation. After that call, the twenty percent was not questioned anymore. Bakewell and Johnson accepted the twenty-percent ownership interest in the cable franchise— no more questions asked. In this case, KB showed they had the power to make Bakewell, Johnson, and Mayor Bradley toe the line.

Councilman Lindsay, who had supported our original application through the loss at the city council meeting in May 1982, later confided to Carl and me that KB did not want to have "the Galloway boys" involved in any meaningful way in a business sense in the South Central cable television franchise.

Lindsay was told by the KB representatives, "If the Galloway boys would not take forty-nine-percent ownership five months ago, why would they suddenly agree to divide twenty-percent with Danny and Channing?"

According to Lindsay, one of the men scoffed, "Those Galloway boys don't like to play ball the way they are supposed to...but Johnson and Bakewell were pushovers. We only had to shake the dollar signs in their faces."

They were right about that. If "not playing ball" meant we left our constitutional rights at the door, we weren't even interested in entering the ball field.

We were interested in a fair game and we were prepared to fight for that opportunity and to protect those rights in the process. We'd been steamrolled by the Los Angeles Mayor, the city council, numerous bureaucratic boards, commissions, city employees, and the friends of the mayor, to name a few.

Bakewell and Johnson would also become twenty-percent owners with American Cable Systems after the transfer of the franchise from Kaufman and Broad. Once again they got a twenty-percent interest in that franchise. The City of Los Angeles seemed to require all cable television license holders of the South Central franchise to have Bakewell and Johnson in their ownership structure.

It was now the city's new mantra that if a cable company did not give part ownership to a black group, they could be branded as racist or exploitative, but the ownership always had the same names, Bakewell and Johnson.

Since neither Kaufman and Broad nor American Cable Systems needed Bakewell or Johnson's money and these mens' values could not have been their cable television experience, what made every applicant accept these two men? Could this twenty percent have something to do with politics? The twenty percent was little more than a nuisance factor for the right to have a monopoly franchise.

The City of Los Angeles has taken great lengths to see that no one is able to access what are supposed to be public records to see how much money was actually made by Bakewell and Johnson from their involvement in the cable industry. I would have certainly expected them to make several million dollars each, at the very least. Political cronyism was simply part of the cost of doing business in Los Angeles.

We rejected the Bakewell group, the "Mayor's Group," and all the other political cronies for their greed and because they were not interested in being in the cable television business. "Only interested in getting some fast money…and selling the future of the South Central community," Mr. Parks said.

Control of our business and our integrity were important factors. As black men, we felt we better represented the interests of the citizens of South Central and the black community. We fully intended to give the black community relevant programming to reach the most economically forgotten citizens in Los Angeles.

It was the ability to air relevant and educational programming within the South Central communities that inspired us to become a part of the cable television industry in the first place. This could only be accomplished by the control of the distribution system for cable television within the South Central franchise. We did not require a monopoly franchise because we believed our programming would separate us from our competitors. After all, wasn't that how the free market was supposed to work?

Chapter Ten

Plain Dealing

We had lost in all our efforts to get into the cable television industry. Carl, I, our board of directors, our families, friends, close associates, and advocates in South Central all thought we should sue. I promised everyone I'd spearhead the effort.

Our legal counsel wanted everything we could get to help them understand exactly what had happened. "You tell us the whole story, put together the paper trail and your witness list...and we'll add the law," they said. "Oh, and you'd better put together something for the media." They checked their yellow pads. "Try talking to your family and friends, it'll help you get your thoughts together." They checked something off the list. "Be sure to give the media some solutions so they don't just look at you guys as crybabies just wanting to get some money from the city treasury."

Get our thoughts together! We'd thought of little else other than the franchise and getting Carl's reputation restored from his slanderous brush with the media.

So I gathered everything and got it organized and written down so people could look beyond the chronology to appreciate our goals and philosophies and see the unfolding of the tragic miscarriage of the bidding process and the injustice we experienced—as well as the excesses and illegalities of the City of Los Angeles.

Beyond the corruption, endless meetings, hearings, and paperwork were many sad stories.

———

First of all, we thought that no other minority-owned bidder, other than ourselves, would be able to win the franchise award, unless they had a stronger franchise application—which didn't happen. Secondly, we knew they could not force us to concede majority control of our application.

All we wanted was a fair shake. There was nothing fair about the experience, except getting to meet more people from the South Central neighborhood and to express the gratitude we felt from their giving us their time and support.

We thought that when we showed we had the business and financial wherewithal to successfully run a cable television franchise, even our adversaries would want to join with us for mutual benefit. But soon into the franchise application experience, we knew we'd have to accommodate some of the political establishment's wishes. We were willing to divide ownership, fifty-fifty, in order to get the right access and programming for the South Central neighborhood.

Of what we saw in the cable industry in Los Angeles and when we investigated the industry nationally, the picture wasn't pretty. Cable television was never a free marketplace as the industry began to grow and prosper. Politicians realized they could use their power to enhance their positions and, often times, line their campaign coffers and pocketbooks.

Cable television became a cash register for elected officials, one of the most glaring examples of the availability of politicians to be wooed by large corporations.

During the 1980s, cable the cable television industry was one of the largest contributors to political campaigns throughout the United States, as well as Los Angeles, falling just short of contributions from oil companies. Politicians sold themselves like a commodity in the marketplace, generally making themselves available to the highest bidder, and the only question was the price they could get for rigging the bids and bidding process. We bitterly remembered getting our bid from Compton back unopened. The politicians were so brazen they didn't even care if we knew they didn't open up the envelopes.

Stable, long-term management and business integrity were the main reasons we refused to give up control to others who were only looking for a multimillion-dollar profit and a quick turnaround. We never forgot the importance of maintaining management influence within the process. This management influence would allow independent selection of useful programming within the community being served.

Instead, the politicians and their cronies used every dirty trick in the book, even changing long-established bidding rules and procedures, to get their way, to get their money, and to leave the mess to be cleaned up by future city administrations.

These cable television franchise opportunities and the cable industry across the country provided contributions to fund the political aspirations of local politicians in exchange for bidding favors and, in return, the franchises themselves, which reaped billions of dollars in monopoly profits. In exchange, politicians shielded these companies from competition within the rapidly growing cable television industry. Could the acquisition of a political favor be inexpensive compared to competition in a free market?

We say yes. We saw it happen.

So we were going to have to fight the City of Los Angeles in court for a franchise because all of our goals as independent black cable franchise owners were continually thwarted by the idea that we wanted control of our company, decision making, and programming for the South Central franchise. We were chagrined to learn that the leading opponents of black improvement in South central were in fact black elected officials in the City of Los Angeles.

We had to file suit and put together a case showing just how wrong and corrupt the government system had become—how far from the ethical and moral standards the City of Los Angeles had sunk. Things were going to get dirty—really, dirtier—as we tried to describe what had happened to us.

Worst of all, the politicians' bungling and greed left the South Central franchise without cable television for ten more years. That's a child's life from first grade to being a sophomore in high school—an educational travesty. After rejecting black cable television franchise applications from the late 1960s, service was partially started on a system for the area in 1988.

In Michael Wolf's biography of Rupert Murdoch, Mr. Murdoch made it abundantly clear that your ability to control the content of media is dependant upon your ability to control your access to the same media. The two are inherently tied.

In a world that didn't have or didn't foresee the Internet, widespread cell phone usage, and personal satellite communication access, having a cable franchise system to help finance and test programming on a local scale, helped in gaining audience and profits for wider-reaching programming goals.

We could provide a market for black and minority writers, directors, and actors along with the technical production staff needed for new programming.

But we never got a fair chance.

Programming and distribution were big goals we wanted to fulfill, but offering the truth through our cable franchise was another.

We thought that in our system of government, which guarantees freedom of speech, it is the job of the media to report on the activities of the local and national governments and responsibly portray the actions and decisions of the government to its citizens.

We needed to get the cable franchise to give the community honest and accurate programming but there were too many examples of cable companies and politicians hiding their mutual collusion. This affected free speech. Would cable owners expose their politician friends who they'd paid to get the franchise? Would they broadcast their politician friends' illegal and felonious behavior for the public good—and risk having the light of corruption pointed in their direction as coconspirators?

How many people knew Mayor Bradley, the city council, and the bureaucratic departments were running amuck? We tried innumerable times to get the local newspapers and television and radio stations to listen to our claims. Some were Bradley and status quo supporters, others were afraid, and still others didn't want to get on the outs of the political machine because they wanted to get, or stay, on the gravy train. How can the citizens of a city, state, and country influence politicians to change rules and laws in the face of all this money, fear, and drive for the wrong-headed goals and objectives?

The fact that the cable television industry was supposed be protected by the First Amendment makes this travesty of free speech even more egregious, dangerous, and important.

Through our dealings with the South Central franchise mess and Carl's dispute with CBS's *60 Minutes*, we learned first hand that the laws and the protection of the Constitution are not the same for all citizens.

In our cable case, local governments like the City of Los Angeles continually changed the rules and regulations regarding a major media industry. In Carl's *60 Minutes* case, we were also finding multinational media corporations like CBS were able to recklessly abuse laws they felt did not apply to them. They used people's names, made accusations, and ruined lives on national television with fewer authentications than the footnotes in a high schooler's English research paper.

No country is truly free when all of the information disseminated in the media is controlled by very few people who run companies that act as monopolies, given power by the politicians who
they've bribed for the privilege. And the politicians won't exercise
any control over these monopolies because the people who run
the companies continue to give them so much money to remain
in office and in power. It becomes an addictive cycle of power and
money—and a desire to ascend the ladder like a video game-
politician "Mario."

———————

Then there was the story—and the problem—of race. We thought
when politicians of any race tried to micromanage situations to
the conclusion they selected, included their cronies in the deals,
and got as much extortion money as they could, they hurt the
people they promised to help and made of a mockery of their
citizens' votes.

We should be able to criticize anybody. Many didn't want to
criticize Mayor Bradley because they would be charged with racism. Others were glad a black man was finally in a high government position, and it looked like from all intents and purposes he
was doing so well in his tenure.

We, as black businessmen, didn't feel so privileged. The
desire of elected officials to force a merger between two competing companies because they are both owned or represented by
black businessmen insulted us and ran contrary to the free market system within the United States. Let the best black company
win—fairly.

The politicians' segregation of blacks into a single franchise
area would allow for the future disparate treatment of that franchise. The results would have a lasting effect upon South Central
by depriving its citizens of access to the technology, education,
and information available to the rest of the city, county, and other
urban areas of the country. Politicians succeeded in limiting competition in the bidding process in cable television by dividing the
South Central-Harbor franchise into three franchises—only for
political gain.

Through the nearly fifteen years we were involved in the application and litigation, we learned elected officials might not be responsible or responsive to the people. The same people with black faces, who merely changed their offices, continually represented the community—like musical chairs. One day they were a councilman, then congressman, then assemblyman, then state senator, and then county supervisor. With this "same-old, same-old" system, had the legislative and judicial systems changed the landscape of the neighborhood to better the lives of the citizens? Had the landscape of their lives improved? Again, we say no. Things continued to deteriorate in the neighborhoods.

A cycle of poverty and illiteracy lead to the crime that existed within the South Central community and continually and increasingly threatened its inhabitants. Did black politicians work for the betterment of the community or did politicians benefit from this cycle? Or were they just accruing power and wealth from the programs and monies aimed at alleviating the suffering and ignorance of these people?

Even when things stayed the same or got worse, what we learned, the hard way, was that some African-American citizens were controlled by their political party and seem hypnotized by the same old tired rhetoric and broken promises. They seemed like a mother whose kid always promises to come through, but never does. Such people were making money off the misery of these poverty-stricken people, as if these elected officials were young children who had the treat bag and made sure they always got the biggest piece.

Take the example of the organization called Brotherhood Crusade, located in South Central. In the cable franchise application process a proposal was made, and contained in the KB application and subsequent DOT reports, allowing non-profit agencies, such as the Brotherhood Crusade, to obtain shares in the KB franchise. How and where were these non-profits going to get millions of dollars to invest in a high-risk venture like cable television?

The non-profits could not invest in this franchise and never did. This alleged use of a community organization was supposed to mitigate the fact the South Central community would have no say over the technology and programming that would have a dramatic impact on all the community and delay the construction of the cable franchise in the community for many years for a few charity dollars thrown their way. This was just another sham promise presented in the application but never fulfilled. No money, no power.

In contrast, although we didn't make an intensive, scientific study, it appeared the lives of the politicians had improved like the old axiom of, "No one leaves politics broke after being elected." We saw this kind of profiteering in our own case. Are we electing the best and brightest or those who wait in service while going along with the scams? Are black citizens of this country receiving proper information about the activities of their representatives or are they told with a wink and a nod that their representatives are getting the same kickbacks and illegal enhancements as their white counterparts? Democracy among thieves.

We were caught in the middle of this nightmare. Community leaders weren't community leaders, and, at this time, some black community leaders were the worst offenders of all.

They exhibited the same behavior and lack of ethics that disempowered our race for generations when the white politicians were ruling things in the South. These misguided thieves had their hands out, just like the white politicians our ancestors had loathed. If we didn't do things "their way," we were out with the same rapidity as their former white politico counterparts. Just because their skin was black, it didn't make them better

This black political elitism and cronyism with the white politicians deciding who got what denied us and this predominantly black neighborhood the economic opportunity and to participate in a free marketplace of ideas and information in South Central—a community poverty stricken not only financially, but also intellectually and emotionally on many levels.

Dishonest black politicians were slamming the door in the face of honest black citizens. If the black politicians thought they were helping or protecting their constituents, the littered landscape of their actions show otherwise. That's another story we needed to tell.

———◆———

As an accountant, I saw it was all in the numbers. The damage caused to low-income communities, by this method of cable television regulation chaos, had an even greater impact. The lower disposable income meant benefits given to the politically favored took a greater percentage of the income in economically disadvantaged communities, like stealing from a blind man's cup.

In movies and television shows, scripts portray a "protection racket" as an illegal scheme by some sort of organized crime organization that preys upon small businesses like mom-and-pop stores—very evil and sinister. And when the criminal is caught in the act, the police arrest him and he is brought to justice. But when the government is protecting its friends, halting all outside competition, and either making the rules or subverting others as they go along, they portray themselves as knowledgeable and politically savvy.

But in the City of Los Angeles protection game, promoting and shielding special interests and politicians was merely the normal and expected day-to-day exercise of government power over citizens in Los Angeles.

So, as we watched, the cable television industry became the "great depriver" or the "great beneficiary," depending on which side of the game you were on. Local governments, as in our application process and subsequent litigation, were willing to spend millions of dollars of taxpayer dollars to prohibit competition. In our case against the City of Los Angeles, the litigation cost to the city was approximately $15 million—or should we say it cost the taxpayers $15 million.

This figure represents a combination of legal fees and the loss cable television franchise fees that could never be recovered because of the delay in providing cable television service to South Central from 1980 to 1990. The total legal fees of the city were nearly $7 million. The lost franchise fees from the lack of cable operations were approximately $8 million.

There's also another price extracted from citizens. The protection game serves to run up the price in any industry where competition is restricted. Specifically, in the cable television industry, prices were twenty-percent higher for cable television service because of the monopoly status.

This information was presented in the deposition of Dr. Thomas Hazlett, Professor of Economics at the University of California at Davis. Dr. Hazlett would go on to teach at such prestigious universities as MIT and the Wharton School of Business. From 1990 through 1991, Dr. Hazlett was the chief economist for the Federal Communications Commission. Dr. Hazlett testified as an expert witness for our case and was deposed by the City of Los Angeles.

Between 1980 and 1999, the total gross revenue of the cable television industry in the United States was approximately $100 billion, according to the National Cable Television Association. Approximately $20 billion of that revenue was directly attributable to the government-protected monopoly granted to cable television companies.

A third price is that neighborhoods like South Central were sold like cattle to the highest bidder for graft to the benefit of the politicians, not the citizens. Citizens, their laws, and the Constitution were being sold.

———

As Carl predicted in 1979, new electronic technology replaced newspapers as the information-dominant media in the United States and so the ability of local citizens to examine the activities of local governments has been greatly compromised. In our case, and many others, being ahead of the technology curve in Black America only brought you high-powered enemies.

The latest demographic information, as we began our quest, clearly indicated that minority communities, like South Central, relied more on television than the printed media for their information. The reasons were quite clear: the high incidence of illiteracy, the lack of alternative resources for information (there were very few libraries and bookstores in South Central) or entertainment (there were no movie theaters or large playhouses in South Central at that time), and newspapers cost money and most newspaper information didn't last much longer than a day. So, for the most up-to-date information and entertainment, they chose television.

So what the people wanted was increased television choices for information and entertainment but the city government wasn't listening or didn't care. In our analysis, we put together four basic premises—as simple as a basic civics class for the "happily ever after."

First, the behavior of government must be constantly monitored by the citizens in a free society in order to protect against the excesses that naturally develop with power. We allege that, during the 1980s and early 1990s, local governments were aided in restricting the flow of information about their activities by virtue of their total control over the cable television operators within their jurisdiction.

Secondly, governments at all levels must also be watched to assure the First Amendment rights of all citizens are protected, not just the person or group most favorable to the elected officials and their positions. Otherwise, governments, like the one in Los Angeles, might be tempted to ignore the laws set down to monitor their behavior. In our eyes, their misconduct and dereliction of duty caused immeasurable harm to us and to the South Central neighborhood.

In fact, the restriction of the purchase of media (in the eighteenth century the media was newspaper and printed material) to those who are in cahoots with existing politicians was part of the reason for the enactment of the First Amendment to the Constitution. Today the restriction refers to the people and media companies who are participating in this egregious and dangerous threat to free speech as well.

Thirdly, there must be some minimum standard of behavior, even for politicians. Our standard for all elected officials and governments in the United States begins with the Constitution of the United States. The purpose of the Constitution was not to restrict the activities of the citizen but rather to restrict the activities of government imposed upon its citizens.

Finally, the Constitution as a document allows for the citizen to live in a system governed by laws controlling the actions of both the citizens and their elected government officials, and citizens having a say in regularly scheduled, free elections to keep or replace those government officials.

Those rights and privileges of our Constitution should never be violated without penalty, especially from the excesses any level of government may unlawfully use against its citizens.

———————

We no longer needed to waste our money or time pretending we were going to have any chance at building a cable television system in Los Angeles, if the City of Los Angeles had its way. We'd been through the grossly unfair franchising process for three cable television franchises in the City of Los Angeles. We no longer deluded ourselves in thinking the current process, with the bureaucrats and rules, could ever be fair or independent. Politicians and "friends" of the current city government continually indicated that no one would do business with "the Galloway boys."

What can you do when you're left with no alternative after your rights and legislative options have been trampled by city government? Few would listen and even fewer would act on our behalf. Our neighborhood activists seemed powerless and the local media only reacted in a lukewarm manner, only interested for short periods of time, and, only then, during the time of the major hearings and council votes.

We've already provided page-by-painstaking-page, describing the abuses within the South Central-Harbor franchise application process. Such abuse and misuse of power should never be allowed in our government at any level, and it clearly demonstrates the over-reaching and corrupt nature of the process that violated our civil rights and the right of free speech.

As a final resort, we looked to the federal court, to seek justice and to protect our constitutional rights. After all, the federal court in America is the last stop for justice in a dispute between citizens and their government. We felt strongly that we had to seek the assistance of the federal court for the protection of our rights and to expose a record of the Los Angeles City government's abuses regarding bias, fraud, and mismanagement.

———

From the beginning, the daunting question facing our intrepid group of entrepreneurs was evaluating our willingness to fight for the rights guaranteed to us by the Constitution. The answer was a resounding yes.

All of us who were working with our company believed in the fight, we believed in our rights, and, most importantly, we believed in our country. To those among us who had fought in the Civil Rights movement, our case was merely an extension of the same issue—our rights as American citizens to exercise our free speech rights.

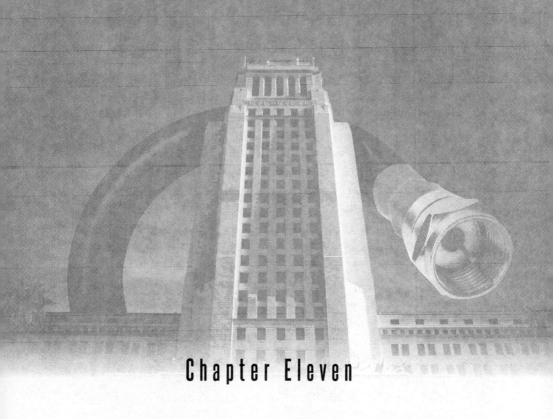

Chapter Eleven

The Justice Hustle—Part One
(US District Court—Judge Consuelo Marshall)

There were a lot of things to consider before going to court. Would we get a fair and impartial hearing in court?

Johnny Cochran had mentioned in his conversation with Dr. Avery that all the black politicians and judges were against us. In considering our litigation decision we carefully evaluated our decision to file suit and go to federal court to protect our rights. In order to defend our rights we were clearly prepared to prove contentions regarding bias, fraud, corruption, and mismanagement.

We had documented the entire process from the early stages of our involvement in the franchise application process as the abuses mounted.

Secondly, Tom Bradley was still mayor. He had access to attorneys, both inside and outside the City of Los Angeles, and tens of millions of dollars in taxpayer funds to finance the city's defense against our case based upon our First Amendment rights and antitrust issues. If he opposed us, he and the City of Los Angeles would be Goliath. Being David, again, in this scenario, meant more time, money, and energy with an uncertain outcome.

Yet, we knew of these abuses and knew they couldn't continue. The illegal stranglehold Mayor Bradley and the city council had on the availability of cable television in South Central negatively affected the South Central community. Other instances of Bradley's misuse of government power needed to end. In our case, the mayor and his friends denied access to technology to those who needed it most. How many lives can you watch get ruined before you try to help?

We knew this process would be expensive and time-consuming. "Let me be clear. The goal of a well-financed defense opponent, like the City of Los Angeles, is to deplete your finances and elongate the process so the case might not be heard," our lead lawyer, Harold Farrow said.

My brother and I felt so passionately about our cause, and now our legal case, continually thinking about the ramifications to us and the South Central neighborhoods. We'd already spent thousands of hours and hundreds of thousands of dollars. We believed if citizens, like ourselves, did not avail themselves in all possible opportunities in a free society, then they will have failed in their responsibility to uphold the very freedoms we are so fortunate to exercise as Americans.

Even before filing our case in court, money was needed for lawyers, research, and figuring out how we were going to keep our respective households financially afloat with the lost time at work for hearings, trials, and depositions. We also had to pay for everything the lawyers needed when, and if, the case went to trial. Then, if we lost the case, we risked judgments against us and having to pay for the court costs of the city's lawyers. We might bankrupt ourselves—including our future earnings.

If we didn't win at the district court level, our lawyers said we needed to budget for filing an appeal at the Ninth Circuit Court of Appeals, which would cost a minimum of $150,000. Again, possibly needing to spend hundreds of thousands of dollars for justice in another court. Another forum for the public to hear the truth potentially required another court case and more energy, time, and money.

Carl and I were going to have to mortgage everything we owned to keep our fight going. So, instead of going to court, we first decided to pursue an alternative strategy to get the rights to build a cable television franchise in South Central. "Let's try a side-step here," I suggested.

"Side-step?" Carl said.

"Yeah. Remember when we were talking about plans to get a county franchise as a foothold, and then trying to get a competitive franchise in South Central?" I replied. I held up a map. "If we can get access to put a competing cable line on the power poles, we can offer ourselves as another franchise in South Central!"

As we developed our alternative plan, there was more legal trouble in addition to our new plan of action. Our original name, Universal Cable Systems Limited (UCS), which we used until 1983, had been challenged by the media and theme park giant MCI/Universal Studios, Inc., because of trademark issues. Pursuant to a settlement in 1981 with Universal Studios, Inc., we agreed to stop using the name "Universal" after the franchising process was completed. We had no interest in getting into a fight with this media giant.

In 1983, we formed Preferred Communications, Inc., (Preferred) and used the new name in all our subsequent business and legal filings. We sold all the assets, including any rights from the time of having submitted a franchise application to the city from Universal to form Preferred in a stock transfer agreement. The ownership of the new company remained exactly the same.

In the summer of 1983, under our new corporate name of Preferred we applied for a license to use public right of ways to build a cable system by adding "our" cable line on the city power poles to gain access to the homes in South Central. In this strategic move to gain access to the South Central neighborhood, we would now be dealing with the Los Angeles city-owned Department of Water and Power.

———◆———

It was déjà vu all over again. According to our many conversations and hearings at the Department of Water and Power, a city-owned utility, they said there wasn't enough room on the several-story-high poles (thirty to fifty feet tall), to accommodate our cable line. The representatives of the Department of Water and Power contended that the addition of another wire to the poles would create a visual urban "blight." The city, at every turn, made it clear there was nothing we could do to satisfy their objections—again.

That was the final straw for us. We could no longer trust or give any appearance of trust in the "system" in the City of Los Angeles or any of its various departments. We needed the protection of the federal judicial system, which has long been the last resort to citizen-litigants, especially blacks in the modern Civil Rights movement, when local government showed itself so clearly biased against citizens trying to exercise their civil rights.

We talked to our legal counsel and we told them we needed to find an experienced trial law firm close to Carl's home. As a doctor, husband, and father of three children, he couldn't take more time than necessary from his family and patients. Besides, we were both based in Los Angeles and needed to work to support ourselves and any impending litigation.

We were disappointed in our efforts. No major law firm in Los Angeles would consider handling the case because of legal conflicts stemming from the fact that they were all being paid by the city of Los Angeles for legal work in other areas.

"Thought it might be that way…but I didn't want to say anything," Harold Farrow said. The city attorney's office is smart and they have the money to involve a good many firms in their legal needs…and it affects the little guys who need representation."

Fortunately, Harold Farrow had a history with us as a consultant and advisor in our application process and he'd seen the abuses firsthand. Mr. Farrow and his law firm, Farrow, Schildhause & Wilson, which was based in the San Francisco area, agreed to take our case. "It's going to give you a lot of long-distance telephone bills and spending a lot time on commuter planes for you, Clint, but it's what needs to be done. You and Carl got a really raw deal down there in LA."

Farrow was the most experienced plaintiff attorney in the area of cable television in the United States. Before he took on our case, he had already won a U.S. Supreme Court case against Boulder, Colorado. The case, decided on January 13, 1982, was *Community Communications versus the City of Boulder Colorado*. The legal issue involved the question as to what extent a city could control the flow of information to the general population. As in our experience, the ability to decide the provider of such information was equivalent to deciding what information would be provided.

People didn't understand the financial burden we were facing with this case. "Don't they just defer all their fees?" Mr. Parks asked.

"No," we replied. "They ask for large retainers for the services they need to put together the case and that's only the beginning!" We didn't want to tell them we had to mortgage everything and make everyday expense decisions based on being able to meet the litigations bills.

Mr. Farrow was very kind and understanding of our financial dilemma. He carried us financially for legal fees by taking the case on a contingency basis and bent over backwards so that we could pursue this litigation despite our meager resources. "I can help you with that end but you're going to have to pay for any additional expenses. Our firm's got bills to pay, too."

By retaining Farrow, everyone knew we were serious about our fight but the expenses he talked about included the cost of expert witnesses, engineers, economists, and more.

———

In our case, we felt, and wanted to prove, that the Los Angeles City legislative and regulating processes violated our constitutional rights.

"You think we're going to get a fair hearing in these courts down here in Los Angeles?" Mr. Parks asked.

"Farrow says we've got a fighting chance if two things happen. One, we've got to get a judge who will listen to our arguments. And two, the judge will have to allow for a jury trial," Carl replied.

"You've got to be kidding," Mr. Watson said with laser rapidity. "All these courts are stacked down here with people from the Democratic Party, who are beholden to one another."

"Al's got a point there," Mr. Parks informed. "Didn't you say you heard that Johnny Cochran said you'd alienated all the black politicians…and the judges?"

"Mentoring blacks in the political system in Los Angeles comes at a price and it's the patronage and decisions those mentors want that's the expected payment," Mr. Watson identified. "I bet lots of favors are being called in and lots of arms are being twisted to be sure we don't get anything close to a 'fair' hearing if we go to court."

"And the price for us will be to see that we get booted out of court as fast as possible?" I asked.

"Faster than the time it takes for the ink to dry on the complaint," Mr. Watson replied glumly.

"But Farrow says we can hope to get a fair hearing at the appeals court level…after the district court," Carl offered.

"If I live that long," Al Watson said sardonically. "We've tried every other way to get justice."

"Here's the last step," I said, trying to be positive about our effort.

———

Several weeks later, we got a phone call from a person who had been a client of mine and also worked with Ted Eagans. "I'm telling you, but never mention my name." This lawyer shared offices with the husband of Judge Consuelo Marshall.

I had previously met the judge's brother at this man's house. We had every reason to believe he was giving us accurate information.

"Don't tell anyone I've told you because it'll kill my career...but you're getting Judge Consuelo Marshall. No doubt. No doubt... at all!" He stopped for a few seconds. "You want to get screwed again? This is going to cost you a pile of money."

This conversation was two weeks before the case was even filed.

According to the law, cases were supposed to be given to judges on an impartial, rotational basis after the cases were filed. Was what Mr. Watson said going to come true?

"They told you the deal in your meetings at city hall to your face," the caller added. "You're never going to see anything...it will all come from behind the doors of the judge's chambers. A lot can happen back there—too much."

In September 1983, our company, Preferred Communications Corp., filed suit against the City of Los Angeles for constitutional violations related to the franchising process for the South Central cable television franchise. Our suit outlined all the facts and issues regarding the egregious and illegal activities we uncovered in our effort to obtain the franchise.

The case was directed to be heard by US District Court Judge Consuelo Marshall. Surprise, surprise.

We did our homework on Judge Marshall. She had degrees from Howard University and a career in the city attorney's office, a few years in private practice, and then a meteoric rise through the state judiciary to her present position as a U.S. District Court Judge.

"Then there's Sam Williams, Bradley's right-hand man, who pushed Judge Marshall's star right to the federal judgeship and she worked for years with Johnny Cochran." Mr. Watson tapped the paperwork I had put together.

"So we're only one degree separated from Mayor Bradley with both Williams and Cochran? Again?" I asked.

"I'd say they're all on the head of the same pin, if you're asking me how close they are," Carl replied.

"And I'd say we better start saving money for the appeal," Mr. Parks replied. "As an African-American woman from Los Angeles seeking a federal judgeship, Marshall's clearly benefited from the friendship and influence of the mayor, and his fraternity brother, Johnny Cochran!"

When we heard Judge Consuelo Marshall was the judge assigned to our case, we wondered about the enmeshed working acquaintances of Marshall, Cochran, Williams, and Bradley. We talked again to Carl's friend, Dr. Avery, wanting to delve more deeply into his case, which was tried by Judge Marshall, and review his past negative comments about her judgeship. Johnny Cochran was his attorney.

Dr. Avery recounted that, several years before, while driving near his neighborhood, he saw his son was lying on the ground surrounded by policemen. His son's car was sitting in an unusual position with the door open. He wanted to investigate and make sure his son was OK. What parent wouldn't? He was told to stay away from his son and leave the scene or he would be arrested. Dr. Avery refused, and this distinguished doctor and minority trailblazer in the medical profession was put in a chokehold and struck several times, leaving him with chronic back and neck injuries.

Dr. Avery hired Johnny Cochran as his lawyer and the case was assigned to U.S. District Court Judge Consuelo Marshall. Marshall had previously worked for Cochran's law firm. Why didn't she recuse herself from the Avery case?

We began to wonder about our case. Two high-profile court cases against the City of Los Angeles filed, in part, by black doctors, both assigned to Judge Marshall?

Dr. Avery and Carl asked me to calculate the possibility of two black doctors in Los Angeles County both being randomly assigned the same black judge with both cases involving black defendants, in a civil rights violation against the City of Los Angeles. The possibility for these events being random became almost astronomical against such possibility.

Dr. Avery shared other disturbing facts. He'd been told by another City Hall insider that he was only going to get $750,000 so the city could save face and "people" would make sure Cochran was rewarded for his help; namely, by being appointed to the Los Angeles Airport Commission.

As his final case settlement, Dr. Avery got $750,000 and Cochran became a Los Angeles Airport Commissioner.

———◆———

Approximately forty-five days after our case, *Preferred Communications versus the City of Los Angeles*, was filed and sent to her courtroom, Justice Marshall dismissed our case with no "leave to amend." The dismissal meant Judge Marshall said we had no legal issue that needed to be resolved by the court. But a dismissal without "leave to amend" was equal to the judge telling you to get lost because your case has no chance of being heard and your case would not be allowed to come back to court using these same issues—a big double "no." Judge Marshall blotted out all the issues and circumstances of our case and told us to go home—as if they had never happened.

It did not come as a great surprise that Judge Marshall had immediately dismissed the case against the city. We already knew of her political ties to Tom Bradley and his close friends, Johnnie Cochran and Sam Williams, which we felt clearly influenced the overall decision-making in this case.

Our attorney, Harold Farrow, was also not surprised by this dismissal. "I'd say it's this court's intention to delay the case quietly for several years by putting it into the appellate process. The court is getting a lot of pressure from the city, I think. But that's not all. Judge Marshall's not giving us the right to amend the case, either. That's really unusual!"

Judge Marshall's ruling, in essence, said that we were forbidden to use most of the information, incidents, conversations, or facts concerning the cable franchise debacle. All the people responsible for keeping the South Central franchise from our company were allowed by Judge Marshall's ruling to avoid being questioned in and out of her courtroom, scrubbing the truth of what happened in the cable franchise fiasco from the public record and away from the community—for a second time. The city undermined us, and now Judge Marshall had too! Black power in two separate branches of government, on both the local and federal level, was halting South Central's access to technology.

———

Perhaps a short lesson might help to illustrate how completely Judge Marshall quashed our case by her actions. In the discovery phase, we as the plaintiffs and the city as the defendant were required to share the evidence "pool" we each had with the other side: give the lists of the people we wanted to call before the court and identify times each side could ask questions of those people in meetings, called depositions, or written statements, called affidavits.

Mr. Howery, the employees of DOT, Councilmen Farrell, Cunningham and Snyder, and the members of the IEDC and BTC would be called by us. We also wanted answers from our competitors, BVT and CTI. Bakewell, Johnson, and Hiawatha Harris would be required to answer our questions. The mayor and his office might not be immune to us if Judge Marshall allowed it.

But Judge Marshall quashed those efforts—and went even further. It is common, for a case dismissed by the court prior to discovery phase, to allow the plaintiff to amend and restate the complaint to indicate to the court their redefined charges and possible cause of action that requires the court's attention. Among the reasons for amending a complaint are the discovery of new evidence, a change in the law, or the correction of a simple mistake within the original filing. Under the Federal Rules of Civil Procedure it would be inappropriate for the court to deny requests as long as there is no undue delay, bad faith, or undue prejudice to the defendant, in our case the City of Los Angeles.

But Judge Marshall cut most possibilities out in her ruling. There was no legal way back to Judge Marshall's court, unless we were willing to pay hundreds of thousands of dollars of our own money through the court of appeals. In laymen's terms, Judge Marshall judicially stripped us of our ability to use this incriminating evidence of mayoral and City Hall corruption in her rulings, and knowingly added years and hundreds of thousands of dollars of financial burden to our case.

"You mean we can't say anything about these issues in Marshall's court or at the appellate level?" Al Watson railed.

"I know you don't think its fair...and I don't either...but that's the law and it's what Judge Marshall has done," Harold Farrow said bluntly. "We won't be able to say much in our case at all now about the DOT, BTC, or IEDC, not to mention Mayor Bradley's office."

Following the monumental trail of continued denials, falsehoods, misrepresentations, and lies outlined in our almost-three-year attempt to gain a cable franchise in the City of Los Angeles, we were told we weren't going to get a hearing and to get lost. If this miscarriage of justice weren't so tragic, it would be farce.

The grievous malignancy of misuse of power, greed, and misconduct of the City of Los Angeles had invaded the judiciary. From our point of view, the purpose behind the dismissal, it seemed, was our opponents' effort to prohibit potentially damaging information regarding the maligned cable franchise process from tarnishing the "good name" of the City of Los Angeles and all its elected officials.

We also knew the politicians in office didn't want public scrutiny or an unbiased, independent evaluation of their actions. We remembered the "savages from Africa" remark made by Councilman Art Snyder.

To say we adamantly opposed Judge Marshall's ruling is the kindest thing we could say. At the very least, this action protected the City of Los Angeles and Mayor Bradley from the economic and political repercussions of stealing the constitutional rights of citizens for the economic benefit of themselves and their political friends.

We felt the ruling perpetrated a sinister, sustained effort to restrain our First Amendment rights by giving absolute power to local governments to subvert and withhold rights of the businessman and citizens pursuant to the United States Constitution. We were trying to seek a legal forum for ourselves and our concerns—and protect future people from the abuses we'd experienced doing business with the City of Los Angeles.

By denying the individual claims we had pursued on behalf of our company at great cost and untold time to ourselves, Judge Marshall, in part, granted the city license to perpetrate mischief over business commerce, its citizens, and unleashed the city to do more harm to more people in business and commerce. How many others, trying to make a positive difference in their neighborhoods, were tossed out as well?

———◆———

Although we knew what Judge Marshall might do, our cable franchise group was depressed, tired, and near broke. Judge Marshall had sunk any chance we had to refer to the cable franchise case in future court filings with the legal "death ray" of no right to amend.

"We got plenty of grounds for appeal with the Department of Power and Water not letting us get a cable wire on the poles for a competing franchise," Carl said with deft precision. The Department of Water and Power was an agency owned by the City of Los Angeles.

"Will that be enough to file an appeal?" Mr. Parks asked.

"Can we win on that and get back to the district court to kick some butt?" Al Watson asked more brusquely.

"We need to try," was all I said. We also needed a pep talk after three consecutive losses, so I took on the coaching role.

———◆———

In our case, our family and friends, and a handful of businessmen and their families and friends, stood behind us emotionally and financially but they also stood on the principle of free commerce and the expectation of a equitable licensing process on the part of the City of Los Angeles and its elected officials, who now fostered an unfair, tainted, and biased licensing process.

It was a crisp Saturday morning in November about a week before Thanksgiving when met we met at Pann's Restaurant on La Cienega Blvd. It was time for a pep talk. We gathered at a large, round table in the back window of the restaurant. As a former collegiate athlete and baseball team captain I had given a few pep talks. You could feel the disappointment and worry. As the youngest person in our group I was particularly sensitive to the feelings of Mr. Parks. His contagious smile was gone and worry showed on his face. He had taken the mistreatment by those he had helped for so many years hard. As a strident civil rights advocate for decades Mr. Parks concern was not for himself but for the community he had lived in for so many years.

Now that everyone was here I told our assembled group about individual rights and two court cases where individuals made a dramatic difference.

I told them there was a reason why the founding fathers of this nation deemed the adoption of the First Amendment to be the first, and hence the most important, addition to the Constitution of the United States. They experienced firsthand a tyrannical, uncaring government that would not listen to its citizens. We were experiencing the same thing—"modern hustle-style"—and we needed to fight against it.

I reminded them that America's strength came from the fact that each one of us could exercise our rights to the best of our ability. If we exercised those rights, by going forward with this court case, we were representing South Central, the people living within one of the lowest socioeconomic neighborhoods in the county, who could not afford to fight for their own rights or, perhaps, were not even aware of the situation at all.

Protecting these rights, which benefited all of us, almost always fell to the hard-fought actions of one individual, one family or one group.

The first classic example I recounted was in 1954, in *Brown versus the Board of Education*, in which a father wanted to fight segregation and have his daughter go to the school in their neighborhood. His landmark case started the integrated schools effort in the United States and affected the future of educational opportunity in the United States.

In 1966, the second case I mentioned was the *Miranda versus Arizona* decision, which demanded that police inform the citizens of their rights as they were being arrested. The Miranda decision would forever alter the interface of police and the American citizen.

The Miranda decision was not meant to limit the legitimate use of power by government, but it represented the rights of every citizen within the United States who would come face to face with a police officer and curb the abuses of police power during an arrest.

When people fought for their own constitutional rights through important issues of government misconduct and mistreating its citizens in the courts, those battles they waged were on behalf of all of us.

When the government exceeded or abused its legal authority, the federal courts were supposed to protect the citizen's rights. So we needed to seek protection of the last resort available to any citizen—the federal courts.

I also told our supporters that I've often heard the protection of civil liberties was the responsibility of each and every citizen within a free society. Therefore, it was our responsibility to challenge the government in all ways possible in our circumstance. So, we would again gather our financial resources and file with the Ninth Circuit Court of Appeals in our effort to obtain justice for our case.

Everyone agreed to continue the case.

—————

Despite our grievances and ill treatment concerning the overt corruption and abuses within City Hall, we came to know and accept that the only way we were able to pursue this matter in a higher court (the appellate court) was to emphasize the constitutional issues involved in our dispute.

"At least we found a strong branch to hold on to after Judge Marshall pushed us over the cliff," Mr. Parks said.

"But the rope pulling us to safety is mighty expensive," Al Watson said. "Have you seen the bills?"

The cost of filing an appeal would be substantial, so Carl and I had to make a decision on how far we were willing to go financially. Farrow told us with a shrug, "It's going to cost at least $150,000." He stuffed papers in his briefcase. "My firm can hold off charging some of the costs, but we've gone about as far as we can go."

Carl was already deeply involved with another costly media case against the CBS television network and their *60 Minutes* news program, which was costing thousands of dollars every month. "What choice do we have?" Carl asked. "I couldn't live with myself if we let the city get away with this."

"To the last breath?" I asked.

"Last breath," Carl replied. "But it's your case. Now let's get going on it."

Knowing I would regret not seeing this case through to the end, I felt reassured by Carl's words. We went forward to the appellate court.

Ironically, Carl's case against CBS and *60 Minutes* was being covered with cameras in the courtroom, making it one of the first cases on cable television broadcast full-time by Cable News Network.

Chapter Twelve

The Ninth Circuit Court Of Appeals
And The United States Supreme Court

We'd fight as long as we could fight given our meager financial resources. We could not accept quitting. As long as we stayed in the game there was always a chance to win.

"Well, you're going farther than most people," Farrow noted. "The appeals process is a time-consuming and expensive process that generally keeps the average citizen from being able to challenge large, well-financed governments. That's what the dirty politicians hope for."

It's the only legal forum available to seek protection of their rights, I thought. But money was a big concern. How many people with strong legal cases but no financial resources lost their day in court? How many sleazy politicians, dishonest bureaucrats and authoritarian personalities got off without so much as a slap on the wrist for abusing the power citizens gave them because of money issues?

We would use every legal avenue available to us to secure our rights and to protect our investment. The ultimate outcome would involve tens of millions of dollars and possible future technology opportunities beyond South Central. But, let's be frank, we risked our homes, personal savings, children's educational savings, and our retirement funds. The defendants were unscathed financially—bankrolled by taxpayer dollars.

———

We took the next judicial road open to us and filed an appeal of the decision to the Ninth Circuit Court of Appeals, which covers the western portion of the United States.

The process included filing a series of briefs (written legal documents) that enunciated our position and gave the legal reasons from past court cases, called precedence, to explain why the appellate court should review the lower court's decision. Each side was expected to file a brief and to make a written response to the brief filed by their opponent.

Farrow was, as we previously stated, experienced in the appellate process, the foremost attorney in the cable television industry, and had a United States Supreme Court victory in another cable television case, *Community Communication versus City of Boulder, Colorado*. He was seeking to protect clients against local governments like the City of Los Angeles and act as a strong advocate for the free market system.

"We'd never be here without our association with Farrow," Carl often remarked. "We'd never have gotten past Judge Marshall."

———

Farrow looked down at his notes. "I'm going to start to frame your case using *Stromberg versus California*.

In 1931, the U. S. Supreme Court case of *Stromberg versus California* highlighted the importance of the First Amendment. Supreme Court Justice Charles Evans Hughes, writing for the majority of the court, stated, "The maintenance of the opportunity for free public discussion to the end that government may be responsible to the will of the people and that changes may be obtained by lawful means is a fundamental principle of our constitutional system."

The importance of Hughes's prescient words cannot be minimized. The fundamental issue raised by the Supreme Court in the time of the Great Depression and that critical year of 1931 was that citizens must have a legitimate means of petitioning the government for change. The First Amendment is the protection guaranteed to citizens to seek a legitimate public hearing for the expression of grievances against the government.

In our experience, we knew we hadn't received legitimate public hearings or the right to express our grievances.

In the absence of these fair and open public meetings, we thought the City of Los Angeles segregated and mistreated its impoverished inner-city communities and deprived its citizens of the best in technological media access. We came to the appellate court to prove our claims.

The appellate court's three-judge panel reviewed the briefs and set a date for a hearing to ask questions and clarify information in open hearings before making their decision. "The federal judges at the appellate level generally have more experience than those judges at the district level," Farrow said. The combined federal judicial knowledge base represented at the appellate court was approximately sixty-five years of experience among the three judges on the panel.

"Unlike Judge Marshall, who had less than two years experience in the federal judiciary when our case ended up in her court," Farrow grumbled. "If she keeps this up, she's going to have a lot of cases appealed. Too many." He shook his head. "The 'poison pill' she gave this case in using 'no leave to amend' will have to be looked at closely."

The hearings were held at the Pasadena courthouse. Even though the appellate court is actually based in San Francisco, hearings are held in local areas nearest to where the parties reside.

———————

It was a warm Pasadena morning on December 4, 1984, when the hearings were held. We were shocked as we entered the courtroom with our attorneys. "Are all these people really here about our case?" Carl asked Farrow. The hearing room was filled to capacity because of the burgeoning public interest in our case and in the cable television industry. The news media came to realize the importance of cable television, the regulation of cable at the city level, and the potential liabilities involved in how the city mishandled the cable application process and its existing monopoly franchises.

"What goes on in this courtroom could easily affect the future of cable television," Farrow replied.

Once again I was awed that a couple of regular guys could have such an influence on such an important aspect of our society as cable television.

———————

The basis of our appeal centered around two critical issues that would determine the legality of the city's franchising process. The primary issue was whether the city could, in fact, for any arbitrary reason, limit access to public right of ways to only one company for the dissemination of programming to South Central. If the city could arbitrarily decide to limit access, just who would be able to exercise the First Amendment rights of that community? Freedom of the press could only be achieved when there is freedom of speech. Placing limits on this new technology of cable television was equivalent to limiting the number of newspapers on a corner to only one newspaper.

It was the policy of the City of Los Angeles to the limit franchise areas to only one provider of service. Even though the laws of the city clearly stated that all franchises were to be non-exclusive, the city took the position that cable television was a natural monopoly, like water and power distribution, and therefore should not be subjected to competitive forces. The city's contention was that a citizen usually only needed one pipe for water to his house and one wire from the poles to his house for his electricity, right? Shouldn't it be the same for cable television licensing? Wrong!

Farrow explained to the court that the only thing a non-exclusive franchise prohibited was the monopoly franchise the city sought to protect for their "friends." The ability to limit the conduits of free speech to your friends and supporters naturally restricted the ability of others to engage in the independent reporting on the activities of government.

Our second position was based on antitrust violations and restraint of trade. Antitrust laws were also called the "competition laws" because they promoted or maintained market competition by regulating anti-competitive conduct. The basis of the antitrust laws in the United States are based upon the Sherman Act and the Clayton Act, which were passed by Congress in 1890 and 1914, respectively. These laws, at the turn of the twentieth century, stopped the oil companies from exerting total control over every aspect of oil production, from drilling to sales of oil products at their gas stations, which they developed in the U.S. using a series of trusts to disguise true ownership of the oil industry and their monopoly intentions.

The Sherman Act stated the intent of the law concerning "every contract, combination in the form of trust or otherwise, or conspiracy, in restraint of trade or commerce...is declared illegal. Every person who shall monopolize, or attempt to monopolize, or combine or conspire with any other person or persons, to monopolize any part of the trade or commerce...shall be deemed guilty of a felony."

Farrow argued the internal machinations between elected officials and their friends eliminated all persons who were not a part of the ruling Los Angeles City political system that had been controlled for many years by the Democratic Party in Los Angeles.

We indicated that cable television represented one of the most important technological changes since the invention of television. Although the educational, business, and other commercial opportunities that developed around and through the cable television industry were growing at a rapid pace during the 1980s and the early 1990s, cable television represented a closer, most personal means of getting information for general use more than a decade before the introduction of the Internet.

We argued that not only was the City of Los Angeles depriving the South Central community from a robust economic, competitive opportunity that would provide dollars and jobs, the city was depriving the community of access to the educational and business benefits of cable television technology as well.

Ed Perez, a deputy city attorney, represented the city before the Ninth Circuit. Perez was a clean-shaven, short man of Latin ancestry, in his early thirties.

"He always looks disheveled, like his suit material doesn't like the heat or humidity," Carl remarked. We'd met Perez before in our battles with the city. "Why does he always have a smirk on his face?"

"Perez has a smirk on his face as if he was impressed with himself and his position," Al Watson remarked. "Guess he's just happy to be arguing before the appellate court? Happy to have a government job."

Farrow interrupted. "I think we have a very strong case. Don't let Perez bother you. Just think of him as one of those guys who always acts as if they are your friend even though he's really trying to steal your wallet."

In their briefs, the City of Los Angeles also contended that it did not have to concern itself with the First Amendment because it was a sovereign city and could thus restrict free markets in the public's best interest.

"If I understand what they're trying to say," Farrow remarked. "They're saying they, as city representatives, have intelligence beyond the citizens who elected them." He shook his head. "In other words, he's saying the citizens are stupid."

As we sat in court, we watched Ed Perez attempting to explain the city's position to the court. Did the city really think this new technology would be too complex and troublesome for laymen? For citizens? Would the judges really believe their argument?

Perez seemed as cocky as his smirk. His arrogance radiated to the second row of wooden benches where we were seated to watch the oral arguments. Perez's attitude and appearance stood diametrically opposed to the six-foot-two-inch imposing statue of the gray-haired Farrow, whose broad shoulders, piercing blue eyes, and broad-shouldered frame were enhanced by his well-tailored, blue pinstriped suit, and crisp white shirt. Farrow's relaxed, confident style demonstrated his quiet confidence, showing that this was not his first appearance at the appellate court.

I looked at the dais and surveyed all the gray-haired heads. "Everyone's got gray hair except Perez."

"Yeah," Carl whispered with a slight smile, "and you can sure tell whose been here before…and who hasn't."

Farrow's argument was clear cut although the issues were complex and the discrimination against us in our cable franchise application could not be fully fleshed out because Judge Consuelo Marshall had cut off our district court trial before we could get depositions and more-finely tuned evidence. We were going to have to make our case using the information and incidents that happened after we were denied the cable franchise application, basing our case now on the Los Angeles Department of Water and Power discriminating against us when they would not allow us to compete as a cable company in South Central by adding an extra cable to the thirty- to fifty-foot power poles.

In this way, we might legally gain access to the South Central area as a competitor to the current franchise owner—Kaufman and Broad.

The Department of Water and Power ruled our company's cable line would endanger the pole structure and cause a "visual blight" on the poles and neighborhoods we wanted to serve.

One wire would cause a visual blight and endanger the thirty- to fifty-foot poles?

As before, we thought this was the city's ridiculous, transparent attempt to deny us business access and free market opportunity in the City of Los Angeles.

Ed Perez, representing the City of Los Angeles, offered a non-sensical argument, stating that cable television was a standardized product, like water and gas lines.

We thought cable television was anything other than a standardized product. Perez's assertion that one type of water being monitored and delivered to the citizen's home was no different than the multi-channeled, multi-faceted cable television industry was absurd.

So Farrow focused attention on these larger First Amendment arguments, the similarities between cable television and the newspaper industry and their identification as "content providers" and "distributors" of their own brand of information on the public right of ways controlled by the city.

In the case of newspapers, the city allowed newspaper dispensers and newsstands on the sidewalks owned by the city. These dispensers and newsstands resided in groups because, by law, the city was not allowed to limit the use of the corner to only one newspaper. The First Amendment to the Constitution allowed for multiple newspapers and therefore multiple dispensers and newsstands for all the newspapers.

Secondly, Farrow argued that telephone poles were also a means of communication and a right of way under the First Amendment. In the case of cable television, the industry used the public utility poles governed by the city through the Department of Water and Power to hold the cable to transmit their signals to the subscriber homes.

Perez railed on about the concept of natural monopoly—a confusing and unsubstantiated economic theory to equate control over water distribution as the same as controlling information and content distribution over the cable television system. We did not agree.

In the cable television industry, the vast majority of programming content had always been controlled by the individual companies, not the cities or municipalities they served. The cities were provided with public access channels that were made available to them and were supposed to be made available for neighborhood and community content. The City of Los Angeles had also required, as a condition of licensing, that certain channels be provided to the city for their discretionary use. These issues had never been a problem in our dealings with the City of Los Angeles. Number of channels—yes. Cable head placement—yes. Change of ownership—yes. Financing—yes. But programming—no. Never.

Farrow identified the programming section of the city's application and asserted that programming delivered to the subscriber was not a concern to the city. Programming was protected by the First Amendment and the city had infringed on that right in denying us a cable license. The city just couldn't arbitrarily decide who got water and electricity and who didn't. But they *were* discriminating with cable television in South Central. The city's "job" was to protect, monitor, and make sure its citizens got uninterrupted water and electricity service to their homes. Therefore, the city's job in monitoring cable television ought to be to make sure reliable cable service got to customer homes, and that they got the public access channels and discretionary channels they required. Nothing more. We felt anything more was unlawful and the basis of our case. When was the last time that electricity or water needed First Amendment protection?

The justices easily flustered Perez when they asked direct questions about the need to protect one company from competition and what, if any, benefit such protection might benefit the public or the city. "Perez doesn't seem to be smirking now that the judges have gotten their teeth into the fallacy of his argument," Carl noted.

———◆———

Numerous "friend of the court" briefs (amicus curiae) had been filed by broadcast stations, cable television companies, cable television trade groups, and various other groups regarding our case. Many of the groups were represented at the hearing by their attorneys and senior executives. All were hoping to get a chance to address the appellate court panel and attempt to make sure their interests were being considered by the court. They all stayed well away from the city's main contention of natural monopoly. One cable company representative even said the concept of natural monopoly had turned out to be laughable, as the cable television industry had grown into the current independent, multibillion-dollar industry.

———•———

Ironically, no national black organizations, black politicians, or black press, print, or media coverage talked about our case or supported our company.

We thought that integrating black society into the mainstream of American economic systems was supposedly a long-stated goal of black leadership. The goal was supposed to be opening up the American free market system to more black citizens so there would be an economic relationship with this country that they'd never before experienced. We expected at least some response or position paper mentioning the issue of our case.

We looked to the prominent national organizations. The NAACP and the National Urban League were often seen as the leadership of Black America. Both these vocal and high-profile organizations received quite a bit of press coverage with high-profile celebrities, politicians, and others who endorsed them. But what about the core issues they defended and believed in passionately? Who did they fight for and when did they just sit back and let things happen?

Both organizations had extensive experience in the understanding of legal matters pertaining to the limiting of civil rights in the United States and had vociferously targeted many issues in civil rights, commerce, and law. None of them came to listen to our story. These organizations never took a position regarding the case of *Preferred Communications versus the City of Los Angeles*.

These organizations certainly couldn't say they were not aware that this case involved First Amendment issues within this, a black community in a major urban market. John Mack, President of the Los Angeles Urban League, had been a director at our predecessor company, Universal Cable Systems!

How could the organizations that purported to be for the benefit of Black America not take any position in a court case involving one of the largest black neighborhoods in the country dealing with civil rights, black commerce issues, and community-building technology being heard at the appellate court level? How could they not consider the importance of the First Amendment case that had been a major thrust of freedom from the beginning of the American Civil Rights movement? Were these organizations not interested in the protection of civil rights but merely giving the appearance of concern?

We felt they could support or oppose our position on the issue. They could not, however, ignore the issue and call themselves legitimate civil rights organizations.

All of a sudden, the great civil rights organizations that existed in America had forgotten about our constitutional rights and the First Amendment. They tried to ignore or defeat a small group of regular black citizens from South Central Los Angeles. We felt they too were living the "liberal lie" of the City of Los Angeles. They seemed to be saying: Don't disagree with us because we've finally got the power, we know what's best, and we're going to make the decisions for you.

The liberal lie is where an organization professes to protect the civil rights of society from the conservative part of society. At the same time the same organization is seeking to deprive the citizens of the most fundamental of civil rights guaranteed by the Constitution.

Arthur Snyder, another nemesis of ours on the Los Angeles City Council, was a conservative Republican, according to the *Los Angeles Times*. Yes, there is also a conservative lie but the liberal lie is so much more hypocritical with civil rights issues. Where were the conservatives when the free markets and free speech were being stripped away from a free people in your city? Your city is probably no different from Los Angeles when it came to awarding a single cable television license. Indifference is one thing and active participation in the deprivation of those rights is another.

We felt we were pursuing a business to provide economic ability within the South Central community and a conduit for information and education within the community. Weren't those good things? How did preventing investment in our own communities, as majority-owned black franchisees, affirm their organizations' purposes or why these politicians were elected? These same civil rights organizations had fought for years for the rights of black Americans. Whatever positions they now held they did not have the courage to stand against corruption and for fair access to the new technology.

We looked to black legislators on the local, state, and national levels. All the black elected officials from 1980 through 1995 were aware of the constitutional battle being fought in this case. They, as shown in their voting records, chose to ignore their principles and block our efforts as local black businesspersons who wanted to make investments in our own community.

At what point would our black government officials involve themselves in addressing the injustices heaped upon black society by the politicians in the City of Los Angeles? Do the wishes of black politicians trump the rights of black citizens who uncover the dysfunctional and illegal behavior of black politicians?

Our reality spoke louder than rhetoric. Our respect for politicians was greatly diminished by their ineptitude. Black legislators' silence and refusal to act or comment was tacit support for positions held by the City of Los Angeles regarding the deprivation of First Amendment rights of black citizens of South Central Los Angeles. Would they refuse to involve themselves because they were servants of a political party and the Galloway boys and their company had run afoul of that political party and their local cronies?

It's also painful to speak about the two-party system of our nation. Most all of our detractors were members of the Democratic Party, and we were told by many that we were definitely on their bad side.

"We're speaking bad about blacks in power...and the Democrats, especially the black ones, don't like it one bit!" Al Watson said. "They're going to freeze us out if they can!"

Getting on the bad side of the Democratic Party in the City of Los Angeles was the political equivalent of getting on the bad side of the Mafia and living in lower Manhattan, it seemed. They would now show us just how powerful they could be—in an ugly, underhanded way. What other choice did we have to remain true to our principles?

There were other meaningful questions to consider. The Democratic Party had controlled black voters since blacks obtained the effective right to vote. Although they had been a mainstay of support for the Democratic Party, had this allegiance provided the best and most lasting economic benefits from that commitment? We'd had many discussions on this topic as we fought for the cable franchise license.

"OK, Al. We've grown up being told about the help the Democratic Party was in the depths of the Civil Rights movement," I replied.

"And I know there were some Democrats who are as racist as can be," Al Watson remarked bluntly. "But loyalty is a strong, strong thing."

"So we shouldn't think Black America can consider alternatives other than the Democratic Party at the local level and consider a variety of alliances in future political dealings and elections?" I asked just as bluntly. "That's racist, too."

"I don't know about either of you but after what we've gone through, I feel Black America should evaluate all potential candidates from an economic benefit standpoint...before casting their votes," Carl replied with a gruff laugh.

Al Watson laughed, too. "Amen to that, brother. Amen to that!"

———

Except for Councilman Lindsay, the assistance of civil rights organizations and black politicians was virtually nonexistent, and the wrath of the Democratic Party cast a long shadow. It seemed that all the civil rights organizations and black politicians were so closely aligned with the Democratic Party and Mayor Bradley that they dared not expose the illegal actions going on behind the scenes of Los Angeles city government.

Not one black elected official in the United States issued a verbal or written position paper relative to the civil rights issues being raised in our case. Could the reason for their silence have been Mayor Bradley's upcoming gubernatorial bid?

All we could hope was that future black politicians and legal scholars would examine the judge's handling of this case, from start to finish.

Without their help, we fought and waited.

———◆———

Black media outlets also ignored us and the South Central cable issue. They joined the "freeze" Al Watson talked about concerning the Democratic Party.

In October 1981, *Black Enterprises* published an article called "Electronic Redlining," which identified that the new technology of cable television was being created and promoted while the entry of black Americans into this market was severely limited. They discussed political and financial reasons of limitations upon black business entry. They did not discuss the Los Angeles cable television market—the second-largest market in the nation! Once again, we were on the outside. They did, however, discuss cable television with Gayle Greer, of American Television and Communications Corporation (ATC), who at the time represented ATC in the South Central franchising process and who was our competitor for the South Central franchise.

The article further discussed the Congressional Black Caucus, composed of congressional black Democrats, and said the "electronic redlining" issue was on its Fall 1981 agenda. The caucus did not discuss the South Central Los Angeles cable television franchise. Again, running afoul of the Democratic Party meant everyone would ignore the issues of South Central and the important economic, technological, and free-speech implications involved in our effort.

Ironically, while black media chose to turn their backs on our case, the national mainstream media was actually interested in our case. Major financial publications, such as *The Wall Street Journal* and *Investor's Business Daily*, published front-page articles directly related to our case.

Other major publications such as the *Los Angeles Times*, the *New York Times*, and *Reader's Digest* covered the story of the regulation of cable television, or lack thereof, by the City of Los Angeles. If such top-rate, national publications reported on our case, on this issue in black America, then where was the black media? If they choose not to cover the issues that are so important not only to our black communities, but to all of us in America, then once again they had abdicated their responsibility to the public.

The truth is, our case had a major impact on the entire country, and these mainstream news sources knew it. Ultimately, we were all affected by the cable television industry's ongoing monopoly protection. It may have started in Los Angeles, but soon almost every American city would award monopoly franchises, while the federal court tried to sort out the concerns to protect constitutional rights to engage in this business, whether it was the amount of cable bills we paid, the available show package lists available, the number of cable companies available to provide cable service, or the very fact that cable television had become the dominant source of our news and entertainment culture. We were all invariably affected.

These national publications knew the South Central decision was important to the neighborhoods, the state, and the nation.

Would this alternative media interest spark something for our case? We hoped and prayed it would.

———•———

Months later, on March 1, 1985, we found out we won our appellate case against the City of Los Angeles and Judge Marshall's court.

The Ninth Circuit overturned Judge Marshall in regards to the First Amendment issues she had summarily dismissed in her courtroom. The Ninth Circuit decided unanimously that cable television was a form of media that was protected by the First Amendment of the United States Constitution.

The wording of the decision left little doubt. The ability of a city to control the right of way on which programming and news would be dispensed could not be strictly limited to a single provider. The decision told elected officials that they could not seek to unfairly deprive citizens of the right to a free flow of information. Once the city allowed one newspaper to use a right of way, to the extent that it was reasonable, the city needed to allow all newspapers the same right of way. How many newsstands are clustered on a street corner? The judges provided the same privilege for cable television.

The ruling indicated that the City of Los Angeles could no longer control and limit access to the cable television right of way to only one person of their choosing. The Ninth Circuit refused to overturn Judge Marshall relative to the antitrust violations. Although the antitrust statute violations were being used in other federal jurisdictions, we would be prohibited from raising this issue in the case going back to Judge Marshall's courtroom.

The case would be remanded back to Judge Marshall for trial, which meant she would be the judge deciding on the outcome of our case—again. Would we get any justice in her courtroom?

The unanimous decision by the Ninth Circuit was a clear rebuke to the inexperienced and recently appointed U.S. District Court Judge Consuelo Marshall. The Ninth Circuit judges all agreed our case was valid and Judge Marshall should have heard our case, which we filed against the city council and should have been heard by the court. "They'll be watching her more closely this time," Farrow said. "That's all I can say."

Other cities were affected by this appellate decision as well. The decision by the Ninth Circuit to grant First Amendment protection to the cable television industry threw numerous cities into a panic. All cities and counties in the Ninth Circuit at that time, including California, Washington, Oregon, Arizona, and Nevada, were now subject to the ruling of the Ninth Circuit—approximately twenty-five percent of the population of the United States.

Newspapers and national magazines began to take notice of the ruling too.

They weren't the only ones to panic. In going back to Judge Marshall's court, the timing and negative potential implications for Mayor Tom Bradley became apparent because he was once again running for governor in a short period of time. The potential implications for him, if we were able to disclose his and his colleagues' actions during the South Central cable television process, would be devastating.

"So what do we do now?" I asked.

"Legally, the city has to decide if they want to go back to Judge Marshall's court or they want to have the Supreme Court hear the case because they think they're still right about their 'natural monopoly' argument," Farrow replied.

"I'd put money on the Supreme Court," Al Watson said. "Bradley doesn't want his problems around town when he's running for governor."

"He'll make the taxpayers pay for his mess?" I asked.

"Better believe it," Al Watson replied. "Like his personal piggybank."

After a short delay, the City of Los Angeles decided to appeal the decision of the Ninth Circuit to the United States Supreme Court. The city filed its appeal and the U.S. Supreme Court decided to hear the case in its 1985-1986 session, held the next year.

Interviews given by city representatives indicated they were ecstatic that the Supreme Court was going to hear the case. We felt they were "ecstatic" because they could delay the discovery process uncovering the city's shenanigans, a possible jury trial to have to pay for their illegal behavior, and, hopefully, as Al Watson said, get Mayor Bradley to the governor's chair before his complicity in this scandal could be uncovered.

The city indicated clearly to the interviewers and the court that they would not go quickly or quietly. In our estimation, a lot of money was at stake and the elected officials were not about to give up decision making and influence without a big fight.

The city had infinitely more money to spend on the court process than we did. The cost of merely preparing an appeal to be heard at the United States Supreme Court required many thousands of dollars. They could do this because, after all, it wasn't their money they were spending, it was the taxpayers'.

We heard the question around City Hall as the politically entrenched bureaucrats wondered, "How could two unknown black men, who were not part of the Los Angeles political community, afford to spend substantial amounts of money to continue a process to protect their rights?"

Our responsibilities were simple and threefold: first, to our respect for the citizens of South Central, who we thought were being ignored and denied their rights; second, to our respect for honest, open information pathways and free market systems; and third, to the loyalty of our army of what we called concerned citizen soldiers who backed our effort with their time, concern, and monies. Once again, we surprised the politicians with our resilience.

We also heard the decision especially worried Kaufman and Broad, who had been awarded the franchise in 1983 without any competition. Now KB, the NYSE company worth more than $1 billion at that time, wanted out of cable television. If they liked the idea of being a single monopoly operator, the Ninth Circuit Court of Appeals decision opening cable to competitors was a concern. Could this indeed signal the end of the single operator? We hoped so.

———◆———

After the decision of the Ninth Circuit Court of Appeals was rendered, Carl and I were summoned to the office of Councilman Gil Lindsay. Councilman Lindsay asked us, "Why are you suing me?" He referred to the fact that he and all the other Los Angeles City Council members were named as defendants in the litigation.

We looked at each other as Lindsay's stern face changed into a wry smile. "I'm just jerking your chain," he laughed.

In the meeting, Lindsay went on to tell us he'd received a call from Kaufman and Broad several days after the decision. Lindsay didn't identify the caller but said the person asked, "What's Preferred Communications' price to drop the litigation and walk away?"

Lindsay said he had a good laugh as he told the caller, "You obviously don't understand the Galloway boys. We've already tried that. They're like alligators, according to Tom Bradley, 'Once they get a grip on you they don't easily let go.'"

Lindsay explained that he was now supporting Kaufman and Broad's application for the South Central franchise because it was the only application pending. "KB is a powerful company, too powerful to get on the wrong side of. You boys know that business is business."

I think by this time we actually understood it, Los Angeles-style. But we didn't have to condone it. This was something else we were trying to change.

———

It was crisp spring day in May 1986 in Washington, D.C., as we approached the U.S. Supreme Court building in our taxi. We had come from Los Angeles on the redeye the previous night. Trying to save money, we'd been able to work the previous day and get cheaper plane fares as well.

We didn't get much sleep anyway because we stayed up talking about our case—*Preferred Communications versus the City of Los Angeles*. The fact that the United States Supreme Court would now review our complaint against the City of Los Angeles seemed surreal.

As the taxi parked, we noticed the long line of people who stood there to personally see one of the most important aspects of the American democracy at work. The people waiting in line were people like us—regular people, regular citizens.

The crowd had come from around the country to witness firsthand the hearings regarding the cases the justices had accepted for that day. To think ours would be one of them!

Like all things in Washington, D.C., the importance of the institution superimposes itself on the iconic buildings the institutions occupy. Carl and I were awestruck by the size and the subtle grandeur of the building—big in size and even bigger in purpose.

"We've actually come to the Supreme Court of the United States of America to have our case heard," Carl said in near-disbelief.

The building represented the very essence of the institution of justice within the United States. These nine robed justices were the final law of the entire country, whose decisions to take cases and give opinions could overturn actions of Congress or even the President of the United States.

"Be glad we're here now. Let's just be happy for us that they're not wearing white robes and pointy hats," Carl joked as we exited the cab.

Carl must have known I was tense because he was being so caustic to make sure I was calm. But all the sad racial recollections and clichés in the world could not describe the great feeling of having your fate before the highest judicial body in the entire nation, but also the pressure of knowing it's your case and your company. "Our fate lies in the hands of these nine justices," I concluded as we looked at the bank of wide steps. "I'm OK," I said to reassure him. "Are you?"

As my brother and I were escorted past hundreds of citizens, on our way up the steps to the Supreme Court of the United States of America, we could not help but be affected by the fact that the highest court in the land was going to hear our case. Our small group of regular citizens had brought the second-largest city in the nation to task before the highest court in the land.

Our case was fairly straightforward and simple: the City of Los Angeles had limited our First Amendment rights as citizens of United States. The decision stood to affect the new technology and the citizens of the entire country.

We felt hopeful about our cause at the Supreme Court hearing since the Ninth Circuit had already ruled unanimously in our favor. We were also resolute in our belief that access to media was one of the most important civil rights and the very foundation of the First Amendment.

The decision by the court would offer our group a final understanding about whether the City of Los Angeles could or could not restrict our entrance into the burgeoning cable television industry. The decision for us would be final and we would accept our losses and move on if the court went against our position regarding the First Amendment. Conversely, we supposed the city would allow us to construct a cable television system in South Central if the highest court in the land ruled in our favor.

Upon our arrival, we met our attorneys, Harold Farrow and his associate overseeing our case, Rob Bramson.

Immediately, Farrow took us to the front of the line and informed the uniformed guard that our case was being heard by the court that morning. After seeing our identification, we were sent to a special security line for processing.

We waited outside the courtroom chambers in the hallway until our case was called. Where we stood was not wasted on Carl and me. The incredible power wielded by the court seemed magnified by the timeless elegance of the rich woods on the walls and the marble floors as we sat down under the forty-five-foot domed ceiling.

"Cases like *Dred Scott*, *Plessey versus Ferguson*, and *Brown versus the Board of Education* had determined the future of an entire race of people in America," I recalled in hushed tones.

We would actually see Justice Thurgood Marshall, who, as the first black justice appointed to the United States Supreme Court, would be there in the courtroom to review our case. We would see this black legal icon who, as an attorney, had argued thirty-one cases before the Supreme Court before becoming a distinguished judge and member of the court. As a younger man, Justice Marshall had argued the case of *Brown versus the Board of Education* on behalf of the plaintiff. The same case I quoted in my pep talk after Judge Consuelo Marshall threw us out of her court. I want to make it clear that the "Honorable" Consuelo Marshall is not any relation to the Honorable Thurgood Marshall.

We talked of the important decisions that affected our lives and opportunities that had been deliberated in these very chambers. We smiled as we were shown to the seats reserved for us as the principals of our case. How many of the people involved in the famous civil rights cases of our times had sat in our seats?

So here we sat. It was a humbling experience to witness the greatest legal minds of our time addressing the very issue we'd already been battling for about six years.

There was a sense of vindication that the highest court in the land had chosen to hear our disputes with the City of Los Angeles.

———

The nine black-robed justices were seated at a horseshoe-shaped, elevated oak podium for the oral arguments. Farrow informed us that the Chief Justice, William Rehnquist, sat in the center seat and the seats closest to the chief were based upon seniority with the farthest seats relegated to the newest members of the court. Seeing and sitting in the presence of nine justices routinely heard about in the evening news felt like watching nine great artists in any field, except we saw them all at once—a daunting sight.

Parties touring the hearings were allowed to remain in the chamber for about five minutes in order to have enough time for everyone to have an opportunity to watch the Supreme Court at work. So their seats were at the middle to the back of the room, to minimize disturbance when the five-minute intervals were up.

The attorneys sat at a table opposite the members of the court at the front of the room. We were seated in a section directly behind our attorneys, next to the section reserved for the press.

Farrow informed us we'd remain for the entirety of the oral arguments in our case—about forty-five minutes. Over six years of our lives encapsulated in forty-five minutes!

———

We were all there to see the Supreme Court justices review, hear the oral arguments, and discuss the findings of the Ninth Circuit Court of Appeals with the lawyers from both sides of our case.

The appellate court agreed with our position. The City of Los Angeles disagreed. And Carl and I were both there to watch Farrow defend our position against the City of Los Angeles's legal team.

Even before this historic day for us, each side submitted a legal brief beforehand, fully explaining why they believed the appellate court decision was correct or incorrect and replying to the brief of their opponent.

Our basic position identified cable television as an electronic newspaper. As newspapers used public right of ways to distribute their product, we felt that cable television, which also used public right of ways, should be entitled to the same protection against government intrusion.

The position of the City of Los Angeles said the city was entitled to limit access to public right of ways for the dissemination of news and information to those who would meet the licensing procedure of the city. Additionally, the city felt it should be able to determine who was entitled to speak using the cable television industry.

The city also continued to maintain that cable television was a natural monopoly similar to that of electric and water companies providing services to the citizens of the city, which meant only one company would be allowed to provide cable television service. The city claimed competition might increase the cost of the providers of the service, which they would pass on to the subscriber and substantially limit access to the cable television market by citizens because of those higher costs.

As in the appellate court case, numerous "friend of the court" briefs were also filed. Those filing "friend of the court" briefs in support of the position of the City of Los Angeles included the National League of Cities, the City of Palo Alto, California, and the City of Sacramento, California. Home Box Office (HBO) was among those that submitted a "friend of the court" brief in support of the position of Preferred.

—◆—

We were ushered in and took our seats. The court clerk called for presentation of oral arguments for our case. Each attorney identified himself and stated which party he represented.

After introductions, the attorney group representing each side of the case was given three minutes to make their opening arguments and to explain or clarify their previously filed brief.

At the Supreme Court, Ed Perez, a deputy city attorney, represented the city. Perez had also represented the city at the Ninth Circuit Court of Appeals. He had been involved in assisting the city with the cable franchise application process since 1981.

———◆———

After the opening presentation, the nine justices asked questions of each party to clarify their understanding of the issues and the relief (what each party wanted from the court decision) being sought from the court.

Chief Justice Rehnquist began the questioning by asking about the natural monopoly theory the city was using to justify granting a cable television monopoly. Justice Rehnquist seemed dubious about stretching the concept of natural monopoly to include cable television.

Justice Sandra Day O'Connor, like Chief Justice Rehnquist, aggressively questioned the city's theory regarding cable television as a natural monopoly. Perez became flustered as he was peppered with questions regarding what we contended all along was a spurious theory by the city used to argue their ability to limit competition in order to protect the public.

Justice Thurgood Marshall asked Perez how the city could classify cable television as a natural monopoly when the majority of residents of South Central would not use this service. This was in contrast to traditional public utilities. Marshall indicated that since cable television was not a standardized product that remained the same every day, like the generic electricity or water services delivered to every house by the city-owned utility, it could not realistically be considered a natural monopoly.

Perez mumbled something about protecting the public's interest, which, given the city's previous actions, was blatantly false.

The content of the cable television system could change every day, or every minute, but the city stubbornly opposed these facts.

Farrow told the court, "The city's own ordinance stated the award of franchise was to be done on a non-exclusive basis, which clearly indicates the creators of the law did not intend cable television be a monopoly."

When questioned on this issue, Perez indicated this clause only gave the city the ability to add franchises in the future but did not require it.

Farrow was adamant the term non-exclusive *excludes* the concept a monopoly. If the city insisted the ordinance term "non-exclusive" could really mean that they will award a single monopoly owner in cable television, they are telling you that black can be white, if they say so. If this most fundamental issue was not clear to the city, then nothing done in the process could be clear to the city.

Perez called the court's attention to the substantial capital requirement to develop a cable television system. To our amazement, Perez told the court that the city was actually doing Preferred Communications a favor by not allowing them to invest in their community because he was sure we would lose all of our investment. He was only protecting us from ourselves.

Several members of the normally stoic Supreme Court snickered at Perez, as he tried to make them believe he was really concerned about Preferred's financial interest. Snickering in the hallowed halls of the Supreme Court!

Trying to respond to questions directed at him, Perez continued babbling his mantra-like argument about natural monopoly—supposedly the basis for the city's legal action from the onset.

"It doesn't look like they are going for the natural monopoly bull," Carl said. "I think Perez is way over his head…and Perez is full of it."

The final question was posed by Justice O'Connor. She asked Perez whether the city had any involvement in the programming being transmitted by cable television. Perez smiled as he responded that the City of Los Angeles did not ask any questions or have any involvement in the programming choices of operators.

Carl and I looked at each other with puzzlement. Carl asked me as we watched, "Does Perez really think that this court is composed of idiots?"

One of the sections in the city's cable franchise application was called "Programming." In this section, the bidder listed what services and channels the company would carry on their proposed system.

The looks on the faces of the justices said it all. They had looked at the briefs and seen the franchise application. They were incredulous someone would so confidently come before them and have no knowledge of the city's own cable franchise paperwork.

Perez was arrogant enough to attempt to deceive the justices of the United States Supreme Court!

At dinner, on the night of the oral arguments, Carl recanted to Farrow about our perception of Perez seeming to "put his foot in his mouth" about the programming issue. We were all amused that Perez thought that the Supreme Court would believe such a blatantly untrue statement. This was the sort of behavior that Perez had used in the earlier hearings we had been through with the city.

Farrow compared Perez's performance to boys in the sandlot trying to play against men on major league baseball teams. "It's the sport of baseball and the rules may be the same, but there is a glaring difference in talent at each level from Little League to the major leagues."

Several months later, on a sunny Saturday morning in June 1986, I was driving south on Interstate 5 with my friend Gene Forte. We had stopped in Paso Robles for breakfast. As we approached the front door of the restaurant, we saw the *Los Angeles Times* newspaper vending rack and went to get a paper. Gene put a quarter in and when he got the paper he grabbed me around my neck and said, "Congratulations, you didn't let those pricks get away."

He then showed me the front page of the *Los Angeles Times*, which said, "Supreme Court Overturns LA Cable TV Law."

I was almost in a state of shock. On Friday, June 10, 1986, the U.S. Supreme Court had issued its ruling in the case of *Preferred Communications versus The City of Los Angeles*. The highest court in the United States had given us back the right that Judge Consuelo Marshall had so conveniently managed to deprive us of for three years.

The paper made note of the unanimous 9-0 decision in favor of Preferred Communications—a rarity on such a divided court. How many unanimous decisions had been rendered by the Supreme Court?

When we later called Farrow, we asked, "How many Supreme Court cases had had unanimous rulings?"

"In this day and age, I'm sure there have been a few...but not that many," Farrow replied, awestruck as well.

Cable television was clearly subject to the protections of the First Amendment and all the justices remanded the case back to the U.S. District Court of Judge Consuelo Marshall for trial.

———————

I called Carl at about nine in the morning on Saturday. "Have you lost your mind?" He said after I said good morning. After he was done scolding me for calling him early on his off day, I told him to get the newspaper and look at the headlines. He read the headline to me and went back to chastising me for waking him so early.

I told him what the headline said in the copy of the *Los Angeles Times* that I had and we could not understand why the newspapers were different. In his Los Angeles edition of the *Los Angeles Times*, the story was on page eight and toned down from the Paso Robles edition of the Los Angeles Times. Front page for Paso Robles, but page eight for Los Angeles, the city most impacted by this verdict?

Carl mused, "This is the same paper, same day, and same story." This was the power of media. This is also the power of politics. This was what we were fighting against.

———————

We celebrated our victory at Carl's house that night, drinking a beer and playing with Carl's kids.

Gene summed it up for the older kids by saying that the results of the battle in court assured Preferred Communications, Carl, and I would be forever contained in the cases of the United States Supreme Court. Like all cases ruled upon by the Supreme Court the effect would be felt by some, if not us, for years in the future.

———————

The Supreme Court ruled unanimously that cable television was a constitutionally protected form of media that was subject to First Amendment protection. The Supreme Court returned the case back to the U.S. District Court of Consuelo Marshall for trial and further development of facts.

It was clear that the city's position of designating only one operator for each franchise area was unconstitutional. We were the only other company who had expressed any interest at the beginning of the development of South Central.

For about a minute, I was able to tell myself that this ruling should make everything quite clear and allow us to move on with the construction of the franchise. Then I thought of the immortal words of Yogi Berra when he said, "It ain't over till it's over."

Two things kept nagging at me. Susan Herman, the head of the newly formed Department of Telecommunications, publicly stated at a May 15, 1985, hearing of the Los Angeles City Council that the city was working to assure that any victory by Preferred Communications against the city would be worthless, because by that time the city would have given any competitors a substantial head start to control the market.

Secondly, I wondered if a Supreme Court ruling—or the Constitution—mattered to Judge Marshall. There was always the chance that Judge Marshall would be vindictive because we had challenged and won at the appellate level. She seemed more concerned about her friendships with Bradley, Cochran, and Williams than any law.

———◆———

Although Judge Marshall had dismissed our case in 1983, not one of the appeals court justices supported her position that cable television was outside the protection of the First Amendment of the U.S. Constitution. The appellate process represented an independent assessment of Judge Marshall's faulty ability and judicial temperament.

Farrow indicated that the unanimous verdict by the United States Supreme Court was extremely unusual because it was invariably a rebuke of the lower court. It was an implicit way of telling the lower court that it was completely wrong, not merely misguided. As Farrow would later tell me, without mincing words, "The court's 9-0 verdict really means, 'You're not only wrong, but you're also stupid!'"

———◆———

After unanimous losses at both the Ninth Circuit and the U.S. Supreme Court, it had even become clear to city officials that Ed Perez was way over his head. The city hired a high-powered, expensive law firm from Washington, D.C., Miller and Holbrook, to replace Perez and take over the litigation—at a cost of several million dollars. Around City Hall the people involved were saying Miller and Holbrook specialized in protecting cities from the "irreparable damage" the city was pretending would occur if cable television competition were allowed.

———◆———

A Supreme Court verdict could only give us so much protection— even a unanimous decision. Unfortunately, these legal battles

247

are fought on local or regional battlefields, where the tentacles of political influence and corruption are more and more commonplace.

To us, the City of Los Angeles was a perfect example of a city government gone completely awry. And make no mistake, in our research, Los Angeles's reputation for its corruption of power was replicated many times over in other cities large and small that looked to the larger, trend-setting cities to define their governing style and what they could get away with.

We saw the blatant corruption in local governments within Los Angeles County. There was Compton, in our case, and now also cities like Bell and Vernon pushed government corruption to the limit.

———

The public and the press are not always interested in looking at government corruption. In times of recession, however, faltering economies frequently expose the underlying results of the financial shenanigans of government officials and the costs involved. Unchecked corruption, allowed to run rampant for decades, highlights waste when citizens want to know where their tax money has gone. Elected officials at every level sell favors for pennies on the dollar—the taxpayers' dollars—which lead to untold future liabilities for those towns, cities, counties, states, and the country.

———

Judge Consuelo Marshall had ruled in 1983 that there was no possibility that we could have a valid action against the city. It had taken two other courts, three years, and hundreds of thousands of dollars of ours and our friends' personal monies just to get the right to ask for our constitutional rights—from Judge Consuelo Marshall. *What price justice? What price freedom?*

Chapter Thirteen

The Justice Hustle—Part Two
(Remanded Back To The "Honorable" Judge Marshall)

The unanimous U.S. Supreme Court decision, in June 1986, remanded the case back to the U.S. District Court and the courtroom of Judge Consuelo Marshall for trial.

Overturning the blatantly unjust decision of Judge Marshall cost us close to a half million dollars. The cost to the City of Los Angeles taxpayers was estimated at about twice that amount— one million taxpayer dollars. All of these expenses for the right to be heard by the U.S. District Court and to have a jury trial!

The unanimous decisions by the Ninth Circuit and the U.S. Supreme Court had made it virtually impossible for the city to win on the major issues in this case. So it was back to the district court and the same judge, Judge Consuelo Marshall.

When Judge Marshall looked at the evidence the first time, we thought she determined an out-of-control Los Angeles city government should be allowed to make illegal decisions and deprive its citizens of rights without penalty. She blocked all legitimate channels within her legal power to thwart our efforts as citizens to seek redress from the government. Did Judge Marshall see her error after two unanimous decisions against her ruling by the appellate and Supreme Court?

———————

"So what do we do now?" I asked.

"Wait for her to start the procedures to get us to a jury trial," Farrow said. "Federal courts have been kind to black business and legal problems like yours, and now we've got the backing of the higher courts." Farrow looked at me and shrugged. "It'll take time but not much longer, I hope."

Black Americans, like us, had long sought the help of the federal courts for protection in places like Mississippi and Alabama. Little did we know that we would need protection from black politicians and the judiciary in Los Angeles, California. Now, here we were before a black federal judge, in Los Angeles, who had summarily and erroneously dismissed our case the first time, and somehow we were supposed to gain justice before this very same black judge. Again.

So, as the umpire would say, in this second half of our judicial double-header, "Let's play ball!"

———————

We started getting phone calls. Several people told us that Judge Marshall would use every bit of her formidable power as a federal judge to delay the process and avoid any jury trial in our case. Our source said, "You've already been told by Councilman Lindsay that there's lots of money against you. The city doesn't like you.

So Judge Marshall won't either, no matter what *any other court says.*"

Another lawyer, who had watched our case closely, said, "Doesn't matter what they say in Washington, D.C. You're in a court in Los Angeles." Would Judge Marshall ignore the rules or change the rules again? Would she attempt to make us pay for having had the audacity to take charge of our rights and appeal her judgment?

"You've got two things in your favor," Farrow said. Two principles were uniformly practiced when a court case was remanded back to the lower courts: the average "discovery period" for cases remanded back to district courts from the Supreme Court was less than two years and the requirement that cases with potential constitutional violations be given precedence in federal court. Nothing could have been more time sensitive than our civil rights in the eyes of the law, we were told. We hoped Judge Marshall would abide by these rules.

Judge Marshall conveniently ignored them all.

———————

We painstakingly rebuilt our case as we started the first step in the process, referred to earlier as the "discovery phase" (in baseball terms, it's getting and evaluating the lineup your opponent will field against you). In the discovery phase, each side puts together its case, gets to examine the materials of the other side, and uses these to prepare and present evidence to the jury. Before the appeal at the Ninth Circuit, no discovery had been allowed in our case because Judge Marshall had wrongly dismissed our case before a trial could occur.

We managed the calendars of everyone to set meetings and tallied the staggering costs of the legal time, administrative staff, typists/stenographers, and gathering witnesses in this costly and time-consuming process. Putting together the documents, depositions, and expert witnesses took a lot of time.

———————

Each time we came to her courtroom, Judge Marshall routinely gave the City of Los Angeles continuance after continuance in the discovery phase of their case, without any judicial explanation or reasoning, dragging the process on month after month.

Time went on and we were not informed of any more need for meetings or depositions as the continuances piled up and more time was wasted.

———————

After proceedings were postponed for the fifth time, Carl whispered angrily. "She's trying to break us again."

"We've got to get out of this courtroom to another judge," I said to Farrow.

"I'll file the papers," Farrow replied. "But it will eat up more time and money. Let's see what we can do." He moved his briefcase. "But I've also got to say, in federal court, they take a dim view of removing judges despite the appearance of bias."

We filed petitions with the chief judge of the district court and also petitioned the Ninth Circuit Court of Appeals to seek relief from Judge Marshall's refusal to move the case forward—but were denied on all levels.

This lack of integrity, under Judge Marshall, seemed corrosive to the very fabric of a democratic society. This wasn't the way the judicial system was supposed to work. Our ability to exercise our constitutional right was separated from the right itself—to the detriment of our case and the constitutional meaning of the word, justice.

———————

While Judge Marshall assiduously continued to prevent our litigation from going forward, the South Central and Boyle Heights cable television franchise areas for which we had originally applied still had no progress in the construction of a cable television system. We tried to publicize these situations but because these areas were predominantly black and Latino there was little concern about this scandal by any major newspaper or television station.

"You know the neighborhoods are changing down there," Carl said sadly.

"More gangs than jobs...and the latest economic statistics are declining, too," I replied.

These are the types of questions we had asked in South Central. These were clearly not the kind of questions on Judge Marshall's mind or those of the officials representing the City of Los Angeles. All we asked for was competence and impartiality, both absent from Judge Marshall's bench and the city.

———◆———

As Judge Marshall held the case in abeyance in her court, the city allowed KB to sell the South Central franchise. KB never finalized original ownership with the city by providing financial documentation, as required by city ordinance, nor did this fact become public knowledge regarding how the city was failing to regulate cable television in South Central. The ability of a defaulted licensee to sell a monopoly cable franchise serving South Central, once again demonstrated the preferential treatment for companies and entities like KB and the Bakewell-Johnson group.

Preferred Communications was one of the companies to express an interest in the defaulted South Central franchise. As we indicated earlier, after we responded to the city's "Request for Information" we never heard from the city about the South Central license again after repeated inquiries—another violation of City law.

We petitioned the court but Judge Marshall refused to review this move by the city to select, without competitive bid, a new builder for the South Central system. The specified process for submitting applications was now eliminated legislatively and judicially, and as before, only for South Central.

As indicated earlier, on January 16, 1986, Susan Herman, general manager of the Department of Telecommunications, issued a report regarding the status of cable television franchises in the city. The report indicated that the Boyle Heights franchise, which was awarded in 1982, and the South Central franchise awarded in 1983 had not begun construction as of 1986.

Despite this unconscionable lack of progress, our company was locked out of the cable television industry while the city spent millions of dollars to protect the monopolies that were not even being built. We failed to see the economic or social benefit of their actions to the community or their city.

Judge Marshall would allow another company, American Cable Systems, which had not even gone through the bidding process, to acquire the franchise. The effect of Judge Marshall's allowing this franchise sale and construction, while at the same time restraining our ability to enter the market, endorsed the city's action to create another unregulated monopoly situation protected in the federal courts—just what the higher courts had identified in their rulings that they didn't want to happen.

Judge Marshall completely ignored the fact that the city had segregated the South Central franchise and was treating South Central in a completely different manner than it had treated all of the franchises within the city. The judge ruled it was irrelevant that the city was not going to use a competitive bidding process to license a company to construct the franchise. Exactly what was relevant to this judge?

———— • ————

During this time when Judge Marshall refused to expedite the case or give us a jury trial, various other litigations were brought by other cities against such illegal cable franchise practices. Citizens and potential competitors charged that the cable television industry and local politicians were protecting each other. The use of large campaign contributions in exchange for the protection of the cable television industry by local governments were one of the great American stories of greed and corruption brought out in these other cases—just like the abuses we suffered in Los Angeles.

Numerous lawsuits were filed across the United States regarding the insider deals given to the friends of politicians in other cities. In Houston, Texas, racketeering charges were leveled against local elected officials during federal jury trials regarding the granting of monopoly cable television franchises. Palo Alto,

California, and Sacramento, California, were also involved in similar litigation regarding the monopoly award of cable television franchises. Both cities were also covered by the jurisdiction of the Ninth Circuit Court of Appeals, who's ruling in our case was now the law covering those cities. While other litigants were getting their day in court with cases filed well after ours, Judge Marshall refused to get on with our trial.

———————

In Los Angeles, with our case, there was no change and no remedy. The discovery process dragged on as the city was granted continual delays in setting a trial date. Judge Marshall's obstruction assured there would be no competition in the cable television industry. The City of Los Angeles, in conjunction with the U.S. District Court, protected monopoly status that allowed the cable television industry to entrench itself in the marketplace with no competition.

Judge Marshall squandered time without apology after the case had been remanded back by the Supreme Court. The first trial date was set on April 1, 1988, with trial due to begin on August 16, 1988. On August 1, 1988, Judge Marshall changed the trial date to November 1, 1988. On October 25, 1988, less than one week prior to the November 1 trial date, Judge Marshall granted the city another delay for trial until April 4, 1989. That was three different trial dates in one year. The April 1989 trial would not be honored either. The delays seemed eerily reminiscent of hearings at City Hall.

Sometimes Judge Marshall changed trial dates, claiming she was too busy to adhere to the trial date, which she herself had set. At other times, she continued to allow the city to request numerous delays in order to seek "additional" discovery evidence, the sources of which were unknown, and our protests requesting the names and importance of these additional sources were continually denied by the judge. Court watchers said, "She's making a mockery of the entire legal system!"

Judge Marshall would continue to express her observations from the bench, deny all our objections, and leave the courtroom.

So, we had all this documented, taken under oath in deposition testimony, and we could not be heard in Judge Marshall's court—or have a trial!

"We can't impeach the testimony of those who lie and distort the facts if we can't get them on the witness stand," Al Watson fumed after another delay.

"Seems Judge Marshall is abusing her court's discretion to delay your trial by prolonging the discovery process," Farrow replied as he shrugged his shoulders and shook his head. "There's nothing more we can do at this point."

We had plenty to say and plenty to show if the time came to present our evidence. There were dozens of blatant examples of irregularities, inconsistencies, and straight-out perjury in discovery information we identified and uncovered under the leadership of our legal team at Farrow, Schildhause, and Wilson. An attempt to list all of the discrepancies that Judge Marshall allowed to be treated as truth would require an additional hundred pages here. To save time, I will focus on only a few of the major issues hidden by Judge Marshall.

One of the most blatant examples of perjury began at the highest levels. William Elkins, a special assistant to Mayor Tom Bradley, stated in his deposition, taken under penalty of perjury, that he had never had any communications with Channing Johnson about the South Central cable franchise.

Our legal team uncovered an April 15, 1983, confidential memo from Channing Johnson to Elkins titled, "South Central Cable TV Franchise Application of ACCESS." ACCESS was the operating subsidiary of KB for the South Central cable television franchise. The memo explained in detail each meeting held between KB and the Bakewell-Johnson group. The meetings occurred from November 1982 through April 15, 1983. Government officials perjured themselves. The memos also addressed Johnson's concerns for the twenty-percent minority ownership and the portion of the franchise they were supposed to receive.

Elkins's deposition testimony directly contradicts that document in the court record.

Judge Marshall was aware of this act of perjury covering meetings in 1982 and 1983 because reviewing depositions prior to her rulings were part of her judicial duties.

Secondly, in order to delay the trial and ultimate resolution of complaints, the city presented numerous reports, none of which had a factual basis. In one erroneous report they submitted against us, they alleged that there was "not enough room on the poles" for a second cable wire to be installed by our company—no room, no cable business competition. Mitchell Kolacinski, a Department of Water and Power (DWP) engineer, stated in his deposition of April 21, 1988, that he knew for a fact that there was insufficient space for a second wire to be installed on the poles.

The judge stated that she would accept this testimony as factual evidence unless we were able to disprove Kolacinski's statements. So we spent nearly $100,000 for engineers to examine the poles and refute Kolacinski's testimony—at which time the city withdrew its claim that there was not enough room on the poles for a second system.

Two years later, in November 27, 1989, Mitchell Kolacinski subsequently recanted his previously sworn testimony from his deposition, effectively admitting that he had lied to the court during his deposition testimony, and that, in fact, there was room on the poles for at least one additional cable television system.

One hundred thousand dollars was lost.

Judge Marshall did two things regarding this issue. She ignored this supplemental declaration and refused us access to the poles or the ability to start a competing cable television business. We were the only other company interested in the South Central franchise. There was space on the poles and we had the financing, expertise, and business plan to start a cable franchise. Judge Marshall also refused to allow any further examination by our attorneys of Kolacinski, just like DOT was protected by BTC, IEDC, and the Los Angeles City Council. A critical figure completely reversed his position and we were prohibited from asking how this occurred.

The testimony was false but would go unchallenged—again. Only in a jury trial could the perjured deposition testimony of numerous city witnesses be challenged. Judge Marshall would allow perjury in her federal courtroom to go unpunished!

In a third example, Judge Marshall also refused to utilize her judicial powers to impose sanctions for the false testimony that had been used by the city to create ongoing delays in our case.

In Judge Marshall's rulings, our company was forbidden from introducing evidence about our dealings with the city regarding the tainted franchising process. Even though Judge Marshall's prior rulings in our first appearance in her court had been unanimously overturned by the Ninth Circuit Court and the Supreme Court, Marshall stubbornly refused to consider any testimony regarding the prior behavior of the City of Los Angeles in the cable franchise process or any information about our prior franchising activities. Judge Marshall ruled that our former company, Universal Cable, which had been combined into Preferred, no longer had legal standing. A mere name change because of litigation by the entertainment conglomerate MCA/Universal made our company and its constitutional concerns invalid? Was this an underhanded attempt to pretend that we had only gotten in the cable television industry in 1983 when the lawsuit was filed? Did she want to wipe out the fact that we'd been involved the cable franchising process since 1979—to the media and to the public?

By this stance, Judge Marshall blatantly ignored two very important facts.

Our legal team strenuously objected at every turn. They argued that our company's entire experience within the licensing process was necessary to ensure equal access of all qualified bidders for commerce in any new technology. Blatant irregularities that occurred during the franchising process in at least three of the fifteen franchises issued by the City of Los Angeles, where we were bidders, deserved to be presented. How could any civil rights issue be established if the judge refuses to allow the prior behavior of the defendant to be deemed irrelevant?

In pursuing our constitutional and civil rights case, our lawyers asked what sort of justice could one expect to receive from a court that refuses to allow introduction of vital evidence that proves gross mistreatment and mismanagement by the government from which we are pursuing your constitutional rights? Being denied a factual historical record of events was the only way to give the court and the jury the information necessary to render a fair and ethical verdict regarding the government's actions.

One example that indicated the utter disregard and lack of clarity the city showed in the cable franchise process was the "Community Antenna Master Plan." This was the document mandating the ownership and community participation of citizens in their community television decisions. Records, transcriptions, and deposition interviews showed this "mandate" was an on-again, off-again proposition, depending on what the city politicians and bureaucrats wanted on any given day—not relying on their master plan.

In the original published Notice of Sale in 1980 for the South Central franchise, the statement that "minority bidders are encouraged to submit applications" was included. The city attorney at that time said the city could not consider such statements that were contained in publicly published documents. Off again, for the decision regarding the original franchise!

"Consideration of the extent of local participation in the ownership and management of the franchise will enhance responsiveness to the cable television needs of the South Central residents" was also a part of the convoluted Los Angeles City Council testimony during the cable franchise mess. On again!

The same city attorney had told the BTC, IEDC, and the full Los Angeles City Council that local and minority participation could not be considered as a factor during the franchising process because no allowance had been made for such participation in the ordinance itself. Therefore, off again!

In our dealing with Judge Marshall's court we wanted to know just when the city had begun being concerned about the needs of the South Central residents and their First Amendment rights.

Judge Marshall denied our requests. Why was this information not relevant in a court of law? Couldn't Judge Marshall see these contradictions?

Instead, Judge Marshall relied on another minority economic theory called "localism" in her rulings.

———————

Localism? During the time of our original application, there was no such term as "localism" ever used or discussed in the analysis, assessment, or award of any cable television franchise in the City of Los Angeles. This new judicial premise with more new definitions and more new rules seemed reminiscent of our experience in the franchising debacle with the city. Was this an attempt by Judge Marshall's court to chip away at our case?

Localism (another term for affirmative action used by the City of Los Angeles) was the process by which the city could require a company to accept minority people as their partners because underrepresented groups (minorities) needed broader economic opportunities within the culture and society. Localism sounded fair and reasonable on the surface, but in looking at our case, the hypocrisy of this argument used by Judge Marshall and the City of Los Angeles was glaringly apparent. We thought the city, in Judge Marshall's court, was spending millions to prevent localism by Preferred Communications.

The shield of localism was not to make sure the best minority-qualified bidder was chosen but acted as another thinly veiled excuse to protect the friends of Tom Bradley and various councilmen who "only give money to my black friends." In our case, the recipients of the City of Los Angeles's localism were Danny Bakewell and Channing Johnson.

We thought the systems of localism and affirmative action in Los Angeles revolved around giving the right amount to the political patronage crowd and the politicians would vote for anything those patrons wanted. Remember the example of Kaufman and Broad having the no-bidding process applied to their application and selling the undeveloped franchise without reopening or reestablishing a bidding process.

How did Judge Marshall deal with localism as a basis for decisions relative to rulings she made in favor of the defendants, regarding providing special financial incentives for localism or obeying the core of the community minority ownership and community participation aspects?

Justice Marshall relied upon unsubstantiated claims and declarations concerning localism on the deposition testimony of Joan Flores, a Los Angeles City councilwoman, one of the defendants in the case.

We were astounded yet again.

According to the Ninth Circuit Court of Appeals and the United States Supreme Court, Los Angeles City Councilwoman Joan Flores, the rest of the Los Angeles City Council, and the city were losing defendants in the major and most fundamental parts of our case. A losing defendant in two higher courts in this very case would now become the expert basis for Judge Marshall's decisions on localism. Not only that, Flores was a councilwoman but not a professor, expert, noted authority, or published author on the issue.

"Your Honor, I don't consider her an expert in 'localism' in the least!" Farrow muttered. "I strenuously object."

Judge Marshall ignored our objections and Councilwoman Flores became an expert despite having a conflict of interest of being a defendant in the very case she was deemed an expert? What sort of bizarre judicial ethics in Judge Marshall's court allowed Councilwoman Flores to become an expert?

How could a judge confer expert status upon a witness when the very concept of expert requires that the expert have no involvement in the ultimate outcome of the case? Flores, as a defendant in the case, clearly had a conflict that precluded her being designated as an expert by Judge Marshall.

Judge Marshall's ruling stated, "Based on the background of Flores in the economics of the South Central area as they related to the operation of a cable TV system, the court finds that her testimony constitutes more than a mere abstract assertion of government interest." What in her background qualified her to be an expert on South Central economics? Councilwoman Flores presented no evidence that she had any understanding of economics, especially in South Central.

Councilwoman Flores's was a defendant, not an expert. It had already been proven Flores was complicit in the violation of our civil rights in two higher courts.

"If she's an expert in economics, so am I," Mr. Watson grumbled. "When it's time for the trial, let me testify!"

On the other hand, Judge Marshall completely ignored the testimony of Dr. Thomas Hazlett, a professor of Economics at the University of California at Davis, who we provided as our expert economic witness. Dr. Hazlett was one of the most knowledgeable men on the economics of cable television in the United States and designated as an expert in the area of cable television economics. Dr. Hazlett would go on to become the chief economist at the Federal Communications Commission during 1990 and 1991.

Nowhere in Judge Marshall's rulings did she discuss the opinion of an economics professor about the economics of South Central. Was the economic information provided by someone with actual skills in the economic field ever relevant to Judge Marshall? With no ability to challenge Councilwoman Flores's testimony in a public forum, such as a trial, the judge continued to pick and choose statements to support her bizarre rulings.

"Thus the court finds that defendant's interest in requiring community participation in the programming and operation of a cable system is compelling." This was nothing more than deceptive posturing to say minority participation in a business was the same as minority ownership of a business—driving a legal wedge in our argument by a false premise given by a non-expert and defendant in the case and making participation and ownership equal terms.

Nothing the city did in relation to the South Central franchise ever provided community participation in the programming or operation of a cable television system. Judge Marshall intentionally distorted the true character of the action of the city to deny true ownership and control of programming to the community.

In Judge Marshall's court, localism became a perverted, dishonest joke.

———

We continued to struggle to get a firm court date and clarify issues like localism as Judge Marshall chipped away at our case.

"The information is supposed to get to a jury," Carl fumed. Carl was right. The factual information of court cases like ours was intended to be determined by a jury. They could look at the facts and determine which party was telling the truth and which party was lying. Judge Marshall's delaying tactics unilaterally decided to what extent we would be able to exercise our First Amendment rights—a clear violation of court ethics and protocol.

Time and trial dates passed.

"Nobody's doing any 'discovery' on the city side," one of our informants indicated. "They're just waiting for you to run out of money and quit. Judge Marshall's their way of doing it."

Until the trial, Judge Marshall could ostensibly do whatever she wanted to do, since all our many efforts to remove her from the case had failed. There was no way to impeach the lies, perjured testimony, or Judge Marshall's suspect rulings during the discovery phase.

Nothing could take the place of a trial of the facts. We and our legal team were disgusted and appalled that Judge Marshall was picking away at the essentials of the court case just like the City of Los Angeles and its administration had picked away at our cable franchising application.

In our humble opinion, Judge Marshall wasn't interested in our side of the court case. One of our consultants said, "Man, you're getting screwed and you're not even getting kissed!"

For those reasons, in addition to the process, we questioned Judge Marshall's entire judicial temperament and her actions. At every turn, she showed a distinct and unerring prejudice toward the City of Los Angeles. It was clear from the initial case, which was filed in 1983 and finally resolved in 1992, that Judge Marshall made every effort to allow the city unprecedented favor in her court, including allowing continuances, delaying her rulings, and changing court dates. Each and all to ensure our case would never receive a fair trial or any trial at all.

We thought, and we told by our legal team and advisors, that disallowing evidence was cheating. In any other endeavor—sports, academics, or business—the system's willingness to disallow, subvert, or suppress all the factual information that supports the grievance would be considered dishonest, certainly not "fair play." We thought the same was true for the federal court. It was plain and simple cheating.

"Just because you wear a black robe and have a title of 'justice' does not dismiss the fact that you are seeking to avoid justice by denying constitutional rights," Al Watson said. "It's inherent in the citizenship of this country, she, err, Judge Marshall, should know and act better…and I'll say it to my last breath!"

If this were a movie set, dust, cobwebs, and debris would have filled the set of Judge Marshall's courtroom.

———

To our dismay, and to the dismay of many court watchers interested in correct court procedures, Judge Marshall would wait five years to affirm the obvious, that the primary issue of monopoly status for cable television granted by the City of Los Angeles was unconstitutional. This was in addition to the three-year delay caused by her original incorrect dismissal of the case—an unbelievable eight years of delays caused by one federal judge.

Fortune Magazine called me in early 1989 and asked how we felt about the continuing judicial delays in the case of *Preferred Communications versus the City of Los Angeles*. In their May 15, 1989, issue I was quoted expressing my views. In my pent-up frustration and disgust I fumed, "I think it would be easier to get a trial in Russia" than from Judge Marshall.

Justice delayed was justice denied.

———

At the same time our civil and constitutional rights were being ignored in Los Angeles, the federal government was beginning to notice the problem of city government corruption in the cable industry. In 1986, several years after our failed franchise attempt, the United States Department of Commerce commissioned a study of the policies of local governments regarding the award of cable television franchises and the potential for a lack of competition in the video program distribution market. The authors of the report were C. William Verity, Secretary of the U.S. Department of Commerce; Alfred C. Sikes, Assistant Secretary for Communications and Information; and the project manager, Anita Wallgren.

In 1988, The United States Department of Commerce issued the report to Congress regarding their findings concerning cable television competition. The report was being generated because of the interest developed nationally after our case of was filed, and because of other widespread malfeasance and corruption by other cities and counties relative to their illegalities and irregularities in cable television franchising.

The report was titled "Video Program Distribution and Cable Television: Current Policy Issues and Recommendations." The report stated, "...diversity of viewer choice has not developed as fully as it might, so that *one cable operator with substantial First Amendment rights* selects, arranges, and markets *all of the program choices* available over the only cable service in town" (emphasis mine).

The Department of Commerce report continued, "The powerful First Amendment speaker is often a financial partner in programming services.... Competition and First Amendment values are closely linked, as suggested by U.S. Supreme Court Justice Oliver Wendell Holmes in his praise of the 'marketplace for ideas' advanced some seventy years ago. That is, policies aimed at fostering diversity likely will yield commensurate public dividends in terms of economic competition."

The report also stated, "Vertical integration of MSOs (multiple system operators) into programming and increasing concentration of cable ownership among the largest MSOs has the potential to harm competition and diversity in video programming. Cable service is increasingly relied upon by more than half of all the nation's television households as the primary source of video programming, yet these households are typically unable to choose among two or more cable providers. Thus, cable operators have come to dominate the local medium of choice for most Americans. Such lack of direct competition risks undermining diversity of program choices, and denies the public benefits resulting from more competitive markets such as better quality of service, lower prices, and more choices." Those hard and biting assessments were exactly what happened to us.

In many areas, the situations we faced were emphasized. We've highlighted some important findings. A main section of the report was called "Politicization of the Franchise Process." The section described the abuses and unfair practices used during the franchising process to enrich politically connected people.

One report section stated, "In the most egregious cases, contestants may have resorted to bribery or blatant anti-competitive conduct. Moreover, however, the applicants have relied upon the tools of a conventional political campaign." Sound familiar?

The report further stated, "One of the most widely used tactics (in franchising) was the 'rent a civic leader' approach, whereby an applicant offered an ownership interest in its system to a politically influential local leader.... Though not necessarily illegal, many of these activities have created an unsavory atmosphere around the franchising process risking loss of public confidence in that process."

In our case, the KB application followed this very plan of "rent a civic leader" by a rumored twenty-percent interest to businesses or charities directly associated with Channing Johnson and Danny Bakewell.

The Department of Commerce report concluded as follows: "For the foregoing reasons, we believe the franchise process, as currently structured, often disserves the public interest. The franchising process eliminates or seriously impedes entry by competitors, imposes substantial costs and delays on franchises, cable subscribers, and the public, which are not offset by countervailing benefits. The public would be better served by municipal efforts to provide a choice of cable service providers rather than extracting costly concessions from a sole provider."

The allegations we had made against the City of Los Angeles were now supported by the report of the United States government.

Judge Marshall did not even consider the report prepared by the United States government relative to the actions taken by numerous cities in the cable television industry—with facts and findings pertinent to our case. Another example of her bias, ignorance, or duplicity in this case?

On January 5, 1990, Judge Consuelo Marshall issued her first court order after seven years of waiting, wading through two other courts, and spending millions of dollars in continuing the fight.

On that day, Judge Marshall used her power as a U.S. District Court judge to say there were no issues worthy of a jury trial in our case, and she ruled there would be no jury trial.

With just a few words, despite the fact that we had spent five years in the discovery process to prepare for trial, Judge Marshall made sure we would never appear in court before a jury of our peers. She decreed that she, herself, as the judge in the case, would make the ruling.

Judge Marshall took it upon herself to decide all of the issues in this case even after being reversed on many issues by two higher courts. She cited four specific sections of the city ordinance that violated our constitutional rights. The most fundamental of these sections was the city's claim that it could lawfully allow only one applicant to get a license to build a cable television system. Marshall found this to be a violation of the First Amendment to the Constitution. Judicially, there was no other choice since this First Amendment issue had been decided unanimously by two higher courts. The Supreme Court decision virtually guaranteed success on our primary issue.

This First Amendment issue did not require five years of discovery or any depositions, interrogatories, or affidavits. This was the key element in the entire litigation. The fact that the city had illegally awarded a monopoly franchise to use public right of ways was a First Amendment issue. All other issues in the case were secondary to the issue of the city's attempt to limit entrance into the cable television market to their friends and political associates at the cost of our and the South Central community's First Amendment rights.

To add insult to injury, in determining the constitutional violations the city had committed, Judge Marshall did not once refer to anything from the discovery process.

We felt the judge used the discovery process to deny the protection of rights that she was sworn to uphold. She stopped protecting the citizens of Los Angeles in 1983, and never displayed any judicial integrity. She also provided protection to an entire multibillion-dollar industry so that some friends of Mayor Bradley could make a few million dollars—even though the Ninth Circuit and the U.S. Supreme Court made it clear in their rulings that there were constitutional implications in the regulation of cable television and favors given from the city to reward such political pandering.

No jury trial also meant the lies told during discovery in the depositions and interrogatories would never be exposed in Judge Marshall's court to give a full view of the complicity of the mayor's office. Judge Marshall allowed perjured testimony given during depositions and other discovery to remain unchallenged.

Judge Marshall denied us and the citizens of South Central the inherent privilege of transparency and impartiality of the jury system rendered in open court, the uncovering of the facts and evidence before an independent group of citizens of the community where the dispute has taken place in a jury trial, and a public determination of which party was telling the truth. Factual information is supposed to be determined by a jury. Judge Marshall denied it all.

Everything detrimental to the City of Los Angeles stayed legally chained to her dais—or behind her own judge's chambers doors.

By refusing to allow a jury trial in our case, the judge unilaterally decided to what extent we would be able to exercise our First Amendment Rights—for a second time.

To further insult our company's efforts, Judge Marshall issued a supplemental court order in September 1991, which provided no relief or monetary damages from the illegal behavior that had been going on since at least 1979, when Carl and I first became involved in the new technology. No damages for stealing our constitutional rights and stalling our cable franchise business—at all.

The second knife in the back was that the City of Los Angeles could continue their corrupt practices. That is, Judge Marshall did not even require the city to change its illegal cable franchising law in any way. In our view, her protection of illegal constitutional violations maintained control of South Central in the hands of Mayor Bradley, the current city council, and the Democratic Party.

"She kept us from building a cable television system for South Central while allowing the city to protect their friends," Carl said.

"Then, Judge Marshall says we can't make an issue of how the city changes the laws for South Central at will," Al Watson added as he tried to express his extreme frustration at the federal process for judicially applauding and condoning the deprivation of our constitutional rights.

The constitutional violations were clear when two higher courts reviewed the case and returned it to Judge Marshall's court in 1986, although Judge Marshall acknowledged the constitutional violations within the Los Angeles law. In what way did the judge protect us from the ongoing violation of our constitutional rights? What is the purpose of the court if it does not protect the citizens from actions by governments that violate our basic rights? Why have a constitutional right if it cannot be exercised?

Therefore, Judge Marshall's ruling restricted the market to one company for the distribution of cable television, which was equivalent to saying that only one newspaper can put its newspapers on city streets. The Ninth Circuit Court of Appeals, in its opinion in this case, stated, "In First Amendment cases, the government always bears the burden of proving the constitutionality of the alleged infringing ordinances." According to the appellate court's order the burden of proof remained with the city to prove that the ordinance did not violate the Constitution. Why was the city given five years to continue this violation by Judge Marshall, and then not asked by Judge Marshall to change their practices in accordance with the Supreme Court and Ninth Circuit rulings?

———————

Through all levels of government, we watched twelve years of our, and the citizens of South Centrals' constitutional rights being suffocated. The "honorable" Judge Marshall went on to determine that she would set the damages and the value of our rights at one dollar. *One dollar?* Yes. One hundred pennies.

All civil rights cases where there is a clear victor requires the payment of damages by the offending party. The one dollar represented the absolute lowest amount of compensation for damages allowed by the courts.

The damages to our company had been calculated by Dr. Thomas Hazlett, one of the leading communication economists in the United States. In his sworn deposition, his calculation of damages for our company from 1983 through 1988, because of the ongoing violation of our civil rights, was approximately *$70 million*.

Judge Marshall whittled down the unanimous verdicts of the appellate court and the United States Supreme Court to one dollar. This is the cost of less than an hour at a city parking meter. Our rights as American citizens and twelve years of our lives valued at one dollar!

Judge Marshall explained that she would not allow a jury to determine the damages to be awarded for the deprivation of our rights because any jury determination would be speculative. Following her logic, in fact, all jury awards are speculative since they are an estimation meant to make up for the damage done by the losing party—a process routinely done in the judicial system many, many times every day.

The increased costs to enter the current cable television industry market were ignored. Not only had the market now realized the value of cable television, but the building costs from 1979 to 1990 had skyrocketed. Judge Marshall ignored these facts as well.

We wanted and deserved a jury of our peers to decide upon an appropriate compensation for the violation of our rights, but instead we were saddled with a judicial "friend" of the violator who decided on our compensation. This was the "justice hustle" Judge Marshall played upon Preferred and the citizens of South Central, and thus on all of America, from her federal judicial bench.

Nothing could provide a greater disincentive to seek protection of our constitutional rights than finding out that twelve years of our lives were valued at one dollar. It brought to mind the Duke brothers from the movie "Trading Places," where powerful businessmen brothers bet one dollar that they could ruin the life of a successful commodities trader to see if they could turn a down-and-out conman into the same type of success as the person whose life they were actively destroying.

—————•—————

After hearing about the one dollar in damages from our attorneys, I remember the deathly smiles that Carl and I gave to each other. At a time when you believe that a gross injustice has been done, thoughts of violence can enter your mind and replace common sense. Because we knew each other so well, we knew that both of us having that smile together could only end in criminal problems. We decided to end the smiling without saying a word. There is something only a person who has literally known you for your entire life can understand by such a lethal, nonverbal signal. In the looks between us, we decided to wait and vent our hostilities and laugh in private as we made sexist and racist statements about the judge and her heinous disregard for justice.

To put it mildly, we were well-beyond-words furious about Judge Marshall's abuses of power. She had issued protection to those who stole our constitutional rights and those of the citizens of South Central, the most impoverished area of Los Angeles. As black citizens representing South Central and its citizens, we felt passionately that Judge Marshall, a black woman, had disregarded and turned her back on South Central and stolen all of our rights to in order protect the status quo, Mayor Bradley, and his friends.

We felt we were acting on behalf of black people and other minorities and were slapped down at every turn by other black people. How was this any different from black-on-black crime, except more egregious?

———

In the years 1980 to 1990, Carl and I estimated we had spent a total of 6,000 and 11,000 hours, respectively, on the application process and the litigation process. The value of our time to protect the civil rights of our entire race did not seem to be a concern to Judge Consuelo Marshall. The judge's ruling was effectively giving the city the right to bypass the Constitution of the United States.

———

"The black and other minority generations of the 1980s and 1990s in South Central are going to be hurt by this...and by a black judge makes it even worse," Carl observed sadly. "Clint, I hope it's not a downward spiral that will kill the gains made by our parents during the 1950s and 1960s."

Throughout our seemingly endless franchising process with the City of Los Angeles, as owners and shareholders in Universal Cable Systems and Preferred Communications, it became imminently clear that the legislative and executive branches of government in the City of Los Angeles were broken and we could not expect any semblance of "justice" trying to work within their systems.

We spent over a decade trying to start a business and get justice. In our estimation as citizens, we felt we deserved a much better judge, in knowledge, ethics, and honesty, who dispensed justice for the greater good and obeyed the law.

A student of civics would define Judge Marshall as the arbiter of "justice," who was charged by her nomination, above all, to serve her constituent community under that law. Any other action would indicate that a judge was biased and had subverted the law, showing ignorance for his or her own unknown purposes. In our case, and many others, Judge Marshall was a dismal failure.

I contend that Judge Marshall's incompetence and surreptitious rulings in our case was equal to the harm done to entire black communities by the white judges using the "harbor" of Jim Crowe laws in the South.

To have a black mayor and a black judge in the 1980s and 1990s in Los Angeles, California, do what the white mayors and white judges did in the segregated South in the 1930s and 1940s, should definitely be called what it is: racist, and an insult to black America.

Black-on-black crime is the legacy of Mayor Tom Bradley, the Los Angeles City Council during his tenure, and Judge Consuelo Marshall.

Chapter Fourteen

Another Day, Another Game—Different Players

We paid our lawyers and investors from the final settlement with the City of Los Angeles. The settlement included fees for our attorneys and court costs and allowances granted by Judge Marshall.

By the time Judge Marshall issued her final ruling in 1991, the cost to build the system in South Central Los Angeles had more than tripled. It would now cost $60 million more than it would have initially cost to build a cable system when we first entered into this blossoming industry in 1979.

We were still prepared to build the system at the higher cost because we could also see potential revenue streams that had not existed in 1979—more channels, more programming, etc.

We wouldn't get the chance.

—◆—

In 1993, shortly after the City of Los Angeles finally reached a settlement agreement with us through our company, the Los Angeles Council City Council changed their minds about cable television licensing yet again. They decided to seek out potential builders for a competitive cable television franchise, but the "change" was that this new franchise would cover all of Los Angeles and not just specific franchise areas. After dealing with "the Galloway boys," it seemed Los Angeles was determined to avoid further trouble with competitive bids.

We then witnessed the ascendancy of another political family after Mayor Bradley left office and how it affected cable television in Los Angeles.

The Hahn political dynasty had been a dominant force in Los Angeles politics since the 1950s. Kenneth Hahn, the father of James Hahn, was a Los Angeles County Supervisor whose district covered substantial portions of South Central Los Angeles. Kenneth Hahn was also a Los Angeles City Councilman in the seat previously held by Councilman Gilbert Lindsay. The older Hahn was highly respected within the black community for the work he had done during the 1960s.

Janice Hahn, the sister of James Hahn, was elected to the Los Angeles City Council in 2001 and was elected as a U.S. Congresswoman on July 12, 2011, in a special election for the 36th Congressional District seat.

This was interesting because throughout the cable television application process James Hahn was the city attorney for Los Angeles. He doggedly defended, at our expense, the concept of a "natural monopoly" as the basis of the city's legal position on cable television competition. We continually identified that this concept had an innate flaw because the law (the city's very own ordinance) specifically stated that the cable franchise was to be awarded on a non-exclusive basis. Still, the city, and Mr. Hahn as its legal representative before the committees, boards, and the Los Angeles City Council, persisted in what we saw as pushing this thinly veiled scheme to limit the use of public right of ways to only their political friends.

In a monumental change in policy from his 1980-1993 stance of staunchly maintaining that cable television was unsuitable for the competitive marketplace, City Attorney James Hahn "became" candidate for Mayor James Hahn, and then Mayor James Hahn. He oversaw the city's "new" position of enthusiastic support for competition with the cable television monopoly they had created—a total flip-flop. Surprise, surprise!

The once-espoused natural monopoly theory was not so natural now. For us and our company, the opportunity to build new cable systems to compete with existing systems was gone as well. The city, in its shortsighted greed and complicit corruption, had destroyed any potential for a competitive market and allowed monopoly cable companies to entrench themselves into the market. Potential competitors would face great difficulty with an existing operator who has been able to gain the financial benefits of monopoly control.

So an arrogant city government on many levels overrode the Constitution, the marketplace, and the free-market system—at will.

———

Furthermore, ongoing complaints from customers about lack of service and high service rates caused by the city-created cable television monopoly policies were beginning to bring the issue to the public's attention, forcing the city to rethink its position about granting unregulated monopolies.

As early as 1997, the city began formal discussions with additional cable companies to build a competitive cable television system for the City of Los Angeles. By 1999, the city began to negotiate in earnest with the nation's largest over-builder of cable systems, RCN Corporation.

An over-builder of cable television systems would build a second system in an area already served by an operating cable television system and were often required to build across an entire city as opposed to only a section of the city as it had been awarded to the original franchise holder. The massive capital required to over-build an entire city such as Los Angeles would be an impediment to anyone seeking to compete in the cable television market. Why weren't the franchise areas as previously specified by the City of Los Angeles allowed to be built separately, thereby encouraging broader participation?

RCN had been able to obtain over-build franchises in such major cities as New York, Boston, and Chicago. When Carl and I heard of these negotiations, Carl said with a smirk, "I guess these cities haven't heard about the 'natural monopoly theory' that exists in cable television."

The city also changed their financing rules. These companies were able to spend hundreds of millions of dollars provided by Wall Street financing. As stated earlier, when our company originally applied for the cable franchise, we were forbidden from using investment banking sources for our funding. Now, not only was competition being encouraged, but the city was encouraging the use of investment banking funds.

In December of 2000, RCN Corp. informed the city that they would no longer seek to build a second cable franchise in the Los Angeles market. High capital costs had taken a toll on RCN. Just as Carl and I predicted, with cable television now entrenched in a monopoly status for so many years, it was difficult for any competitor to gain entrance into the market against an unregulated government-protected monopoly.

———◆———

Shortly after RCN walked away, the city began negotiating a new franchise agreement with Western Integrated Networks (WIN). There was no bidding process initiated in this instance either. This new company was to build a second cable television system to cover the entire city. WIN was yet another company that received a substantial financial injection from Wall Street.

Unfortunately, as in all other situations concerning cable television in the city, the South Central area was the last area scheduled to receive the new "competitive" cable television service.

Meanwhile, Los Angeles began the evaluation of WIN to determine the company's financial stability. The estimated cost of building a second franchise, covering the entire City of Los Angeles, was estimated at approximately $600 million. Even with the tremendous entry fee into the industry, the City of Los Angeles refused to allow for a competitive bid for the licenses that they wanted to issue.

Once again, the city made clear its commitment to prohibit minority participants from applying for the franchise by creating an exorbitant entrance fee. The entrance fee would now be $600 million of financing required as opposed to the $90 million that it would have cost to build just the South Central franchise area at this time. The city only denied the use of investment banking for capital development in the most impoverished area, South Central. Perhaps, as we said, this is the reason why impoverished areas remain locked out of the economic system. Governments have repeatedly blocked investment within these communities for their political benefit and not for the benefit of the citizens of the community, leaving the most needy people unserved or underserved?

There was always special treatment for the South Central franchise.

———————

In July 2001, WIN was awarded a franchise to build a second system to cover the entire City of Los Angeles. They proposed to construct a new fiber-optic system to provide the new technology of high-speed Internet service, telephone service, and cable television service.

We had recognized, years earlier, that cable television would be much more than just an entertainment medium. Once again, with meddling and bungling, government involvement had destroyed the free-market mechanisms protecting the economic system. The limitation on competition would subsequently impact the coming Internet revolution as well.

———————

279

We later discovered that WIN and its executives made substantial contributions to the mayoral campaign of James Hahn when he was elected mayor in November 2001.

As we said, Mayor Hahn represented the ultimate hypocrisy, becoming a leading proponent of building a competitive cable system while conveniently forgetting the fact that his vigorous, unapologetic defense of the monopoly would doom our franchise attempt and the very competition he now supported. No apology or recriminations. It appeared to us that the supposed principles of government were up for sale or barter.

But during his campaign for mayor, James Hahn depended heavily upon the citizens of South Central to provide votes in support of his candidacy through the primary and general elections. Tragically, the inability of the South Central community to obtain information, such as candidate Hahn's record of blocking economic development and the resulting jobs that were lost for South Central citizens, allowed him to receive a substantial black vote from an uninformed populace. This is precisely why we didn't want the powers at City Hall to control the reins of all the First Amendment information outlets.

As we predicted, the South Central community did not have any influence within the media that would provide the information from which they would make informed decisions. The result was the election of a mayor who formerly had aggressively fought capital investment within his own community. Without competition, who would tell that part of the story to the black community?

Eventually, WIN filed for protection under Chapter 11 of the U.S. Bankruptcy Act. They would not successfully emerge from bankruptcy. WIN never built one inch of cable in the city of Los Angeles. Once again the city had selected a potential cable operator that did not have the financial ability to fulfill the contracts that they had signed with the city—one of a field of at least five licenses issued by the City of Los Angeles to companies who could not financially perform in the cable television market. WIN had managed to make major political contributions before its demise.

Hahn served only one term. His attempts to seek statewide office as the Attorney General of California were defeated. But in 2009, Hahn was appointed as a Los Angeles Superior Court judge by Governor Arnold Schwarzenegger—son of a councilman, city attorney, Mayor of the City of Los Angeles, and a superior court judge. This was another example of the relationship between politicians and the judiciary.

James Hahn had come full circle in the political spectrum. Would he be independent when it came to decisions about his political friends?

The judicial path might not seem as independent a part of our government as we might like—just another giant pension for favored politicians.

Time was not kind to cable television system competition.

In answer to the call against local government manipulation of cable television franchising, the state of California took over cable television regulation.

In our estimation, it was too little, too late. Cable television now supposedly competed against the recently deregulated, former monopoly-entrenched telephone companies. The cash-rich telephone companies came back in the game along with media companies using the same poles and cable access we as citizens paid for with our taxes on the first go-around.

By destroying competition for the commerce in cable television, Los Angeles severely hindered the evolution of electronic technology to many minority communities. Numerous cities followed Los Angeles's illegal actions. The ability to provide information to minority communities so that they can make informed decisions about government and elected officials had been altered—and not in a good way. In our estimation, the failure of the South Central community to gain access to the information and resources available to other communities had contributed to a continuing downward spiral within the entire community. And in how many others?

The behavior of the mayor and the Los Angeles City Council looked very similar to old-time Chicago. The politicians acted in their own self-interest and those who interacted with them soon found out they had two choices—to go along or to try to fight against it. Most simply accepted the dysfunctional system until the leaders retired from office, died, or the behavior became so blatant that the sleazy politicians were forced to resign for their spurious activities. Such unethical governments always "said the right things" and made promises; but their actions and outcomes were as dismal as the ones in Los Angeles.

Politicians spoke glowingly of the competitive marketplace and allowing the free market to make the decision for the consumer, saying a free marketplace requires competition. Instead, they set up unnecessary monopolies where companies were not required to be responsible to the citizens and their monopoly could not be modified.

They were protected from competition by the very government funded by taxpaying citizens, thus increasing costs for services used by the citizens every day. There were other costs to each citizen. Crooked, deluded politicians used public monies in unethical ways. They used taxpayers' money against the best interests of the citizens, even as they claimed they needed more tax dollars. Tax dollars were the war chest used to fight lawsuits questioning officials, political decisions, and activities.

Unethical politicians also flagrantly enrich themselves, their friends, and their reelection coffers by giving access, promoting business interests, and making unsavory deals without looking at the effects such actions will have on the infrastructure, lives, and laws concerning the citizens they were sworn to protect.

The blatant hypocrisy displayed by the City of Los Angeles in our cable franchise efforts and court case are examples to all citizens who to deal with government. In their legislative responsibilities, the concept that the law was the same for all persons was simply a lie and part of the hustle. Expecting fairness and integrity from them is simply deluded thinking, making the concept of equal protection under the law another fallacy. Such hypocrisy helped create a dual standard in the application of laws in the cable television industry.

Our form of government was built on the premise that government service was a sacred privilege to allow civic-minded people to serve their communities—and go home.

We've seen elected officials control the actions of government for overly long periods of time, often for generations, turning elected office into an economic grant for their own personal enjoyment and enrichment. Day after day, politicians are arrested and jailed at all levels of government while trying to take advantage of their position for personal financial benefit. This doesn't begin to cover the many benefits the politicians have granted themselves in terms of salary, benefits, and retirement with bloated golden parachutes for being elected officials.

Golden parachutes funded by community tax dollars.

———◆———

Nationally, Congress was getting involved in the cable television mess, and not in a good way.

If meddling by local governments wasn't disappointing and shameful enough, the United States Congress got involved with squelching First Amendment rights. In 1993, Congress passed the Communications Act of 1993, which eliminated the potential for damages against Los Angeles and all other cities for civil rights violations in the award of cable television franchises.

Congressional representatives and senators suddenly realized, as court cases were filed, that potential damages created by the illegal awarding of monopoly cable television franchises could bankrupt cities. This was another instance of government efforts that might impede information and withhold the benefits of a jury trial. The press might not react to the undeniable theft of citizens' rights. Now, it seemed, court cases and awarding damages would subsequently require the approval of the United States Congress.

———◆———

The FCC changed as well.

In 1989, Alfred Sikes, one of the authors of the 1988 U.S. Department of Commerce report regarding cable television, would become chairman of the Federal Communications Commission. While Sikes was chairman, the FCC did nothing to support the First Amendment rights being deprived by local governments throughout the nation. Although Sikes helped to identify the problems of an unrestrained monopoly cable television industry while working for the Commerce Department, the FCC refused to develop competition in cable television despite its knowledge that local minority communities were being locked out of the technological advances available through cable television.

The FCC took no action in Sikes's tenure except to allow the telephone companies to enter the market. The entrance of telephone companies into the cable television market had previously been labeled anti-competitive by the FCC.

Everything old is new again.

Chapter Fifteen

What Does This All Mean To You?

Records show that local governmental protection by the local politicians offered the cable television industry the chance to obtain outrageous monopoly profits with almost no control over the service—a costly maneuver paid for by the public and the cable subscribers. The cable companies were allowed to charge whatever they wanted without any competition for more than twenty years, and the local municipalities looked the other way.

In contrast, consider the competitive forces that drove down the price for numerous services that were once monopolies, including telephone service. The competitive market always has caused greater pricing alternatives.

The restraint upon the development of competitive cable television aided the current situation of a few companies controlling all the media in the United States. The same people own the cable systems and the networks that go on the cable systems. Has restraint upon the construction and ownership of competitive cable systems led to true restraint upon the free press? Can it be free if you cannot access the medium without meeting the unreasonable demands and additional unreasonable barriers of the local government?

The obscene profits made by the cable television industry during the monopoly license period were supposedly from the free market risk and reward. That would be untrue because there were no free market forces that controlled the cable television industry at that time. It was simply a classic case of government corruption allowing the cable companies to charge consumers hundreds of dollars extra, annually.

These cable television franchises, based on political contacts and contributions, offered with it a chance to steal from every community, including the low-income communities because there was no one to protect them.

How much? As we said before, our expert, Dr. Thomas Hazlett estimated that as of 1985, twenty percent of all cable television income was a result of monopolistic protection provided by governments at taxpayer expense. Twenty percent! This represented billions of dollars annually protected with the collusion of local governments.

When cable television finally came to South Central, it cost citizens hundreds of dollars more annually, became a greater burden upon low-income communities, and required a substantially higher portion of the income of the average person in lower-income minority communities.

———

We felt outraged. I continue to be outraged.

My brother Carl and I were kicked out of the competitive market by the City of Los Angeles and the U.S. District Court. We knew that if the government was able to violate our constitutional rights with the support of Judge Consuelo Marshall, then the Constitution became just meaningless words, wherein those "rights" were nullified. Such abuses continue.

And how does a government start to muzzle opponents when citizens' rights are being violated? In our case, they set themselves up as the only gatekeepers to information distribution, a simple approach to squelch alternative viewpoints and dissent within a society.

Therefore, we believe all of society, whether they know it or not, pays a heavy price when the fundamental economic system is allowed to run for the benefit of powerful politicians, their friends, and moneyed contributors.

In our case, with their intentions to gain power and business for themselves, their friends, and political contributors, their greedy action restricted private enterprise and free speech as well. A free society must allow for the dissemination of information to all of its citizens.

I believe in private enterprise. I believe private enterprise can provide the economic impetus to develop communities as well as supply resources for any community to participate in the overall economy. Yet, the local government, in our case and in cases involving cable television franchises around our nation, systematically denied the concept of self-reliance, trying to restrict First Amendment rights and free markets.

In illegally altering the cable television franchise process, the City of Los Angeles wanted to give former employees and friends the rights to cable franchises for personal gain. In addition to that, governments might have a more sinister goal: the goal of restricting the media and its flow of information—information about their shady practices and cronyism.

As a result of these actions, citizens were deprived of knowledge they needed to take part in the very government that they elected. In our case, there can be no doubt that when a government controls its citizens' access to the media, the ability to evaluate the performance of that government is invariably compromised. Few media outlets were interested in our story because of fear of reprisals or being cut off from access to information or other news stories in the city administration and management aspects or city courts.

As the dominant news media moved from newspapers to electronic media, the City of Los Angeles placed itself in a position to possibly filter what news would get through to its citizens. Favors were owed by the "friends" who got the franchises. Like a quasi-totalitarian government, those political favors could directly affect the media and information distribution.

Thankfully, the Internet has come along and has given greater access to individuals all over the country and world to additional information sources without the interference of local governments. But those who cannot afford the price of a computer or hand-held device are once again vulnerable even in this technology age.

Even with the Internet, cable television continues to play a huge part in the distribution of information because of its delivery of broadband, high-speed Internet service capabilities. The lasting influence of cable television reinforces the absolute importance of gaining access to technology at its inception.

Currently, cable television has become a dominant gatekeeper in the information universe. The ability of each cable system to determine how much information may be received by a subscriber and at what speed the information will be delivered invariably has an impact on the nature and content of information that the Internet delivers.

Also, countless industries have been influenced by the cable television industry since its inception. Programming, advertising, the Internet, cell phones, and e-books are just a few examples.

It has become all too clear to me that the founding fathers did not intend for the government to establish "gatekeepers" for information to be disseminated to the public regarding the activities of our government. Otherwise, they would not have created the First Amendment to the Constitution. In the Constitution, free speech doesn't have a subscriber cost.

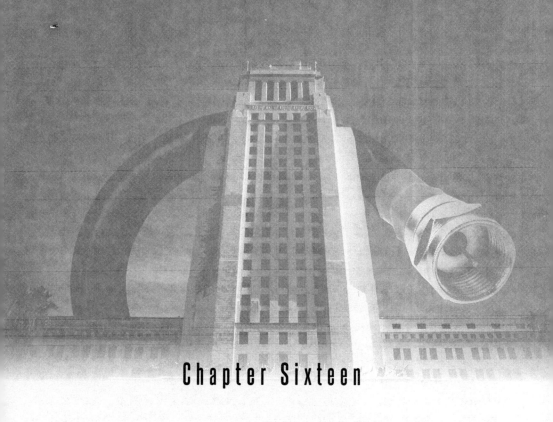

Chapter Sixteen

Citizen Soldiers And The Aftermath

There was a large cost for us, and for those who believed in us, our business, our court case, and our cause.

Our families, investors, and board members who volunteered their help did not have the financial resources to fight against the meddling, unethical politicians, judges, and their friends. We needed the help of friends and concerned citizens.

As we looked at our dilemma, the bureaucrats, boards, and committees were changing our bids and subverting the law. The simple three-letter word, "law," is a very powerful word. It seems eerily similar to another simple three letter word, "war."

Every battle needs soldiers. Typically, a soldier is defined as someone who fights for his or her country as well as the beliefs and laws the country provides to its citizens.

But, there exists a different kind of soldier as well: the citizen soldier. We thought of ourselves as citizen soldiers.

On a global scale, we, as a country, defend our American rights against foreign entities by maintaining a standing army with all the resources necessary to protect our citizens and defend ourselves against all enemies. Inside of our country, we've created a legal system of people sworn to protect our rights and provide remedies when those rights are violated.

Our enlistment was not one based upon conscription to a military service but rather based upon citizen conscription to fight for a principle or right guaranteed by the Constitution. We were fighting for the upholding of the laws, which limit the government's ability to control the actions of the citizens. We were fighting to defend the rights guaranteed by the Constitution and the Bill of Rights. Every right needs to be practiced with care and respectful conduct, and beyond that, every right that's threatened needs to be defended to continue and thrive.

The American democracy is supposedly kept under control by a system of checks and balances. This means the various levels of government composed of the legislative, executive, and judicial branches of government are supposed to protect the citizen against excesses and be scrupulously independent from one another.

The system also provides a method for the citizen to protect themselves against the excesses of government. When the legislative or executive branches have exceeded their authority by passing laws that violate the Constitution, it becomes the citizens' obligation to take up the battle against such excesses, either by the ballot box, information media, or the court system.

We can never assume our government and its elected officials will protect our constitutional rights or police itself, human frailty being what it is. Finding and identifying the truth are battles fought between citizens and their government every day. We've all seen firsthand the actions of government officials who have protected their friends and themselves instead of defending the rights of their citizens.

Our battle as citizen soldiers is different only in size and scope from military tactical maneuvers. Ours are more peaceable fights of issues, legal briefs, and our rights as citizens under the Constitution, the Bill of Rights, and federal, state, and local laws.

In South Central, the future of an entire neighborhood and its predominant race of people was given away for the political expediency of unethical politicians. We felt this jeopardized the flow of information into the black and other minority group population in those neighborhoods and was done to maintain control of minority votes and electoral success on the local, state, and national level.

———

In considering the judicial branch, the judicial system is neutral and cannot act to correct the behavior of a government unless a citizen files a complaint. Our judiciary branch of government allows for citizens to contest the actions of the legislative or executive branches by hearing their grievances in an "independent" court of law. A significant responsibility of the judicial branch is to provide the citizen with a legal alternative for resolution of disputes between the citizen and various levels of government.

———

Our citizen battle involving cable television started more than thirty years ago. The battle has been as real as any fought with guns and bullets. We felt the City of Los Angeles sought to dictate both the civil rights of the South Central community in respect to cable television media licensing and to pick exactly which company would get the license in clear violation of its bidding process procedures.

The toll in war fought with regular army troops is the blood and lives of real-life casualties. Carl and I believed the ultimate effect of allowing our government to escape its responsibility to the Constitution of the United States, has created numerous lawless and poverty-stricken communities, like South Central—effects as real as any war. Ours was a war for education, self-awareness, and economic independence.

We sought a peaceful forum to address our disputes and fought to bring attention to a city government that could not or would not regulate itself, and, at the same time, excused itself from all due process. Our battle was fought with writs, motions, and injunctions—weapons of courtroom battles. This is the battlefield of the politician and the citizen. These battles are real, very costly, and they often feel like a matter of life and death.

Our gravest challenge when we were fighting for our rights as citizens was to match the financial resources of the governments, which are funded by the near-bottomless coffers of tax dollars. As citizens, we were at a perpetual disadvantage when our opponent was able to extract his resources by virtue of taxation.

<hr />

This book has already introduced some of our soldiers.

Our oldest soldier was Perry C. Parks, Jr., a seventy-one-year-old retired postal supervisor when we met him in 1980. His son, Henry, shared legal offices with Ted Eagans, a long-time member of our legal team.

Mr. P., as we called him, had boundless energy for his age and enjoyed being involved in local politics. At six feet, two inches tall, he was always the essence of grace enhanced by his gray hair. His imposing presence, sincerity, and gentle smile warmed all who met him. He liked to attend as many political meetings as he could, had been a community organizer and volunteer for most of his life, and was widely recognized and highly respected for his community activism.

This tall septuagenarian became one of our greatest assets. Mr. P. was born in Atlanta and attended college in Texas, growing up in a segregated society, so he knew what happened to a people when they were deprived of their rights: illiteracy, poverty, social injustice, and violence. The mere mention of his name in the neighborhood and City Hall would get our group a meeting with almost any elected official in the Democratic Party and other places as well, including the offices of our adversaries.

When asked about why he would fight with "those Galloway boys" instead of aligning himself with elected city officials, he said he was too old for the money to matter and right was right no matter what anyone said. Mr. P. told anyone who would ask about the potentially huge impact of cable television and how it could transform the landscape of South Central forever—and it needed to be implemented as soon as possible to spread its beneficial effects across his deteriorating neighborhood's landscape.

Like any black man of his age, who had been born in Georgia and lived through the Great Depression, he had seen his share of racism and how black Americans were constantly being denied their civil rights. You would never hear him speak negatively about anyone even when those whom he trusted for many years refused to allow him to exercise his hard-won civil rights in these cable television issues. He was too much of a gentleman.

Mr. P.'s primary interest in cable television was for the benefits such technology could bring to the South Central community, in which he lived. As Mr. P. explained it, he had waited for years for an opportunity to provide tangible benefits to this community through his political involvement. Unlike the younger members of this organization concerned with the potential business plans and monetary aspects involved from involvement in cable television, his genuine love of the people of South Central kept everyone's views in the proper moral and cultural perspective for this venture.

Very early on, the Department of Transportation had taken the position that an investment in South Central cable would be a money-losing proposition. Mr. P. felt differently. He saw it as an intellectual and information imperative for his neighborhood and believed it was the responsibility of black citizens to provide this important service to the South Central community regardless of the lies the DOT sought to perpetrate.

Another soldier, Al Watson, whose vital information and wit has already been described here, was in his late 60s when we met in 1980. Al was a client of Ted Eagans. Al owned and operated Al's Boning Company, a meat-processing and -packing company in South Central, and the largest black-owned meat processor west of the Mississippi, employing over two hundred people. As a successful businessman in the community, Al not only worked and lived in South Central, he proved indispensable to us for his profound knowledge of business within the South Central neighborhood. I'll always remember his tart, acerbic wit kept us sane and on course in the most stressful times.

Al introduced us to the well-renowned Councilman Lindsay, who believed in our efforts and tried his best to help us. Lindsay had been a councilman since 1962 and Al's friend long before Lindsay's public service.

Al's business was in Councilman Lindsay's district and his relationship with Lindsay greatly enhanced our ability to apply for the original cable television franchise. It did not take long for us to realize that without an elected official in your corner in City Hall, you had no realistic chance of participating in the cable television bidding process—or any business controlled by the city process for that matter.

Al was only five-foot-five, but he was physically quite strong from the rigors of processing tons of meat each week. He walked with a pronounced limp, also attributed to his life of hard, long work hours and business ownership. Al was very proud of his trademark handshake, like a vise grip, and made sure anyone he met would become equally impressed in shaking his hand and feeling its strength.

Unlike Mr. P., Al was a businessman, keenly aware of the financial benefits that might accrue for the owners of a large cable television franchise. As a result, Al was vehemently against any attempt at appeasing the Bakewell-Johnson group. The simple fact was that Mr. Watson and we had no trust in Channing Johnson or Danny Bakewell. Both men seemed to be concerned only about the amount of money they could get out of the cable franchise license on a short-term basis. Our goal as a company was to provide a long-term platform for educational, health, business, and other minority-needs programming that would enhance the community and provide opportunity information where none currently existed.

Al was as rough and tumble as they come. He made it absolutely clear on many occasions that he would be more than willing to resolve our differences with our adversaries in a physical manner—despite being twice the age of most of our opponents. He had what some would call "black chutzpah" and we were thrilled to have him on board.

They had different demeanors and approaches but both Mr. P. and Mr. Watson were from the South and had seen the effects of abusive and tyrannical government. They were equally infuriated at the prospect that cable television franchises, such an important piece of community economic and technological infrastructure, would be thrown about like a political football for the benefit of a few elected officials and their friends.

Russell and Donna Grisanti were close friends of mine and behind-the-scene soldiers. Russell and I had worked together at Coopers and Lybrand (now part of the company PricewaterhouseCoopers), an international accounting firm, in the San Francisco office. In conjunction with the financing submitted with the original application, Russ had worked with me to make sure of our financing arrangements. I consulted with Russ often about the extensive financial planning and arrangements involved in the franchising process. Russ and Donna proved to be even better friends than I ever could have imagined.

Judge Marshall's indifference to the truth would show how just one small piece of false testimony, the supposed lack of availability of pole space, would end up costing us approximately $100,000 to prove the truth.

Because the Grisantis had been familiar with our cable television involvement from the beginning, they were aware of the financial strain of trying to fight the city. They came to me, without being asked, as if they knew what was on my mind, and said, "Clint, we will not allow you to drop this case simply because you've run out of money." They went on to provide us with tens of thousands of dollars based only on my word that their funds would be returned at the end of litigation *if* we were successful. At times like this, when your funds are running low and your faith is waning, you learn who your friends are.

Both Russ and Donna were fully aware that ours was an uphill battle, not because of the content of our case, but because the black federal judge ruled in favor of the city and backing up the black politicians fighting on its behalf and stalling in every way possible to make us quit. Russ and Donna invested in our case because, as they put it so simply, it was not right that the government could steal our rights because they were able to outlast us financially.

When you are in battle your comrades in arms are the only people that you really trust.

Russ had served in the Air Force during the Vietnam War. As a veteran, he said, "What the hell do you think I was over there fighting for?" The city was challenging all Americans and not just Carl and me. Not just Preferred. Not just South Central. The city was challenging *all* of our rights.

———————

During the early negotiations with the mayor's circle and the Bakewell-Johnson group, I asked a college friend, Gene Forte, to attend some of the sessions with our competitors. Gene was from a small town in central California and I brought him along because I was afraid I was being inflexible in my unwillingness to cede control of the company Carl and I had created.

Gene was a successful Beverly Hills stockbroker with a major Wall Street firm, but in our negotiations we never introduced him as a financial backer. We felt it best that our competitors did not know what contacts and resources we had available. I simply introduced him as a friend of mine whom I had asked for assistance. Not only were we college friends, but we'd both chosen careers in the investment banking industry. And we were both doing well in our careers.

Gene's tenacity and support during this battle was immeasurable. Gene offered us access to his largest clients from his investment banking clientele as potential investors in our cable television system. Gene spent numerous hours working with us to arrange backup financing after the city, without notice, unilaterally reduced our financial rating without any testimony or support, which would have scuttled our financing package.

———————

Harold Farrow provided the legal support necessary to battle a major municipal government that had gone out of control. Without his and his firm's expertise we would have been lost. Harold Farrow, Rob Bramson, and the other associates of the firm of Farrow, Bramson, Chavez, and Baskin allowed us to compete in the judicial forum. Without great sums of money or a very supportive legal team willing to absorb some costs and wait for payment in others, we would have been in deep trouble in our fight against the Los Angeles city government.

The contributions by the citizen soldiers ranged from financial resources to political contacts to moral support to simply listening to us as we shared our story. We had some great friends who were willing to fight with us, for us, and against this imposing government attempting to stifle our rights. Thankfully, our allies were not intimidated; they continued to rally at our side. And the truth is, we needed them—not just financially, but also for moral and emotional support. Any soldier grows to love his brothers in arms and we needed more and more soldiers to continue our fight and to keep up the dream of winning. They all put themselves on the line for Preferred Communications.

———————

Even with limited resources, in our eyes and minds, this battle had to be fought. And if we were waiting for the government to limit their actions and constitutional violations, that would be the definition of futility. In the elapsed quarter-century since our original battle with the government, I have watched as politicians have continued to expand their rights incursions and increase the protections afforded to elected officials, while the rights of the average citizens have been systematically eroded.

As a soldier, there can be no surrender until the battle has been won or lost. We exhausted all potential judicial remedies in an effort to recover our civil rights. We pursued all legal and administrative remedies for the excesses of government that stemmed from the "regulation" of cable television.

Even in losing this case, we were able to return to our professional lives and to continue making decent livings despite a collective feeling of being persona non grata in Los Angeles.

This battle for defending our rights may have technically ended—but at tremendous economic and physical cost to my brother and me. The costs of the overwhelming stress of investing all of our resources, the years of our lives, and ultimately, putting ourselves on the line, took its toll.

But the price we would have paid for not defending our rights was even higher. It may seem old-fashioned but shining a light on corruption and defending the Constitution of this nation are still worthy goals. Character, integrity, and honesty are worth the cost.

Because every branch of government in Los Angeles seems to rest in the control of the same elected faces year after year, it's been easy for politicians to go unchallenged. Their confidence increases because of public indifference and inactivity as our rights slowly erode under multi-generational governmental tenure. Where is our responsibility? What is happening? And why didn't more people care? The lack of access to media would assure that Black America would never have knowledge of the behavior of its elected officials until those officials were arrested. If they were arrested.

We felt like we were screaming into a tunnel and only our brothers in arms could hear us. The government was deaf and, more than that, they covered their ears as they laughed at us. The public was deaf and interested in anything else, it seemed. We would have liked to think of the events as a nightmare that would go away when daylight breaks, but this was a real and tragic event. Waking up didn't alter anything.

Unchecked government mistreatment and mismanagement are only tested during times of economic crisis, truly out-of-bounds civic behavior, or scandal. Discomfort promotes activism.

In our estimation, the Los Angeles city government demonstrated utter incompetence in managing the economy and marketplace. This franchising process prohibited the free market from performing its function to control supply and demand of goods and services.

Disregarded laws, make-rules-as-you-go policies, lining political pockets, and graft littered the course of our cable franchise process. Failed government policies such as these are at the core of economic mismanagement and fiscal crisis. Could anyone defend or predict the course of illegality we encountered in the franchise process?

The lack of available independent information to the public is another significant factor in city fiscal and management crisis. No one would listen to our complaints or concerns as we tried to illuminate the corruption in Los Angeles. In the cable industry as a whole, this has been exacerbated by the reduction in the ownership of all media outlets to a few conglomerates. Sensible, middle-of-the-road solutions never come to the public's attention. Extreme views might sell "programming product," but citizens need information before their street, town, or city are the subject of these sensational reports. Then we hear the cries of, "Why didn't anybody tell me?" Too few outlets and too few viewpoints?

How long will the average citizens suffer these kind of traumas or a twenty-first-century American depression? I don't think that the average citizen will have the patience to wait decades for the government to recognize its failings and to correct them.

While the rest of America suffers from corruption and recession, Black America is suffering a cultural depression as measured by unemployment and financial resources. Black America had plenty of economic issues that have only been served with expensive and short-term band aids with little getting to the needy people themselves.

I am blessed to live in a country that allows me to challenge the government when it attempts to steal our rights. I love this country and that is precisely why I have fought so long and hard to defend what I know to be right. The Constitution and its applications to the citizens of this country are certainly worth fighting for. I cannot forget those who have died in pursuit of these very rights.

But as much as the battle exhausted us, we were kept alive and strong by a large circle of friends, our brothers and sisters in arms, who protected us and supported us as we continued to fight. Perry, Al, Russ and Donna, Gene, and Farrow—every one of them fought this battle with whatever resources they were able to garner.

Margaret Mead, the world-renowned anthropologist, once said, "Never doubt that a small group of thoughtful, committed citizens can change the world. Indeed, it is the only thing that ever has."

———

There are casualties of war, even in civil battles. Even having won some battles, there were others to fight, especially for Carl. Less than one year after we had received our settlement from the city to end our litigation, Carl was diagnosed with leukemia and was given less than a year to live.

In the ten years prior to his diagnosis, Carl fought two major pieces of court litigations with national implications: our cable case, and the court case suing CBS and *60 Minutes*. In my opinion, the resulting stress from the two major cases and the blatant injustice heaped upon him were major factors in his contracting this deadly illness.

Like everything else in life, Carl fought the illness with a tenacity and cleverness admired by everyone who knew him. His one-year death sentence turned out to last more than fifteen years.

Nine months after Carl was diagnosed with leukemia, I was diagnosed with a brain tumor. We had both contracted serious illnesses within a short period of time following our involvement with the legal system. I was fortunate that my tumor was benign and was removed in a ten-hour surgery. After that, Carl always liked to joke about my good luck of only getting a brain tumor, because they could remove it.

None of our other four siblings ever had any serious medical issues.

Stress is factor for all soldiers in battle. The battle may be fought with rifles or writs but the effects of stress are still the same.

It was the cruelest of ironies that a black federal judge and a black mayor would be the root causes of this stress—each also so influential in assuring the deprivation of rights to a substantially black population in the City of Los Angeles.

Carl was heartbroken to find that it was black politicians fighting to prevent Black America from exercising the freedoms guaranteed under the Constitution. He shook his head and said, "So this is the progress we made."

We had come so far, but we still felt so far away from true freedom.

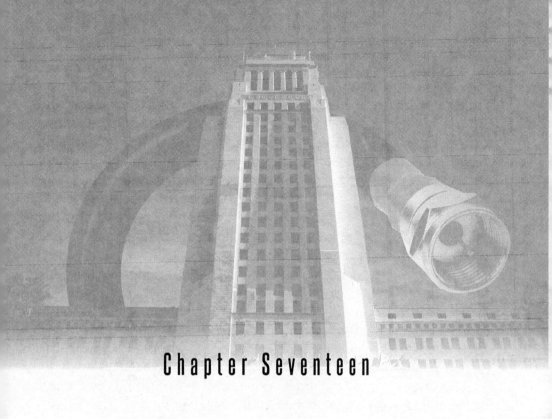

Chapter Seventeen

The Myth Of Black Leadership

According to Wikipedia, leadership is a "process of social influence in which one person is able to enlist the aid and support of others in the accomplishment of a common task."

This lack of interest by leading black publications continued to point out that many minority communities did not then, and do not now, receive the relevant information about politicians and the effects of these political actions upon them. In a free society it is the free market that is supposed to allow the communities to best determine the issues that most represent the concerns of that community. We briefly discuss five of our concerns.

1. Violence in Programming. First, the importance and power of television was made abundantly clear in 1982 when the National Institute of Health issued its report titled "Television and Behavior—Ten Years of Scientific Progress and Implications for the Eighties." This report established the direct relationship between television violence and aggressive and violent behavior displayed by children. The factors were determined to be more prevalent in minority communities because of the tendency to view more television than in society in general. The report further indicated that, "Television is also said to mold children's attitudes, which later may be translated into behavior. Children who watch a lot of violence on television may come to accept violence as normal behavior."

Those relationships of television and behavior established in 1982 by the National Institute of Health have been upheld and strengthened in many other psychological studies through the intervening years.

The findings can be directly correlated to urban minority communities, where people watch more television, and the violent activity that has engulfed these communities. South Central is a classic example of the effects of media to inundate a community with violent images. While major corporations profit from the display of violence, the community is forbidden, in violation of the Constitution, from providing programming that it deems suitable for its community.

Where is the leadership to address this important issue that had destroyed millions of lives by allowing programming that encourages violent behavior for a profit? There is no black leadership on this issue because black leadership is just a myth and those posing as black leaders are merely shills for the Democratic Party.

The inverse correlation between television and education has been known for decades but steps taken by black citizens to improve their communities have been terminated by the actions of local governments. These local governments have significant minority participation but this representation is little more than an apparition.

The National Institute of Mental Health has identified television as a major health issue because television's power and ability to cause behavior modification for better and for worse. We have seen the worse in South Central. Would black leadership involve itself if people were being given poisoned food? The results of poisoned programming have the same effect—continuous violent programming desensitizes children to such behavior and actions. Regarding children's attitude toward violence, the report concludes, "Looking at violent scenes for even a very brief time makes young children more willing to accept aggressive behavior of other children. This acceptance of aggression makes it more likely that the children will themselves be more aggressive."

2. Free market access. By denying our constitutional rights, Los Angeles acted against the free market system and the First Amendment rights of the citizens of South Central. It is difficult to understand why the political leaders would seek to deprive poor people of the economic resources that would make jobs available—jobs created by the capital investment of people from their own community.

If our assertions are true, civil rights organizations, claiming to be looking out for the best interests of Black America, have abdicated their responsibility in order to curry favor and perpetuate the interests of their ruling political party. That begs a third question, then: who, in fact, looks out for the economic interests of Black America?

We feel, as black citizens, we have been failed, by our political leaders, as a group of people, to capitalize upon the resources available to us to invest within our community. This investment could improve the lot of the residents of our urban minority communities. In our experience, we have been shown that black politicians failed in leading minority communities in accessing and utilizing economic power in South Central. Black organizations cast a blind eye to our efforts and the economic corruption perpetrated by black politicians in Los Angeles.

3. Black organizations. We feel any organization that does not discuss economic activity within the poorest communities in

America, cannot in good conscience claim to represent the best interests of a socioeconomically disadvantaged community.

If these organizations won't fight for equitable treatment by local government, these organizations allow local governments to withhold the constitutional rights as well as the ability for economic development within impoverished communities. They are parties to strangling long-term economic development and their minority communities' ability to participate in the economic development that determines its ability to provide growth and wealth within that community.

Look at the activities of civil rights leaders. Look at the ongoing "begging" apparatus that continually seeks short-term solutions with government involvement in the economic needs of the community. We feel the needs are best met, financed, and fostered by our own growth within the society.

Informed decision-making requires valid information with which to make a decision. Without any ability for the community to be informed and hold their leaders responsible, the community has received irresponsible leadership.

4. Economic factors. Any economy, whether local, national, or international, is dependent upon the recirculation of funds within that economy to provide jobs and services to the community with money attached by business activity. The continual outflow of money from minority communities serves to reduce the amount of jobs and services available within the community. The jobs will follow the money and the money leads out of town for South Central.

There is a substantial amount of capital that flows out of Black America without consideration of the economic impact such outflow of capital. It is only through reinvestment to develop the community that continued economic growth would provide opportunities within disadvantaged communities.

When valuable economic resources, such as cable television, are all removed from community control, then the jobs, information avenues, money, and options go with them. No community can be expected to provide employment and better conditions for its people if it is not allowed to utilize the economic resources produced for the benefit of the development of its citizens.

We have failed to reap the benefits that go with the ability to access capital and capital markets for the development of local communities. The development of economic enterprises stabilizes the community because of the reduction of unemployment. With that economic "engine," statistics show decreases in unemployment and increases in educational levels and decreased crime.

5. Media companies. Media companies have failed to provide the black community with the information resources necessary to drive an open economic market. Black media, especially, have failed to properly report upon the activities of elected officials on behalf of the public, with a few exceptions. This failure to provide the information necessary for black Americans to responsibly participate in the economic system of this nation has been simply disregarded. For every hour of solution-based programming there is one thousand hours of fictional and factual depictions of blacks in violent, illegal, and poverty-stricken activities. Black media has obsessed itself with providing a showcase for celebrity, entertainment, and sports personalities. Few attempts have been made to provide relatively important information regarding education, financial structure, health, and building or rebuilding communities.

From the beginning, Carl and I both felt that it was our collective responsibility to make programming a prime objective of our business plan. We saw the use of electronic media as a teaching tool that offered a brand-new opportunity for this struggling community to receive enhanced educational programming—instead of the massive quantities of infomercials and pornography that permeate most cable television systems today.

Unfortunately, it's also a story of a real place with real people who have been badly abused and neglected—South Central and its citizens. Instead of economic progress, economic depravity has continued to ravage South Central, which is now called and designated by the city as "South Los Angeles." This was done because South Central has such a negative image in the mind of

307

the public. Whatever the area is called by the City of Los Angeles, more gangs, more violence, and more staggering unemployment have produced more despair and more crime. It seems that only visible and continually negative stigmatizing, high-profile music and movies have developed to publicize this morass.

That brings to mind my sadness of not being able to intervene in making educational and other types of programming available to South Central through cable television. We've only witnessed the continual failure of the educational system in the City of Los Angeles, which has accelerated the downward spiral of the inhabitants in South Central, still Los Angeles's most impoverished neighborhood. The failure is clear by any standard of measurement. The failure persists because those who are supposed to be leading Black America still seem more concerned with their image over the true circumstances in their community.

Public school student skill levels continue to sink. It is difficult to effectively compete in any market or game when your skill level is substantially below all your academic competitors. Could we have helped? We'll never know.

It is not our place to figure out why the public education system is failing. Rather, it is to publicize that our opportunity to help make the changes necessary to compete in the new age of technology was snatched from us. Without education and economic and academic resources, how is Black America supposed to make decisions that will integrate them into the larger and more prosperous economic system of the United States? While there are many black Americans who now work within the larger system, a significant black population has yet to participate in the investment and economic development that has made the American economic system the envy of the rest of the world. Instead of participation in the broad American economy, South Central is riddled with problems of the gangs and the illegal drug economy, lives changed by incarcerations, and the explosion of single-parent households.

During our involvement in the franchising and judicial process we met with numerous elected black officials. We met with Maxine Waters in early 1982, and we were supremely disappointed in our conversation. She is currently a U.S. Congresswoman and has been in office since 1991.

At this time she was a member of the California State Assembly and represented a portion of South Central. She explained that she would not take any steps to protect the rights of South Central from the City of Los Angeles.

According to Ms. Waters, elected officials in each branch of government don't get involved with the business that goes on in the city because otherwise they might start stepping on each others toes. It was inconvenient to secure the civil rights of her constituents. Never mind that the citizens of South Central were being stomped on by the City of Los Angeles in more than just cable television. We'd heard it all before. Was this some contemporary unwritten code among all politicians—or just black politicians?

Congresswoman Waters closed our meeting by suggesting that we make some stock in our company available for her husband, Sidney Williams. In 2011, Water's was under investigation by the House Ethics Committee for allegedly providing inappropriate interference for a bank partially owned by her husband.

During early 1982, I was introduced to Mervyn Dymally by his son, Mark. Mark had been an accounting client of mine. Dymally had been Lieutenant Governor of California during the late 1970s. He had also represented sections of South Central in both the California State Assembly and the California State Senate from as early as 1963 through the late 1970s when he became lieutenant governor.

Dymally explained, "Tom Bradley is little more than a front man for the interests of the real estate and media tycoons from West Los Angeles." Dymally explained that we had become a problem for the Democratic Party of Los Angeles County because of our making the mistreatment of South Central an issue. In 1982, Dymally was elected to the U.S. Congress, and he was one of the politicians who refused to speak up about our court case. Once again, he, as others, were not concerned with the constitutional rights of South Central.

Although Maxine Waters and Mervyn Dymally have been representing portions of South Central for the better part of four decades, the plight of South Central has continued to deteriorate. They were only two of the many black elected officials with whom we met, and who were members of the Democratic Party of Los Angeles County. The answers were the same from all the elected officials. They minded their business and let the City of Los Angeles and County of Los Angeles do as it pleased in their political sphere of influence. This was a disservice to everyone.

———◆———

I've spent a substantial portion of my adult life engaged in a battle for civil rights that affect us all and that we need to maintain freedom. This is especially important to me when only several generations ago my ancestors were slaves.

I'm proud of the gut-wrenching journey that my ancestors made, so that amazing opportunities like building a cable television system could be presented to my brother and me. Opportunities like these have come to the rest of my family as well, and for this I am eternally grateful.

An examination of my own family's success in obtaining professional standing clearly indicates the tremendous achievement that is possible in America for any group of people. This is the essence of America—the ability to transcend your station in life within your lifetime and to accomplish lofty goals against great odds.

As a young man in a big family, I was always a part of the ongoing mischief. I can remember that when we were misbehaving my mother would always say to my father, "Tommy, these children are acting like fools."

My father's straight face response was often, "They're not acting." His implication was that the behavior was representative of the child displaying it. In other words, we probably *were* fools.

The same goes for the government. We are all witnesses to the way the government works. If they act the fool, then they are the fool. If they act the scoundrel, then they are the scoundrel. There is available proof. The records of the City of Los Angeles show the illegal support and protection afforded to politically connected friends while politicians reaped contributions in campaign coffers. The ongoing availability of supporting documentation in the court records of the United States District Court, United States Ninth Circuit Court of Appeals, and the United States Supreme Court shall serve as evidence to anyone who seeks to verify or contradict the contents of this book. I have also made most of the documents and information discussed in this book available on the Internet at the book's website, www.cablecomestosouthcentral.com.

———◆———

What shall become of my people?

We felt personal heartbreak to witness and experience that a major cause for the crippling problems facing black Americans was the black leadership. It seems they've managed to keep a boot on the neck of black Americans who are trying to rise up in society.

Please do not think that this corrupt activity described in this book is limited to black or poor or any other specific group of people. Minority communities merely serve as the testing ground for government abuses. By using the power of media, Los Angeles has simply put a better facade on the face of its corruption. The politicians became more adept at presenting a distorted view of the true activities that exist in this city.

The poor and the minorities, they are most often the unprotected, the unsafe, the forgotten. It is easier for the government to abuse these vulnerable people.

For all the great liberal dogma of the Democratic Party, they have failed urban blacks and economically disadvantaged communities for the past three decades. They've spent the public's money protecting their friends from the American free market system. And it is this very system that is in great danger as America seeks to pay for the trillions of dollars that have been squandered by incompetent and corrupt government, at all levels.

Black America needs a dramatic change of leadership. No team—be it athletic or political—will continually allow itself to lose without contemplating a change of leadership. Black leadership is a consistently losing team and we had better consider replacing our leadership. Competent black leadership is entirely possible in this country.

At this time, without constitutional rights, active participation in the American economic system, and engaged, compassionate leadership, Black America seems hopeless. And as Gore Vidal once said, "A leader is a dealer in hope." I am sure you can better understand the skepticism of black youth today.

We will only find hope in a new and honest leadership—unlike the current faces in power and unlike our past experience. The new black leadership must not hinder our growth by trying to convert all community assets for their own benefit. They will not lead the charge to deprive us of our constitutional rights. We cannot let them close the door of opportunity to the citizens for the benefit of their political patronage.

A December 18, 2008, *Los Angeles Times* article was headlined, "NAACP Gives a Stern Warning to TV." The NAACP spoke of its concern for a lack of diversity on television. Not "a day late and a dollar short," but "a quarter century late and a billion dollars short." They are not going to bring the boat back because you missed it.

Chapter Eighteen

Final Thoughts

I believe that I have earned my right to these final thoughts—at a cost of millions of dollars and thousands of hours in pursuit of a cable franchise.

A conundrum exists in America today. The founding fathers recognized the dangers of limiting the free press and, as a result, they instituted the Bill of Rights and the First Amendment to the Constitution. We saw government trying to limit and control the freedom of cable television and news for their own benefit and the benefit of their cronies, and we sought to publicize this problem. The attempts of the government to deny the citizens unfettered access to media in our democracy is threatened. To limit its citizens' access to the media, and thereby free speech, threatens our democracy.

In keeping with the Constitution, government is supposed to leave media alone. Cable television was not supposed to give gifts or curry favor with the government, making an unholy alliance that has threatened the independence and credibility of both.

Trouble becomes unleashed when the media acts as a shield, allowing for the unrestrained avarice that has taken over our government, our economy, and our financial markets. The results of a disinterested and profit-driven media and a "shielded" government, allows both to abdicate their responsibilities to the general public in favor of indifference and malfeasance.

Whether we like it or not, the power of the American media to shape our minds is at an unprecedented level—media industries and a culture awash in instant entertainment and information. This power is magnified in the black community, which watches more television than any other ethnic group.

Information can be viewed or interpreted in any way by reporters and network executives. Should we be paying more attention to the latest Hollywood scandal or to larger social, economic, and cultural issues? Should the airwaves act like nothing more than a horseracing handicapper or a tout for talking heads?

Which voices are you listening to today? Are these voices strong and independent, and are they impeccably reporting the truth? Are news sources paying attention to the government as a whole or slanted to who they like? Have citizens been lulled or guided toward indifference?

———

The futures of many people were decided by the actions taken in our case. Specifically, the futures of the youth living in South Central have been limited by the resulting lack of access to technology. But the restraint on our First Amendment rights was not limited to South Central; it was placed upon all citizens in the United States.

It's a cause-and-effect proposition. You cannot limit a person's civil rights, granted by the First Amendment, and expect that it will not affect every American citizen. Limiting one person's rights limits every person's rights. In a democracy, we are all in this boat together.

———————

I have written this book in part to make you all aware of the dangers when governments are allowed to operate without the restrictions placed on them by the Constitution. The truth is every government needs to be checked by the citizens at some time. Government and individuals all need restrictions to an extent. But when government officials are allowed to act indiscriminately and circumvent the restrictions of the Constitution and federal judges refuse to perform their judicial responsibilities, we are left unprotected from the excesses of government. When the citizen is left unprotected from the government it is called tyranny, and the boat is compromised.

Freedom does not exist in a vacuum, but in the air we breathe as we exercise our freedom openly and with pride. We must always remember that the Constitution was developed to protect us citizens from our government—to protect our freedom, not the other way around.

In 1979, we started on a journey to provide meaningful programming to the citizens of South Central because their needs were substantially different than the needs of those living in other parts of Los Angeles. South Central was composed of approximately half a million people of predominantly black and Latin ancestry. This community represented the lowest economic level that existed in Southern California. We wanted to enrich it both intellectually and financially. If we could have changed the crime rate or the graduation rate by just one percent, how many thousands of lives could have been improved or saved?

In Los Angeles, we were being deprived of the rights guaranteed to us by the United States Constitution. While government officials and employees were concentrating on lining the pockets of powerful political contributors, and even themselves, we were trying to open the minds of poor people, to give them a chance.

Subsequently, the federal courts and the FCC also encouraged the consolidation of media in the hands of a few powerful friends of politicians. This has accelerated the deterioration of American democracy. We are all in it together now.

This book is timely—now, and whenever freedom of the press or media is compromised. Americans are witnessing on a grand scale what Carl and I witnessed on a more intimate scale almost thirty years ago. What we experienced in Los Angeles then is happening to our beloved country now.

Some cable television companies seem awash with profits, so much excess cash that the principal shareholders in one company would take an extra couple of hundred million for themselves. Members of the Rigas family, who were the principal owners of Adelphia Cable, one of the five largest cable television companies in the U.S., were convicted of improperly diverting over $200 million from Adelphia for their own personal use. The father and son were convicted and sent to prison. How much money does a company need to generate to siphon off a few hundred million dollars?

The shady and corrupt practices known in the cable television industry exist in numerous other industries controlled by the government. The blatant corruption that takes place in real estate development and the allocation of government contracts cannot be challenged in court under most circumstances. These abuses have a price in lost revenues and tax dollars. We look at the decrease in the average person's lifestyle and increase in the lifestyle of the elected official and say from our experience that this is not a coincidence.

Let's consider the three major financial calamities we've experienced since 1980 in the financial markets. During the 1980s the savings and loan debacle cost the taxpayers billions to protect the high-risk ventures aided by the legislative actions and contributions by those who "own" elected officials. The failure of media to adequately address the issues that cause the financial market collapse was allowed because of lack of competition for media access.

The turn of the twenty-first century saw the "dot.com" meltdown, as media was used as a powerful sales device for Wall Street interests. The losses to the general public amounted to hundreds of billions of dollars because no one in the media was willing to question the outrageous valuations of unprofitable companies, suckering investors into companies with little prospect of making any sustained profits or any profits at all. Could Wall Street spending large sums for advertising on television stifle criticism of its behavior? Media "needs" these advertising dollars to survive at their current corporate levels.

The latest financial crisis was partially caused by unrealistic real estate pricing in the marketplace and financing methods stimulated by government officials loosening credit requirements so hundreds of thousands of unqualified people could obtain loans. These methods encouraged "gambling" in the real estate market by offering cheap money to buy houses and rental properties in a Ponzi scheme of one property paying for another property. Did the large sums spent by real estate sales and financing companies on television advertising cause the media to limit its criticism of the dangerous price rises and easy financing that supported an overpriced market?

The monetary losses in cable television, due to forced monopoly control, seem small in comparison. But as a country, the price we've paid is the corruption of local governments.

———

My brother and I never started with the intention to fight City Hall. We have all been told that you can't fight City Hall. We were also surprised that we would have to combat the government over our constitutional rights to speak in our own community.

Once the battle began there was no turning back. Once we began to challenge the actions of politicians and community leaders where they had drawn a line in the sand, we were dared to cross it. Everything the politicians at that time stood for was the exact opposite of what we'd been taught to believe by our close friends, neighbors, schools, churches, and parents.

We may have lost the battle, but the war is far from over. The many new, electronic sources for the delivery of information are creating new opportunities and resources. Still, the government and large media will try to limit the growth of alternative media outlets, but progress cannot be stopped. The question still remains about the degree of control that cable will be able to exert over broadband transmission facilities. The election of Barack Obama was due in large part to his campaign's use of the Internet to gain adherents and enthusiasts in a wide and varied audience. We are truly standing at the cliff of a new media age. Will we scale to new heights or walk off the cliff like lemmings?

And from this striking new vantage point, we can see for miles and miles into the promising, yet unknown future and back to the lucid folds of the past. We now see that the cozy relationship between government and business has led to the most damaging economic crisis in America since the Great Depression. How many lives will be destroyed during this economic crisis? Millions? That does not seem like an outrageous estimate at this point.

The financial devastation heaped upon the average American is not a result of short-term bad government decision-making but rather the result of the government's callous, long-term disregard for the laws of this nation, laws they are able to ignore in order to maintain their power and ability to continue to enjoy the legal and illegal benefits of their office.

We were fighting the power hunger and greed of government officials on behalf of South Central in the '80s. The Los Angeles politicians stole the few remaining media assets that were left from the citizens of South Central. The entire process seemed little more than a large governmental bully kicking us any time they got a chance.

We were fighting for the truth. We *all* need to fight for the truth. Allowing for the consolidation of media in the hands of a few wealthy individuals has contributed to the death of the independent press in America. But this shouldn't end the quest to obtain independent sources of information to tell us the truth about what is happening in our beloved country.

We believe that more information is better—but quality and integrity determines its usefulness, not the quantity.

In 2003, the Los Angeles City Council voted to change the name of South Central Los Angeles to "South Los Angeles." As Wikipedia stated, "South Central had become synonymous with urban decay and street crime." Do they really think changing a name is going to change the economics and the poverty of this community? Once again the City of Los Angeles is the master of rhetoric versus reality. The politicians of Los Angeles are culpable in the rampant crime and decay within South Central.

Each citizen must take responsibility to affect real change in this country. Each citizen must protect his or her own rights. I have long since stopped believing that elected officials will do this for us.

———

As I stood in an elevator of a high-rise office building in downtown Los Angeles, I overheard a conversation between two well-dressed, mid-level bank managers. The younger of the two stated, "These politicians act like they are some sort of royalty and own the country."

I could only smile as I thought of the words that my father had said on so many occasions in our simple household. "They're not acting."

We may have lost our battle but the war is never over. As long as even one citizen is willing to risk it all to preserve our rights guaranteed by the Constitution, then the war continues. Look what it took to stop our simple group of citizens. Our opposition included the Mayor of the City of Los Angeles, a United States District Court Judge, numerous Los Angeles City Councilpersons, city attorneys, district attorneys, community leaders, and some Fortune 500 corporations.

———

Approximately two thousand years ago, Longinus, a Greek philosopher, said, "In great attempts it is glorious even to fail."

My departed brother and comrades in battle can feel proud of their courage for having shown the fortitude to confront such great odds. I, for one, am proud of all of us. Our fight was not in vain, not if one citizen reads this book and decides to fight for what makes this country so extraordinary.

Cable television, as we foresaw it, was an opportunity for South Central Los Angeles to have an impact on the programming that is brought into their living rooms, hearts, and minds and to promote the betterment of an entire race and other minorities—a lost opportunity.

In South Central, opportunity knocked softly and left after being mugged by City Hall.

Index

CPSIA information can be obtained at www.ICGtesting.com
Printed in the USA
LVOW13s0057250713

344448LV00007BA/766/P